D0302946

RECEIVED

- 8 AUG 2005

Creativity

AND THE

BRAIN

Creativity
AND THE
BRAIN

Kenneth M. Heilman

Psychology Press
New York and Hove

Dementia Services
Development Centre
University of Stirling
STIRLING FK9 4LA

Published in 2005 by
Psychology Press
Taylor & Francis Group
270 Madison Avenue
New York, NY 10016

Published in Great Britain by
Psychology Press
Taylor & Francis Group
27 Church Road
Hove, East Sussex BN3 2FA

© 2005 by Taylor & Francis Group
Psychology Press is an imprint of the Taylor & Francis Group

Printed in the United States of America on acid-free paper
10 9 8 7 6 5 4 3 2 1

International Standard Book Number-10: 1-84169-425-8 (Hardcover)
International Standard Book Number-13: 978-1-8416-9425-2 (Hardcover)

No part of this book may be reprinted, reproduced, transmitted, or utilized in any form by any electronic, mechanical, or other means, now known or hereafter invented, including photocopying, microfilming, and recording, or in any information storage or retrieval system, without written permission from the publishers.

Trademark Notice: Product or corporate names may be trademarks or registered trademarks, and are used only for identification and explanation without intent to infringe.

Library of Congress Cataloging-in-Publication Data

Heilman, Kenneth M., 1938-.
    Creativity and the brain/Kenneth M. Heilman.
        p. cm.
    Includes bibliographical references and index.
    ISBN 1-84169-425-8 (hardback : alk. paper)
1. Creative ability.   2. Neuropsychology.   I. Title.

QP360.H435 2005
153.3'5—dc22
                                                    2004009960

Taylor & Francis Group
is the Academic Division of T&F Informa plc.

Visit the Taylor & Francis Web site at
http://www.taylorandfrancis.com
and the Psychology Press Web site at
http://www.psypress.com

Contents

Dedication

This book is dedicated to my geometry teacher, Mr. Abraham Goodman, who taught at New Utrecht High School in Brooklyn, NY, and who in 1954 first introduced me to the joy of discovery and creativity.

This book is also dedicated to many of my former students, residents, and postdoctoral associates who helped this joy grow into a passion. Some of these include John Adair M.D.; Jeff Anderson Ph.D.; Anna Barrett M.D.; David Beversdorf M.D.; Lee Blonder Ph.D.; Dawn Bowers Ph.D.; David Burks M.D.; Charles Butter Ph.D.; Anjan Chatterjee M.D.; Jean Cibula M.D.; Cindy Cimino Ph.D.; Timothy W. Conway Ph.D.; H. Branch Coslett M.D.; Greg Crucian Ph.D.; Steve DeKosky M.D.; Todd Feinberg M.D.; Eileen Fennell Ph.D.; Glen Finney M.D.; David FitzGerald M.D.; Shep Fleet M.D.; Paul Foster Ph.D.; Shawna Freshwater Ph.D.; David Geldmacher M.D.; Georges Ghacibeh M.D.; Robin Gilmore M.D.; Mike Gold M.D.; Leslie Gonzalez-Rothi Ph.D.; Margaret Greenwald Ph.D.; Brenda Hanna-Pladdy Ph.D.; John Hughes M.D.; Dan Jacobs M.D.; Yong Jeong M.D.; Jocelyn Keillor Ph.D.; Manho Kim M.D.; Drew Kirk M.D.; Mathew Kodsi M.D.; Carol Kooistra M.D.; Lisa Lu Ph.D.; Linda Mack Ph.D.; Lynn M. Maher Ph.D.; Victor Mark M.D.; David McFarling M.D.; Kim Meador M.D.; Mark Mennemeier Ph.D.; Jose Merino M.D.; Jeannine Mielke Ph.D.; Bayard Miller M.D.; Tomoyuki Mizuno M.D.; Mary Morris Ph.D.; Maria Mozaz Ph.D.; Duk Na M.D.; Steve Nadeau M.D.; Cindy Ochipa Ph.D.; Michael Okun M.D.; Steve Rapcsak M.D.; Stacie Raymer Ph.D.; Robert Rhodes; Alonoso Riestra M.D.; David Roeltgen M.D.; Heidi Roth M.D.; Ron Schwartz M.D.; Steve Sevush M.D.; Paul Shelton M.D.; Brian Shenal Ph.D.; Joel Shenker M.D.; Jeff Shuren M.D.; Beth Slomine Ph.D.; Lynn Speedie Ph.D.; Reva Tankle Ph.D.; Rudolf Taubner M.D.; H. Gerry Taylor Ph.D.; Jack Tsao M.D.; Daniel M. Tucker M.D.; Thomas Van den Abell Ph.D.; Mieke Verfaellie Ph.D.; Kytja Voeller M.D.; Robert T. Watson M.D.; Eli Wertman M.D.; David J. Williamson Ph.D.; and Kyle Womack M.D.

About the Author

Kenneth M. Heilman received his M.D. from the University of Virginia. He is currently the James E. Rooks, Jr., Distinguished Professor of Neurology and Health Psychology at the University of Florida, and he serves as director of the university's Memory and Cognitive Disorder Clinic and its Alzheimer's Disease Center. He is also Chief of Neurology at the Malcolm Randall Veterans Affairs Medical Center.

Heilman's primary clinical and research interests are Cognitive and Behavioral Neurology with special interest in attention, emotion, and skilled movements. In the past 30 years, he has written more than 400 articles, chapters, and books. Heilman is a past president of both the Cognitive Behavioral Neurological Society and the International Neuropsychological Society. Heilman received the University of Florida Research Foundation Professorships and the Clinical Research Award, and he also earned the Outstanding Achievement Award from the Society for Cognitive and Behavioral Neurology for his research and educational contributions to neurology. Heilman's clinical skills have been recognized in multiple editions of the *Best Doctors in America* and *America's Top Doctors*.

Preface

For more than 25 years I have been the supervisor of a postdoctoral fellowship program. Our fellowship program is designed to prepare neurologists, psychologists, and speech pathologists for academic careers. Each year I receive several applications for a limited number of openings. An academician needs skills in four domains: clinical care, research, teaching, and administration. The people who apply to our program have already completed their clinical training (e.g., an internship and neurology residency) and most are already superb clinicians. Although we attempt to increase their skills as cognitive and behavioral neurologists, those are not the skills that our fellowship is primarily directed at enhancing. We also attempt to increase their skills as educators, but, being a terrible administrator, I do little to help their skills in this domain. Most of my efforts, therefore, are directed to developing and increasing their skills as investigators.

When interviewing the candidates for this fellowship, I like to know which candidates would most benefit from our research training program and develop into the best investigator, but how is one to know who has the greatest potential to be creative? Although there are some psychological tests that have been designed to assess creative potential, the validity of these tests for people who want to perform neuropsychological or cognitive neuroscience research has never been established.

Creative neuroscientists are usually highly intelligent and all of our candidates are extremely bright, but my experience has taught me that all are not equally creative. In addition, these fellows' teaching or clinical skills are not always good predictors of their creative potential.

Acts of creativity are not limited to humans. For example, chimps like to eat termites. To harvest termites, the chimp inserts a stick into an opening in the termite mound, allows the termites to crawl on the stick, withdraws the stick, and then eats the termites off the stick. Jane Goodall filmed a chimp that found a large termite mound, but in the vicinity of this nest there was not a stick that he could insert into the mound. The chimp, however, did find a branch of a tree that had fallen to the ground, but from this main branch there were multiple side branches that would have prevented the chimp from inserting it into the opening of the mound. After examining the main branch, this chimp broke off these side branches, inserted the main branch into the mound, withdrew the stick, and enjoyed his snack.

The chimp's production of this tool was a creative act. This historic observation suggests that creativity is not limited to humans and can be observed in some of our closest ancestors, but generally creativity does not have a great influence on the lives of apes or other animals. In contrast, even in the past hundred years, creative people have revolutionized our lives. My father was born in 1904 on Staten Island, NY, which at that time could be reached only by boat. From the time he was born to the time he died at the age of 93, the world had dramatically changed. His father was a saddle maker because Ford had not yet developed the mass production of cars. Thus, automobiles were expensive and rare. The Wright brothers first flew a plane a few months before his birth, but airplanes were not commonplace. There were no televisions, no computers, and not even antibiotics. These changes were not caused by Darwinian principles of random mutation and survival of the fittest. These changes were brought about by the inventions of creative people such as the Wright brothers and Alexander Fleming. Thus, the human is the only organism in which we can study creativity.

I have been studying brain-behavior relationships in humans for more than 30 years, but I realized that perhaps I could not decide which candidate for our fellowship might be the most creative because I knew little about the brain mechanisms that lead to creativity. I, therefore, used several computer search systems such as Medline, PsycInfo, and PubMed to see what I could learn. Although I did find a few articles and chapters that addressed certain aspects of the neurobiology of creativity, I found no comprehensive or major work that attempted to synthesize this information or to develop a neurobiological theory of creativity. Thus, I decided to write a brief article about the neurobiology of creativity, which was published in *Neurocase* (Heilman, Nadeau, & Beversdorf, 2003). Although that article had some of the same ideas that are presented in this book, they had to be limited because articles published in journals must be brief. In addition, since submitting the article, I have been continuing to learn about the relationships between the brain and creativity. Hence, in this book I write about many topics not covered in the article.

After I finished the first draft of this book, I was sent a page-proof draft of James E. Austin's (2003) book, *Chase, Chance, and Creativity: The Lucky Art of Novelty.* In this book Austin quotes Jung, who said, "Creative man is a riddle that we might try to answer many ways, but always in vain, a truth that has not prevented modern psychology from turning now and again to the question." Although the neurobiological basis of creativity still remains a riddle to me, some prior investigators have had some ideas about the brain mechanisms that might be important for creativity. In this book I discuss some of these theories and have added some of my own. Thus, the purpose of this book is to share some of the knowledge that I have gained and to develop some testable hypotheses with the hope that this book will serve to help elicit and encourage further inquires into the neurobiology of creativity.

One of the most creative people of the 20th century, Albert Einstein, said, "Things should be made as simple as possible, but not simpler." I hope that there are people from a variety of disciplines—and not just neuroscientists, neuropsychologists, and neurologists—who might have an interest in understanding the brain mechanisms underlying creativity. Thus, I have attempted to follow Einstein's suggestion and make this book succinct and as simple as possible, but not simpler. To help people who have little background in neuroscience read and understand this book, I have included some simple diagrams. Throughout, I present some personal anecdotes. I included these because I felt they would make reading this book more enjoyable and relevant. I hope that you enjoy reading it, that you finding it stimulating, and that reading this book will encourage you to partake in creative endeavors.

I dedicate this book to Mr. Goodman, my 10th-grade geometry teacher at New Utrecht High School in Bensonhurst, Brooklyn. Until I took Mr. Goodman's geometry class, I always felt that school was drudgery and imprisonment. I was left back in the 3rd grade because I could not spell and when reading aloud I made frequent errors. In my grade school class, one of the activities to which the kids looked forward was the spelling bee, but I was such a poor speller my teacher told me not to bother standing up. All I seemed to do in school was memorize, and I never found that memorizing was fun. Worst of all was having to sit at a desk all day, look out the window, and count the hours before I could go outside and start playing stickball, Brooklyn's number one sport.

In my first year of high school, I was failing Spanish because I still could not read the words aloud exactly as they were written. I was doing poorly in English because I still could not spell. I was also taking geometry class, which everyone thought was very hard because there were all these theorems that had to be memorized. Mr. Goodman taught the geometry class to which I was assigned. This class was different from any other class I had ever taken. First, he taught us about different forms of thinking (inductive and deductive) and taught us the beginning of logic. I later learned that the Greek word *logos* has many meanings, including the study of a subject (i.e., -*ology*) and a means of reasoning. He showed us how we could use systematic thinking to solve theorems, and he tried to teach us how to solve these theorems by using knowledge and reason (logos) without having to memorize them.

One of the strongest memories I have of high school is the time Mr. Goodman asked two young women and me to go to the blackboard and solve a problem he gave us. I had known these two women since grade school. They were extremely smart, could recite poems from memory, could read Spanish flawlessly, and could spell almost any word correctly. Thus, I was certain that I would again end up looking like the class idiot. After about a minute or two I was able to calm down, and I wrote all the steps to the solution and came to a conclusion that looked correct to me. For the first time in school I had an "aha" experience. When Mr. Goodman asked us to sit, I noticed that I was the only person to complete the problem. Mr. Goodman looked at my solution, corrected a couple of spelling errors, and then said, "Very nice, Mr. Heilman. You did good." Then he told the women who had been at the blackboard not to worry because this problem and the solution was not in our book.

After this episode, I looked forward to geometry class each day and even enjoyed doing my geometry homework. I enjoyed doing the homework because I enjoyed the challenge and the feeling of discovery. I enjoyed the thinking and the addictive joy that comes with problem solving. I do not recall a lot from that geometry class that I took about 50 years ago, but I did learn that I wanted to continue my education and wanted a career where I could solve problems. In my high school yearbook, next to my name, it states, "Kenny plans to attend an out-of-town college and then enter the field of medical research." I knew back then that I was addicted to the joy of discovery, and it was Mr. Goodman who taught me about this joy.

Unfortunately, I have been so busy fulfilling this desire for discovery that I did not stay in contact with Mr. Goodman. Thus, I do not know if he is still alive or, if he is, if he will see this dedication, but I still want to say to him, "Thank you."

I am also dedicating this book to some of my former and current students, residents, and postdoctoral associates with whom I did research. If I wrote all the wonderful attributes of each of these people, there would be no room in this book to discuss creativity. Most of these people have had and are having creative careers, and observing these people succeed has brought me much joy. Their curiosity and inquisitiveness have been a source of inspiration to me, and I want to use this dedication to thank them for coming to Gainesville. Finally, I want to thank Melvin Greer M.D., and Norman Holland Ph.D., for their suggestions, support, and encouragement.

1

Definitions

When I was in public elementary school (P.S. 103), my fifth-grade teacher Ms. Carole tried to increase our Brooklyn vocabularies, which consisted primarily of four-letter words, by asking us to define words. One day she asked me to define the word *loquacious*. I remember saying to her, "I know what it means but I cannot tell you now." She, of course, said, "If you knew what the word means you would be able to give me the definition." About 35 years later I saw a retired engineering professor who was probably suffering with Alzheimer's disease. To test his naming I gave him the Boston Naming Test (Goodglass & Kaplan, 2000). The test consists of a series of 60 drawings of objects that range from common (e.g., bed) to rare (e.g., abacus). This patient scored extremely well on this test, correctly naming 59 of the 60 objects. These results suggested that this degenerative disease did not destroy the memories or representations of the word sounds that are associated with these objects. In contrast, if you put two of these pictures before him (e.g., bed and abacus) and asked him to point to one of these objects ("Point to the object in which you would sleep."), he would frequently point to the incorrect object. Although he could repeat sentences, he did not understand conversations, and when he spoke spontaneously he used well-articulated and correct English words, but his sentences had no meaning. In our clinics we see other patients who, unlike this man, cannot name many of these pictures, but in a roundabout manner (circumlocution) they can describe these objects and understand conversations. Observing these two different types of patients led me to believe that the brain, like a dictionary, contains several independent stores of word knowledge. When you look up a word in a dictionary, there is a phonological description of how the word sounds. Following this, there is an explanation of the word's meaning. There is a place in the left hemisphere of the brain that stores memories of how words sound. This store is called the phonological lexicon. Although this phonological lexicon stores word-sound knowledge, it does not store the meaning of these words. There is, however, another place in the left hemisphere that stores meanings, a conceptual-semantic field, but does not contain information about the phonological composition of words. Had I known in fifth grade what I know now, I would have told Ms. Carole that I have a lexical representation of the word and I know it is a good English word, but I do not have a semantic representation of this word. In the fifth grade I confused familiarity with understanding. She was correct: I did not know what the word *loquacious* meant.

In this book I write about creativity, but until I started to read more about this construct I am not sure I fully understood what this term meant. Behavioral scientists and laymen often use psychological terms such as *attention, emotion,* and *creativity.* Most people feel that they know what these words mean, but these terms are often difficult to define. Many books and articles have been written about creativity, but most of them never offer a definition. Before we discuss the neurological basis of creativity, I will attempt to define this word. *Webster's Dictionary* (Soukhanov & Ellis, 1988) defines *creative* as having the ability to create. It defines *create* as "to bring into being . . . or to produce." Pregnant women bring children into being, and people produce products in factories, but neither of these acts is what we mean when we discuss creativity. A second definition of *create* is "to produce through artistic effort." This definition appears accurate, but scientists, inventors, business people, and others who are not artists can also be creative. Another definition of *creative* is "marked by originality." Unfortunately, I do not believe any of these definitions fully capture what we mean by this term that we use to describe the work done by many of our well-known scientists, authors, composers, and artists. It is true that creative people often produce original works, but there are many original paintings, sculptures, novels, poems, scientific theories, and inventions that are original but not very creative.

A person who is very creative, and well recognized for his or her creativity, is sometimes called a genius. The term *genius,* however, has many definitions. Samuel Johnson, the founder of the first English dictionary, wrote that "the true Genius is a mind of large general powers" (Simonton, 1999). People who score more than 130 or 140 on an intelligence or IQ test are sometimes called geniuses. Lewis Terman from Stanford University performed one of the most famous studies of high intelligence. Terman (1954) collected a group of children who scored very high on IQ tests and identified these children as geniuses. These highly intelligent children were followed as they matured to adults. Most of them turned out to be very successful, but this group did not have many people who were noted to be extremely creative. One of the children who was tested by Terman, but not included in this group because his IQ was lower than the criteria set by Terman, was William Shockley. Shockley later won the Nobel Prize in physics because of his invention of the transistor. Thus, it appears that many people who have very high IQs do extremely well in school and may be successful in life, but many of these people with high IQs are not very creative, and there are many extremely creative people who do not have extremely high IQs.

In chapter 2 I further discuss the relationship between intelligence and creativity. As I discuss in chapter 3, many people who have been considered to be geniuses have learning disabilities. It is doubtful that these people with verbal or math learning disabilities would have scored higher than 140 in IQ testing. Two of perhaps the most creative scientists in the modern era, Einstein and Darwin, demonstrate the relationship between learning disability and creativity. Einstein had trouble with learning to read (developmental dyslexia) and in doing arithmetic (developmental dyscalculia). In his autobiography Darwin wrote that, compared with his younger sister, he was very slow to learn, and his teachers considered him as a very ordinary boy who was below the common standard in intellect. Children with developmental language disorders including dyslexia often have problems learning foreign languages. Like Einstein, Darwin might have had a developmental language disorder because he wrote in his autobiography that he was incapable of mastering any language. In addition, he states that even as an adult he was not quick witted. When reading, he had trouble fully understanding the meaning of the text and, to understand these works fully, he had to read books repeatedly. There is a society called Mensa that boasts that to be a member one must be a genius with an IQ higher than 130. It is doubtful that people such as Einstein, Darwin, and Shockley would have applied for membership, but if they had, and their membership had been based on their IQs, they might have not been admitted.

Several dictionaries, such as *Webster's,* define *genius* as "the possessor of an inclination or talent." Most intelligence tests assess a variety of skills. For example, the Wechsler Adult Intelligence Scale (Wechsler, 1981) assesses domains such as language (e.g., definitions), visual-spatial skills (e.g., block design), and working memory (digit-span and digit-symbol tests). There are high-functioning autistic people (savants) who have much better working memories than do normal people but have low IQs because they perform poorly on other parts of this test. There are children with developmental language learning disorders who often perform much better on the visual-spatial tests than they do on the verbal tests. To be creative, a person has to have skills and knowledge in the domain in which she or he is creative, but in other domains his or her skills may be average or below average. Most important, the possession of special skills or talents does not ensure that a person will use these skills in a creative manner.

Francis Galton (1869/1978) in his classic book *Hereditary Genius* defined *genius* as eminence or enduring reputation. In his book *Origins of Genius* (1999), Dean Simonton supported this definition, but noted that although eminence is the criteria, this eminence should be associated with creativity rather than leadership. The reason he excluded leadership is not clear, because many leaders have been very creative. Simonton also likes this definition because it avoids the problem of the "so-called unrecognized genius." And according to Simonton (1999), "A scientific article that no one cites or a musical composition that no one performs cannot qualify as a creative product." Howard Gardner, who has a strong interest in creativity, has written several books that deal with this subject. In one of his more recent books, *Intelligence Reframed,* Gardner (1999) appeared to agree with the position of Mihaly Csikszentmihalyi (1996), who suggested that creativity does not emanate from the mind or brain of an individual but rather depends on communal judgment. Although from a historical perspective he might be correct that it is society that decides who is declared a creative genius, creativity as defined here is the product of an individual's brain and not the judgment of society. Recognition or eminence does not directly depend on the level of creativity. During their lives many artists who are now considered geniuses, such as Van Gogh, were not recognized or eminent. Does that mean that only after their death they became geniuses but were not geniuses when they lived? What would happen if Van Gogh were never discovered or if all his paintings were destroyed? Would he be any less of a genius? Thus, based on the previous discussion, there are no clear criteria for a creative genius. In addition, many creative acts are performed by people who never achieve eminence, and although some might consider many of these acts minor, it is important to learn about and understand the brain mechanisms that allow creative acts, large or small, because the difference between major innovations or what Thomas Kuhn (1996) called paradigmatic shifts and minor creative acts may be a matter of degree rather than type.

My goal in writing this book was to learn about the brain mechanisms that might account for creativity. Eminence is something that society bestows on someone who has been creative, and the purpose of this book is not to learn how society makes these decisions. In addition, almost every human is capable of creative acts. Although some are recognized by large populations, others are recognized only by some family members or friends and some are recognized by no one, not even the person who performed the creative act. Although few people would call these latter examples of creative people geniuses, it is my purpose to discuss the brain mechanisms that might account for creative behavior, both great and minuscule. It is, however, well-known that some people perform acts that are more creative and of higher quality than the creative acts of other people, and, thus, I also discuss the differences between people.

As I briefly mentioned, many psychologists have noted that a person's full-score IQ does not entirely predict his or her creativity (also see chapter 2) and several psychologists searched for another psychometric method of predicting creativity. Guilford (1967), who introduced the psychometric approach to predicting creativity, thought that divergent thinking was a critical element in creative thinking, thus he developed Alternative Uses Test, in which participants devise alternative uses of common objects, such as a brick. Other tests of divergent thinking include (a) the titles task, in which participants are asked to provide titles for a plot; (b) the consequences test, in which participants are scored by the number of consequences and their novelty; (c) projective tests, such as the Rorschach Inkblot Test and the Thematic Apperception Test, in which the number of original responses are counted; (d) anagram tests, in which participants are presented with words whose letters are scrambled and must find the word as quickly as possible; and (e) the word rearrangement test, in which participants are provided with 50 words and they have to use as many of these words as possible to tell a story. On the basis of Guilford's work, E. Paul Torrance (1974) developed a test battery called the Torrance Test of Creative Thinking. In addition to the Alternative Uses Test of Guilford, one of the subtests in Torrance's test asks how a product can be improved. Another subtest shows the participants a scene and the participants write out questions that they would like to ask about this scene. These tests are scored by originality (the rarity of the responses), fluency (the number of relevant responses), flexibility (the variety of responses), and elaboration.

Torrance (1988) conducted validity tests by giving this test to children in high school and then following the participants until they were adults (i.e., 12 years after the tests had been given). He then assessed the quality and quantity of their creative achievement, using blinded judges as raters. Torrance found that these test scores significantly correlated with measures of creativity and that these creativity tests were much more predictive than were IQ scores. Critics of this psychometric approach note that a robust discriminative and predictive validity has not been clearly demonstrated (see Plucker & Renzulli, 1999, for a review and for additional references). Although there are many suggestions as to why this test might not have robust predictive validity (e.g., creativity is domain specific), the Torrance test came under heavy criticism because the skills that it is measuring are not considered to assess the critical dimensions of creativity (Amabile, 1983) and it does not assess some of the processes that we define as creativity in this chapter. Creativity, as defined in this book, is a combination of divergent and convergent thinking. When presented with data that is explained by a series of ad hoc theories (e.g., the Ptolemaic planetary system) the creative thinker (e.g., Copernicus) had to diverge from this theory, develop a new theory, and then provide the converging evidence to support this theory (e.g., the solar system theory of Copernicus and Galileo).

To gain an understanding of nature, one has to be creative, but *understanding* and *creativity* are not synonymous. Perhaps one's means of finding a definition of creativity is to make a list of famous creative people whose work led to a greater understanding of nature and then learn how his or her work is similar. This list could include people such as Copernicus, Galileo, Newton, and Einstein. All these people were scientists. Some people would define science as nothing more than the collection of facts; after all, that is what many of us did in our science classes. Although some people working in scientific endeavors do little more than collect facts, the creative scientist's analysis of facts allows him or her to gain an understanding of nature and to develop testable predictions. Thales of Miletus (ca. 580 BCE) was perhaps the first to suggest that there must be unity behind what appears to be plurality, and the creative scientist is one who discovers unity in the variety of nature.

There are many reasons why creativity is important to society. People have always had the desire to control nature. Humans desire to control nature so that we can meet our needs (food and water), prolong our life and the lives of people for whom we care, control our fears, and reduce pain and suffering. In the medieval era, magicians searched for a spell that they could cast over nature to control its power. In the absence of control, religious zealots ask the Creator to change nature according to their requests. History has taught us, however, as noted by Jacob Bronowski (1972), that "man masters nature not by force but by understanding."

In the second half of the 20th century, the advance in medicine that overall might have influenced our health the most was the discovery of antibiotics. Paul Ehrlich, who received the 1908 Nobel Prize in physiology or medicine, introduced the basic concepts of this work. Ehrlich suggested that medical investigators search for "magic bullets," or synthetic compounds, that would kill the infectious agents that cause diseases without causing serious damage to the person who has the disease. Ehrlich pioneered the systematic study of the structure of synthetic drugs and their biological effects. He introduced the first successful treatment of syphilis when he introduced arsenic treatment (arsenic 606 or salvarsan). Ehrlich's theories, however, really came to fruition with the work of Alexander Fleming, who discovered the first antibiotic, penicillin. Chemotherapeutic agents that are used to treat cancer use the same principles, but many of these agents cause serious damage to the people who are treated with them and have been, in most conditions, only a modest success.

In addition, chemotherapeutic agents and antibiotics do not cure degenerative diseases, and much of the human suffering that we now see in our clinic is related to these degenerative diseases. In the future, many diseases, such as cancer and degenerative diseases, will probably have genetic treatments, and thus, in the next several decades, one of the sciences that may influence our lives the most is genetics. Genetic research started with the work of Gregor Mendel. During the 19th century many monks made copious records of natural events and stored this information in their notebooks and ledgers. Most of these records were never read by anyone other than the monks who collected these data. Because most of these data did not lead to a better understanding of nature, they had little or no influence on science. One of these monks collecting data, however, was Gregor (Johann) Mendel. Mendel had grown up on his father's farm where he worked in the orchards. After being ordained he attended the University of Vienna and wanted to be a high school teacher. He took the teacher's certification examination several times but repeatedly failed, getting his lowest mark in biology. Mendel lived in a monastery that had a small garden, where he planted peas. Mendel observed that some peas looked different from other peas. Some were tall and others short. Some had wrinkled seeds and other had rounded, smooth seeds. Peas, like people, reproduce by a sexual union when a sperm fertilizes an egg cell and a seed is formed. Mendel collected facts by breeding and crossbreeding these peas because he wanted to learn if he could predict the height and seed type based on how the parents looked (phenotype). Because he could eventually predict a pea's phenotype based on its parents, he suggested that phenotypic traits are controlled by heredity and that heredity was lawful. He thought that each pea seed receives two controlling elements for each trait. These elements are now called genes. One of the elements comes from the sperm and the other the egg. If both of these genes carry the same characteristic (e.g., tall) the pea will be tall. If each parent provides the seed with two different genes (e.g., one tall and the other short), then one of these two will determine the phenotype. This gene is called the dominant gene. The one that does not determine the phenotype is called the recessive gene. If one looks at a tall plant, one cannot know if this plant has two tall genes (homozygote) or one tall gene and one short gene (heterozygote). If a heterozygote plant that has one tall gene and one short gene gives off an egg or sperm, this egg or sperm can have either a short or a tall gene. If this plant gives off a tall gene, its offspring will be tall, but if it gives off a short gene, the offspring can be either tall or short, depending on the genotype of the other parent.

We can see from this example that Mendel was able to see unity in the variety of nature. He made observations, formed hypotheses, and then started to perform experiments based on these hypotheses. Just as Mendel's peas need fertile soil to grow, creativity often requires a fostering environment. Fortunately, the monastery where Mendel performed his research contained a rich library on horticulture, farming, and botany. He also had many colleagues who were interested in his findings and encouraged him. After his pioneering discoveries, Mendel was elected to be the abbot of his monastery, and this concluded his scientific productivity.

Scientists like Mendel develop scientific theories to help explain the means by which phenomena that appear to be random are actually orderly and lawful. In his book, *The Structure of Scientific Revolutions,* Kuhn (1996) stated, "Discovery commences with the awareness of an anomaly, i.e., with the recognition that nature has somehow violated the paradigm-induced expectations that govern normal science." Thus, the observation of an anomaly by a scientist suggests that the scientific theory that attempted to explain the order in a system is inadequate and a new theory that accounts for this anomaly must be devised. The development of an entirely new theory based on the awareness of anomalies would be what Kuhn called a "paradigmatic shift."

Although this discussion, so far, has primarily addressed scientific creativity, scientists are not the only creative people. Painters such as Van Gogh, Picasso, and Rembrandt; composers such as Beethoven, Mozart, and Tchaikovsky; writers such as Vonnegut, Fitzgerald, and Steinbeck are also creative. Coleridge, as quoted by Bronowski (1972), provided an explanation of artistic creativity that is similar to the one discussed about scientific creativity: Artistic beauty is "a unity in variety."

When I first read this definition of artistic creativity I had some trouble understanding what this meant, but then I recalled listening to a conversation between fine artists when I was sophomore in college. I was a chemistry major who wanted to be a theoretical chemist. I met a wonderful artist, Aviva, whose world and thinking was very different from mine. During one college break we met some of her artist friends in a coffeehouse in Greenwich Village. Between listening to beat poets, who often sounded like Lawrence Ferlinghetti reciting his *A Coney Island of the Mind,* these painters got into a discussion about the most difficult part of painting. Although I expected them to discuss technical problems, they seemed to agree that the most difficult part of painting is knowing when a painting is completed. I was naive about oil painting, and I thought, *Why is this difficult? When you have covered the entire canvas you have completed the painting.* Luckily, I listened to them speak rather than offering my opinion because in their conversation they started to speak about "closure."

I was reluctant to ask any questions during these artists' conversation, but later that evening, while taking the F train to Aviva's home in Queens, I asked her what she and the others meant by closure. She asked me what I thought it meant, and I told her that initially I thought a painting was complete when the entire canvas was covered. Before I could tell her that I understood this naive concept was incorrect, she asked, "Is a novel complete when the author runs out of pages? No, the novel is complete when the story has been told. When people use oils they often paint over areas they previously painted. Closure is when the painting is complete." I told her that her explanation was circular. She said, "Tomorrow let's go to the Met. I will show you."

The next day we went to the Metropolitan Museum of Art, and fortunately the Met was having an exhibit of the impressionists. One of the first paintings she showed me was Renoir's *The Bathers.* She showed me that although each individual figure in the painting was complete, together the women formed an oval shape that both complemented each woman's shape and tied all their figures together. She also showed me how different patches of color complemented each other. She then asked me if I thought the painting would have been better had Renoir painted more of the scenery around these women. I shook my head from side to side. She asked, "If he added more

women or left out one of the women, would the painting be better?"
Again I shook my head and said "No." She then said, "See, the picture
has closure." In retrospect I think she was trying to illustrate what Coleridge so succinctly stated, that artistic beauty is "a unity in variety."

Renoir's and the other impressionists' paintings we saw that day
were beautiful, and although each had its different style, all had unity
in variety, or what she termed *closure.*

After we left the impressionists exhibit, Aviva took me to a room
that had modern paintings. Although I had no problems seeing the
beauty expressed by the impressionists, I did have some trouble
understanding why people thought that these paintings were beautiful.
She told me that she thought I did not think these paintings were
beautiful because they were not representational. She explained that
modern art freed the artist from the representational constraints. Artists did not have to paint someone or something but could be free to
use forms and colors as they wished and still achieve closure. I, like
many other people, still have trouble seeing the beauty in nonrepre-
sentational art. I think Bronowski (1972) attempted to address this
issue when he wrote,

> How slipshod . . . is the notion that either art or science sets out
> to copy nature. . . . Science like art is not a copy of nature but a
> recreation of her. We remake nature by the act of discovery. . . .
> And the great poem and the deep theorem are new to every
> reader and yet are his own experience because he himself re-cre-
> ates them. They are the marks of unity in variety; and the instant
> when the mind seizes this for itself, in art or in science, the heart
> misses a beat.

Although most great artists have never studied the brain and how it
functions, they appear to have implicit knowledge about how the brain
functions and they use this knowledge when painting, allowing the
people who view their art to obtain closure. For example, Banich,
Heller, and Levy (1989) noticed that most paintings are right-left
asymmetrical. These investigators wanted to learn if the right-left
position of the objects in the painting made a difference in how people
would judge the quality of the painting. They photographed many
paintings by respected artists. These painting, however, were not well-
known to the general population. They made slides from these photographs and showed them to people who had never seen these paintings
before the study. They showed one half of the participants a slide of
each painting as portrayed by the artist and the other half of the participants saw a mirror image of each painting, so the right-left was

reversed and the objects on the left in the actual painting were now on the right and vice versa. They asked the participants to judge how well they liked each painting they saw on the screen. Banich's group found that, in general, most people liked the painting more when it was shown as it had been painted by the artist than when viewed right-left reversed. When the investigators analyzed how the mirror-image slides of the paintings were different from the slides that depicted the painting as painted by the artist, they noticed that when there were multiple objects in a painting, the major object would usually be on the right side of the canvas. When looking at a painting, like reading a sentence, most people scan from left to right. Some people have thought that we probably scan in a left-to-right direction because that is the way we are taught to read and write, When reading or writing Semitic languages such as Hebrew or Arabic, however, people read from right to left, but when these people scan their environment or perform acts other than reading and writing, they scan left to right just like people who read and write European languages. When scanning paintings in the natural left-to-right direction, a viewer who sees the major or dominant object of the painting before seeing what led up to the dominant object might feel that not seeing these antecedents detracts from their preparatory value. One can liken it to having fore-play after the climax. If a climax comes too early in a book, sym-phony, or painting, these works of art can lose their closure and the aesthetic sense of fulfillment that one gains from having everything come together.

Margaret Livingstone (2002), who is a neuroscientist at Harvard and performs vision research, wrote a wonderful book called *Vision and Art*. In the book she gives other examples of artistic creativity. For example, on page 38 of the book there is a copy of Monet's painting titled *Impression Sunrise*. In this painting the setting sun appears to shimmer when it reflects off the water. While the sun reflecting off the water is painted orange, the water is painted a greenish blue. The sun and the water are different colors, but the sun appears to shimmer because the sun and the water have the same amount of luminance (the amount of light that is reflected back to the eye). To demonstrate that the reflectance of the sun on the water and the water itself are of equal luminance, Livingstone took a black-and-white photograph of this painting. Black-and-white photos show only differences in lumi-nance, and in this photograph she demonstrated that the sun is almost not visible in the reflection off the water. White reflects much more light than gray, and gray reflects more light than black. Livingstone noted that it is primarily change in luminance (and not color) that allows us to detect objects, see their shapes, and know their location.

She also noted that the neural system that detects color is located in a different part of the brain from the part that detects luminance. In addition, the parts of the brain that determine locations are in the dorsal portions of the occipital and parietal lobes (see Figure 1.1), and the parts that process color are in the more ventral portions of the occipital lobes. The portions of the brain that determine location derive most of their information from changes in luminance, not color. Thus, because the sun is of equal luminance, this part of the brain has difficulty determining the sun's location, and so the sun appears to shimmer on the water.

Some of the impressionists must have also known (most likely intuitively) that luminance and color were independent, thus they could produce shadowing and depth by increasing and decreasing luminance independent of color. This knowledge allows the artist to represent an image and even give it depth without having to use the object's actual colors. With this freedom they could select a color based on aesthetic values, while maintaining the representational qualities of the painting.

Livingstone gave another example of the creativity of great artists when she wrote about Leonardo da Vinci's *Mona Lisa*. Art historians have repeatedly commented about Mona Lisa's facial expression, which appears to change, making her appear as if she is alive. In her book, Livingstone quoted E. H. Gombrich, who stated in his book, *The Story of Art,*

> What strikes us first is the amazing degree to which Lisa looks alive. . . . Like a living being, she seems to change before our eyes. . . . Sometimes she seems to mock at us, and then again we seem to catch something like sadness in her smile. All this sounds rather mysterious, and so it is; that is so often the effect of a great work of art.

Livingstone noticed that when she focused on Mona Lisa's mouth she seemed to have a serious expression, but when she focused on another part of the picture, that smile that so many people have written about became apparent.

The eye's best acuity is when images fall in the center of the retina in a region called the fovea. When images fall on parts of the retina that are not part of the fovea; there is a loss of acuity; the farther away from the fovea these images land on the retina, the poorer the acuity. Thus, when one looks directly at Mona Lisa's mouth, one can see the fine details of her lips, but when one looks at a different part of the painting, one cannot see the fine details of her lips and, instead of

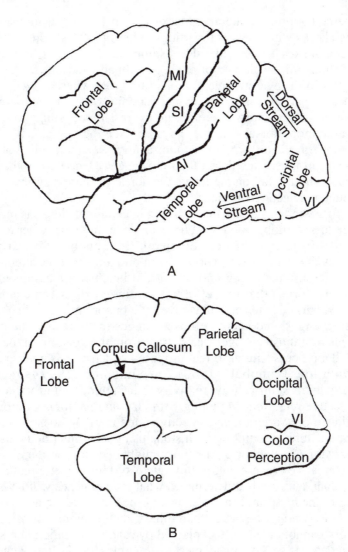

Figure 1.1. Diagram demonstrating the lateral view of the brain. (A) demonstrates that the parts of the brain that determine spatial location are located in the dorsal (top) portions of the occipital and parietal lobes (dorsal stream) and the parts that determine identity are in the ventral portions of the temporal and occipital lobes (ventral stream). (B) demonstrates that the parts of the brain that process color are in the ventral medial portion of the occipital lobes. MI = primary motor cortex; SI = primary somatosensory cortex; AI = primary auditory cortex; and VI = primary visual cortex.

seeing the precise lateral extent of her lips, one fuses the shadow of her cheeks with the lateral portions of her lips. This increase of lateral extent makes her look like she is smiling.

Studies in our laboratories (see Heilman, Nadeau, & Beversdorf, 2003, for a review) have demonstrated that whereas recognizing a specific person is mediated by the ventral ("what") temporal-occipital system, recognizing an emotional expression depends more heavily on the more dorsal ("where") system (see Figure 1.1). When using peripheral vision, which has poor acuity, we can localize objects in the environment and detect their movement. Hence, when these facial images do not fall on the fovea, the dorsal ("where") system might be better at detecting emotions.

Artists often suggest that working in certain mediums is more diffi-cult than working in others. For example, it might be easier to sculpt a model from clay than chisel a work from marble. Similarly, some artists think it is easier working with oil paints than watercolors. The reason clay modeling and oils might be easier than chiseling and watercolors is that in the former mediums artists can change their work, but the latter mediums give little opportunity for change. Mak-ing changes, and keeping those changes that enhance the goal and removing those changes that detract from the goal, might be consid-ered a process similar to that proposed by Charles Darwin to explain evolution. Campbell (1960) and Simonton (1999) suggested a Darwinian approach to creativity that includes blind variation and selective retention. Modeling with clay and painting with oil paints allow more variation and selective retention than does painting with watercolors or sculpting with stone using a hammer and chisel. This Darwinian metaphor of creativity might account for some aspects of the creative process, but in biological systems genetic mutations are random, and survival determines what mutant genes will be transmit-ted to the offspring. In the creative process, however, although some solutions might be better than others, the development of a creative work cannot be entirely explained by random variation and selective retention. If so, how many pieces of marble would Michelangelo have to sculpt before he decided to keep his masterpiece, *David*? This the-ory also does not explain why the same cognitive systems that allow selective retention cannot also influence the boundaries of variation.

The major problem with the Darwinian postulate of creativity as espoused by Campbell (1960) and Simonton (1999), however, is that in biological evolution it is survival that retains and propagates the best genetic programs, but in creative endeavors it is not entirely clear what survival means. Certainly, with some creative inventions, pragmatic utility (designing a better screwdriver) ensures survival, and, because beauty enriches the beholders' quality of life, we ensure the survival of great works of art. But these pragmatic and aesthetic survival mechanisms cannot explain why theories such as those of Copernicus, which had no pragmatic value for hundreds of years, survived.

In his book, *Consilience,* Edward O. Wilson (1999) wrote about what he called the "Ionian Enchantment." According to Wilson, this term means "a belief in the unity of sciences—a conviction, far deeper than a mere proposition, that the world is orderly and can be explained by a small number of natural laws." Wilson called this the Ionian Enchantment because the roots of this concept go back to the 6th century BCE and are attributed to Thales of Miletus (one of the Aegean cities in western Asia Minor that were part of the Ionian Confederation). Many of the greatest physicists, such as Einstein, believed not only that the universe is orderly and lawful ("G-D doesn't play dice") but also that what appears to be diverse phenomena often share the same physical laws. Although the laws of electromagnetism, radiation, and gravity appear specific for each force, Einstein and others recognized that there are also similarities (e.g., the force decreases as a function of distance) and they attempted to develop a unified field theory "to find the thread that links." Artistic creativity and scientific creativity require different skills and talents, but there are also some elements that both forms of creativity share. In this book I write about how creativity in different domains might be mediated by different brain mechanisms, but I also attempt to develop consilience by discussing the brain mechanisms shared by all creative acts.

Helmholtz (1896) and Wallas (1926) suggested that creativity has four components: preparation, incubation, illumination, and verification. In the first stage, preparation, a creative person acquires the skills and knowledge that allow that person to develop creative works. For example, Einstein developed superb skills in physics and math before he made his great discoveries, and Picasso learned to draw forms and mix colors before he painted his masterpieces. Eysenck (1995) in his book, *Genius*, noted that before you can solve a problem you need to recognize a problem, and he believes there is a stage of problem finding. He noted that to find a problem a person must have extensive knowledge in the field where the person wants to find a problem. Darwin's son, when describing his father, noted that he had a quality of mind that appeared to be very important in the making of scientific discoveries. Charles Darwin thought that exceptions were important, and he never let exceptions pass unnoticed. Eysenck would have called this behavior "problem finding." I have often told my research fellows that you have to know almost everything there is to know in a domain before you know the questions that must be asked.

Having extensive knowledge in a domain also allows investigators to find anomalies, and anomalies allow a person to recognize that prior investigators have not entirely found the thread that unites. Problem finding, however, is still part of the preparation stage.

One of the best examples of Pasteur's dictum that chance favors the prepared mind (*"Dans les champs de l'observation, le hazard ne favorise que les esprits preparés."*), is the story of Alexander Fleming. One of the greatest advances in medicine in the 20th century was the discovery of antibiotics. Although some believe this discovery was made entirely by accident, it was a discovery made by a prepared mind. Alexander Fleming, a Scottish physician, was interested in the clinical aspects of infectious diseases and antiseptics and was actually performing bacteriological research. Fleming was growing the virulent bacteria staphylococci in his laboratory. These bacteria were being grown in little, clear, glass plates called petri dishes. Fleming was not a meticulous person. He left his laboratory for a few days and did not properly store these cultures. He also left his laboratory window open, and the petri dishes with staphylococci remained uncovered. When he returned to his laboratory he noticed that a mold had been blown in through the window and landed in a petri dish with the staphylococci. In those areas where the mold landed the bacteria were dead. The mold was penicillium, and this phenomenon led to the discovery of antibiotics. This finding, to use Kuhn's term, was an anomaly, but it was the "prepared mind" of Fleming's that recognized the importance of this phenomenon.

Knowledge alone might not be adequate for creativity. There are many brilliant people with large stores of knowledge in a domain who never develop a creative work. It could be argued that these people might have not made great discoveries because they were not in a position to see critical accidents of nature. Unexplained and anomalous phenomena, however, are abundant in all domains, and these "whispers of nature" are all around us, but the prepared mind needs more than knowledge to hear these whispers.

Creativity—the ability to understand, develop, and express in a systematic fashion novel orderly relationships—requires that the brain manipulate stored knowledge. Wallas (1926) called the process in which people subconsciously manipulate knowledge "incubation." The solving of a problem Wallas called "illumination." Wallas's terms of *incubation* and *illumination* have received much criticism. For example, Weisberg (1986) suggested that creativity does not require great leaps (e.g., illumination) and that the processes that lead to many great discoveries might not be subconscious incubation, but rather a series of conscious steps. Even according to Wallas, illumination, rather than being an independent factor, appears to be the culmination of the incubation process. Thus, instead of discussing incubation and illumination as independent processes, we will call the development and understanding of new principles "creative innovation." Creative innovation is based on either the conscious or the unconscious manipulation of knowledge. This incubation process can lead to the development of a hypothesis that might be a great leap, which Kuhn called a "paradigmatic shift," or a small leap, which Kuhn called "normal science." A hypothesis that is the product of creative innovation can be tested by either an accident of nature or a devised experiment that is part of the verification process. It is possible that Fleming discovered that the penicillium mold killed the staphylococci because he had already developed the hypothesis that in nature there are natural agents that can kill bacteria.

In contrast to Helmholtz (1896) and Wallas (1926), Sternberg and O'Hara (1999) suggested that creativity requires a confluence of several distinct resources: intellectual abilities and knowledge in the domain in which one is creative (which Wallas includes in the preparation stage), as well as thinking styles, motivation, and environment. The next chapter contains a discussion of the preparation stage, which is heavily dependent on intelligence and acquired knowledge.

2

Intelligence

There are many definitions of *intelligence*. Some psychologists, who do not like the construct, jokingly define *intelligence* as the score one obtains on a test of intelligence (IQ test). Others define *intelligence* as the ability to do well in school. But to most psychologists, and as defined in *Webster's Dictionary* (Soukhanov & Ellis, 1988), intelligence is the measure of a person's ability to acquire and apply knowledge. Sternberg and O'Hara (1999) suggested several possible relationships between intelligence and creativity: (a) they are the same; (b) one is a subset of another, for example, creativity is a subset of intelligence; (c) they are unrelated; and (d) they are overlapping but independent sets. If intelligence is the measure of a person's cognitive ability to adapt, creativity is the gift that might allow one to better adapt; this would be true of certain forms of creativity (e.g., medical science), and not true of other forms (e.g., painting).

The founder of intelligence tests, Alfred Binet, must have initially thought that creativity and intelligence were the same or closely overlapping because in the first intelligence test he devised in 1896, he used inkblots to explore the imagination of children. Later, according to Sternberg and O'Hara (1999), he discontinued this inkblot test because he was unable to develop a means of scoring it.

Guilford and Christensen (1973), one of the first to study and help generate psychologists' interest in creativity, said that creativity was a subset of intelligence. Guilford attempted to develop psychometric tests that could measure creativity. These tests are similar to those developed by Torrance (1974). Most of these tests assess individuals' ability to develop novel uses of common objects. For example, as mentioned previously, participants would be asked to name in a fixed time interval the different ways in which they might be able to use a brick. Guilford found that students with a low IQ consistently performed poorly on these tests, but for those students with a high IQ, performance on creativity tests did not highly correlate with their performance on IQ tests. After reviewing the relationship between intelligence and creativity, Torrance (1975) suggested that IQ and creativity are only moderately related.

Another means of studying the relationship between creativity and intelligence is to study creative peoples' intelligence. Barron and Harrington (1981) studied architects and found a weak relationship between the creativity of these architects and their IQs. They concluded that for those people with an IQ of about 120 or higher, the IQ does not predict creativity as much as it does if the IQ is below 120. These observations suggest that there might be an IQ threshold: A person's IQ needs to be higher than this threshold to have sufficient intelligence to learn enough about the domain of his or her creativity and to acquire the skills needed to be creative in that domain. Thus, intelligence is a necessary but not sufficient component of creativity.

Other investigators also have studied populations of known creative people and attempted to learn if there is a strong correlation between their estimated eminence as creators and their intelligence. Simonton (1994) and other investigators, such as Herr, Moore, and Hasen (1965), also found that the correlation between intelligence and creativity is weak. This weak correlation, however, might be related to the test that was used to measure intelligence.

Cattell (1963) posited that there are two types of intelligence, which he termed "crystallized" and "fluid." Whereas crystallized intelligence is primarily declarative memories, such as knowing that Albany is the capital of New York, or lexical-semantic knowledge, such as knowing what the word *impale* means, fluid intelligence is the ability to solve problems. Most intelligence tests, such as the Wechsler Adult Intelligence Scale (Wechsler, 1981), test both crystallized (e.g., vocabulary definitions) and fluid intelligence (e.g., similarities such as "How are a fly and tree similar?"). Cattell thought that although crystallized knowledge is important in creativity, it is fluid intelligence that determines creativity. Although fluid intelligence may be the best predictor of creativity, I know of no formal studies of this relationship. There may different domains of fluid intelligence, such as solving mathematical, rhyming, or imagery problems. In addition, there has been little written about the brain mechanisms of fluid intelligence and cognitive flexibility.

The major purpose of this book is to discuss the brain mechanism that might be important for creativity, and because intelligence appears to be a necessary component, I want to mention some of the brain mechanisms that might be important for intelligence. Unfortunately, the brain mechanisms that account for intelligence are not well understood. According to Donald Hebb (1949) the critical element in learning is the ability to change the strength of the connections between neurons. A corollary of this hypothesis might be that the more neurons with which a person is endowed, the greater the ability to learn. Some intelligence tests were primarily developed to predict how well a student would perform in school, and a student's performance in school is heavily dependent on the ability to learn. Thus, a highly intelligent person might have more neurons than someone who is less intelligent, and this difference could be reflected in the size of their brains. Partial support for this hypothesis came from the work of Rosenzweig and his coworkers (Rosenzweig, 1972; Rosenzweig & Bennett, 1996), who found that rodents who were put in an enriched environment at a young age and who subsequently could learn better than the animals not exposed to an enriched environment (controls) had brains that weighed more than the brains of the control animals and even had larger heads. Studies of humans reveal that diseases that reduce the number of neurons are associated with a loss of intelligence and that people who have extremely small heads often have below normal intelligence. Measuring head size to estimate intelligence would save society a lot of money. Except for the extremes (e.g., microcephaly), however, there is only a weak relationship or no significant relationship between IQ and the size of the head or brain (Tramo et al., 1998).

Although there is no simple relationship between head size or brain size and IQ, Rosenzweig (1972) found in his classic enrichment studies that the animals raised in enriched environments were more intelligent. On postmortem examination, they found that when these experimental animals, which were raised in an enriched environment, were compared with control animals, the experimental animals had an increase in the thickness of their cerebral cortex. This increased thickness might reflect an increase in the number of synaptic contacts. On microscopic examination, he found that the number of dendritic spines (see Figure 2.1) was also greater in the experimental animals,

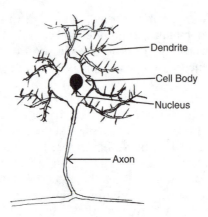

Figure 2.1. Diagram of a neuron, demonstrating cell body, axon, and dendrites.

thereby providing support for the connectivity postulate of intelligence. This increase in neuronal connectivity could increase the potential for the development of the neuronal networks that are important for learning and the storage of knowledge.

Charles Spearman (1905), one of the founders of the psychometric approach to intelligence, noted that, independent of the cognitive tests that he and other investigators used to measure intelligence, performance on that one test strongly correlated with performance on other cognitive tests that measure mental ability in different domains. On the basis of this predictability, Spearman posited that in addition to specific abilities that are needed to perform on test (s factor) domains, there is a general intellectual ability that he called the g factor. Concordance studies of twins and siblings has revealed that monozygotic twins reared apart have IQs that correlate more closely than siblings reared together. This positive concord suggests that there may be a biological factor or factors that determine general intelligence other than environmental exposure.

Carly, Golding, and Hall (1995) reviewed research of the biological factors that might account for differences in human intelligence and noted that the results of event-related potential (ERP) studies suggest that people with high IQ test scores show faster responses in some test conditions and might have less variability in their ERPs. This ERP data would suggest that high intelligence is related to faster neural conduction speed. Carly et al. also noted that functional imaging studies suggest that people with higher IQs have lower cerebral metabolic rates during mentally active conditions. This finding suggests that brighter people have more efficient brains. Carly et al., however, concluded that despite some well-replicated findings in the search for the biological basis of human intelligence, there is a dearth of explanatory accounts to link differences in cognitive performance with variance in brain mechanisms. Although the biological basis of general intelligence, or the *g* factor, has not been determined, there are some candidates.

Central nervous system proteins called nerve growth factors could influence the degree of neuronal connectivity, and the degree of connectivity might be a possible determinant of intelligence. For example, in a study of the effects of environmental enrichment on levels of brain nerve growth factor, its receptors, and their relationships to cognitive function, Pham and coworkers (1999) found that animals placed in the enriched condition had significantly higher levels of nerve growth factor when compared with the control animals housed in unenriched environments. Thus, it could be posited that one of the biological controls of the *g* factor is nerve growth factor. The brain levels of these growth factors are probably influenced both genetically and environmentally. To my knowledge, however, no one has demonstrated that the differences in human intelligence are related to the size or number of synaptic contacts, or differences in nerve growth factors, because the methods to study these variables are still not fully developed.

Recently Duncan and associates (2000) attempted to determine the neural basis for "general intelligence," or Spearman's *g*, using positron-emission tomography (PET). These investigators physiologically imaged participants' brains while they were performing spatial, verbal, and perceptuo-motor tasks that have high *g* involvement and also had participants perform other matched control tasks that have low *g* involvement. They reported that, in contrast to the common view that *g* reflects a broad sample of major cognitive functions, high *g* tasks were not associated with the diffuse recruitment of multiple brain regions but instead associated with selective recruitment of lateral frontal cortex in one or both hemispheres. On the basis of these results, Duncan et al. concluded that "general intelligence" derives from a specific frontal system important in the control of diverse forms of behavior.

Functional imaging and brain lesion studies have repeatedly demonstrated that the lateral frontal lobes play a critical role in what has been termed "executive functions," such as managing the allocation of resources, mediating goal-oriented behaviors, as well as working memory. Thus, it is not surprising that in many cognitive tasks these frontal areas would show activation. On the basis of studies of patients who underwent frontal lobotomies for the treatment of mental illness, researchers have repeatedly demonstrated that ablation of the frontal lobe does not severely influence performance on standardized intelligence tests (Valenstein, 1973). Thus, factors other than frontal lobe function might be important in the neural basis of intelligence.

It is also possible that nonstructural factors might also influence the g factor of intelligence. If, according to Hebb's law (neurons that fire together wire together), learning and memory are based on modifications of synaptic strength between neurons that are simultaneously active, an increase in the sensitivity of synaptic coincidence detector would lead to better learning and memory. The N-methyl-D-aspartate (NMDA) gated ion channel is a neural depolarization coincidence detector (detects when neurons fire together) and the influx of calcium through this channel enables an increase in synaptic strength. Thus, the enhanced NMDA gated ion channel activity could enhance learning and memory. Tang and coworkers (1999) demonstrated in transgenic mice that overexpression of the gene for the NMDA receptor in the forebrains of these mice, which leads to an increase in NMDA ion channel density, is associated with superior learning ability, as assessed by various behavioral tasks. Thus, differences in the NMDA gaited ion channels might represent a unifying mechanism for associative learning and memory. These observations suggest that genetic control of cognitive attributes such as intelligence can be mediated neurochemically.

Since the pioneering reports of Paul Broca, studies of patients with discrete brain lesions suggest that a person can have specific cognitive disabilities. Developmental disorders can also be associated with specific cognitive disabilities. For example, there are children with specific disabilities in reading, math, drawing, music, and route finding. Some of these children become creative geniuses. For example, as previously mentioned, there are many great artists, such as Picasso, who did not do well in school because of language disabilities and, as it was noted in chapter 1, even mathematical geniuses such as Einstein have had language learning disabilities. Thus, the g factor alone cannot explain specific disabilities or specific talents, and several theorists have placed more of an emphasis on special factors. For example, Howard Gardner (1985), who popularized the concept of "multiple intelligences," had worked with neuropsychologists and behavioral neurologists such as Edith Kaplan, Norman Geschwind, and Harold Goodglass at the Jamaica Plain Veteran Administration Medical Center in Massachusetts. These clinician-scientists knew the classical localizationist papers that were published in the late-19th and early-20th centuries by clinician-scientists such as Paul Broca, Karl Wernicke, Kurt Lichtheim, and Hugo Liepmann. They not only resurrected the contributions of these pioneers but also advanced our knowledge about the modular organization and localization of different cognitive functions. On the basis of this knowledge, Gardner (1985) suggested that people have multiple intelligences. Although Gardner's concept of multiple intelligences had a great influence on educators, this concept was not new when he described it. For example, in 1938 Thurstone criticized Spearman's (1927) theory of intelligence. Spearman suggested that intelligence is a single entity, but Thurstone instead suggested that intelligence consists of several primary abilities and these primary abilities, were separate and distinct. In Gardner's first book about multiple intelligences, he listed seven abilities: linguistic, logical, mathematical, musical, body kinesthetic, spatial, and interpersonal. In his 1938 book, Thurstone also suggested that there were seven major "vectors" of the mind. In a more recent book, Gardner (1999) listed several more (e.g., spiritual) but has not reached the 150 forms of intelligences posited by J. P. Guilford.

There are many forms of creativity. Whereas some depend on language skills, others might depend on visuospatial or musical skills. Thus, if creativity in a certain field were related to intelligence, it would appear to be related to a specific factor or a special form of intelligence. In the next chapter we discuss what might be the neurological bases of these special talents.

3

Knowledge and Talents

Creativity is a product of the brain's activities and, to understand the basis of the creative process, we have to understand the brain. Before people can perform creative acts they almost always have to spend several years developing their stores of knowledge and developing their talents. Thus, to understand how the brain might mediate creativity, we must first learn about its organizations, because functions such as the storage of knowledge and the development of talents are dependent on brain organization.

Cellular Organization

The fully grown brain weighs only about 3 pounds. The brain can be divided into two major components: the structures that perform the mental computations and the supportive structures. About 100 years ago Santiago Ramón y Cajal revealed that the basic units of the computational portion of the brain are individual living cells called neurons (see Figure 2.1). The human brain has about 10 million neurons. Most of the neurons in the cerebral cortex have a cell body that gives off branches similar to those of a tree. These branches of the neuron are called dendrites. In some neurons these dendritic branches are given off on one side of the neuron's body. On the other side of the body, the neuron has a single long branch called an axon (see Figure 2.1). Some dendrites in the cortex of the brain gather information from nerves that bring sensory information to the brain, and other dendrites gather information from other neurons in the brain that are close neighbors. Some axons leave the brain and are important in motor control. Other axons connect with other neurons. Thus, the neurons in the brain have a rich network of interconnections. There are more than a trillion of such connections. Neurons are not physically connected together but, when activated, they can communicate with each other by giving off chemicals. The areas where one chemical is given off by an axon or a dendrite and excites or inhibits another adjacent neuron is called a synapse (see Figure 3.1). The chemicals given off at synapses are called neurotransmitters, and depending on the type of neurotransmitter that is given off, neurons can either activate (e.g., glutamate) or inhibit (e.g., gamma-aminobutyric acid or GABA) the adjacent neurons that receive this chemical information.

Most of the brain's neurons are found in the cerebral cortex; that is, the mantle that covers the brain. The cerebral cortex is about 3 millimeters thick, and if one looks at the cerebral cortex in the microscope, one can easily recognize that it has six layers. At the turn of the 20th century, Korbinian Brodmann examined these six layers and noticed that in different parts of the brain one or more of these layers was

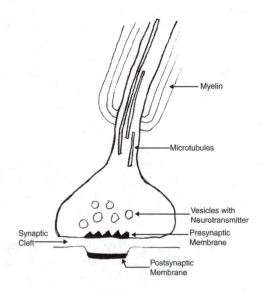

Figure 3.1. Diagram of a neuronal synapse.

either thicker or thinner than the same layer in a different part of the brain. The microscopic differences he found in different anatomic regions of the brain was related to how dense the neurons are in each layer and to how the neurons in these areas are connected to other parts of the brain. Some neurons bring sensory information into the brain (afferent) and others send messages out of the brain (efferent), like those that control movements. Most neurons in the brain, however, communicate with each other. Thus, neurons in the brain gather information from the outside world and from one's body. They also send information to and receive information from other neurons, and it is the strength of connections between these neurons that stores knowledge.

Neuronal Representations—Knowledge Stores

In the first chapter I mentioned Thomas Kuhn's proposal that discovery commences with the awareness of an anomaly or the recognition that nature has somehow violated the paradigm-induced expectations that govern normal science. Thus, the observation of an anomaly suggests that the scientific theory that attempted to explain the order in a system is inadequate and a new theory that accounts for this anomaly must be devised. A corollary of Kuhn's hypothesis would be that to be able to recognize an anomaly, one would have to have a large store of knowledge in that cognitive domain. Many of the most exciting scientific discoveries appear to happen almost by accident. An example of how important stored knowledge is to scientific discovery is the story of Alexander Fleming, who, as I mentioned previously, noticed that the penicillium mold that accidentally had blown into his bacterial cultures killed the bacteria. Prior to this accident, Alexander Fleming was performing bacteriological research and was interested in antiseptics and how the body fights infections. Thus, Fleming had a mind that was prepared for this discovery. This finding, to use Kuhn's term, was an anomaly, but it was the "prepared mind" of Fleming that discovered the importance of this phenomenon.

Because knowledge and skills are lost or degraded when the cerebral cortex is injured or degenerates, we know that knowledge is stored in the cortex. To be creative one has to have excellent stores of knowledge. In the next two sections, I discuss where knowledge is stored and how it is stored.

There have been two major theories as to how the brain stores information. Some researchers have believed that the storage of knowledge is distributed over almost the entire cerebral cortex (mass action hypothesis), whereas others believe that different forms of knowledge and different types of thinking (e.g., verbal versus visuospatial) are mediated by different parts of the brain (localizationist or modular hypothesis).

Franz Gall first put forth the modular or localizationist hypothesis in the latter part of the 18th and early part of the 19th centuries. He thought that intellect was mediated by the two cerebral hemispheres, united by the corpus callosum, and that the brain stem was important for controlling vital forces such as respiration. These major hypotheses were subsequently all shown to be correct. He also proposed that the brain was organized in an anatomically distributed modular fashion such that different human faculties are located in different anatomic areas of the cerebral cortex. Gall also reasoned that if certain brain functions are mediated by specific anatomic areas, then the more brain tissue a person has devoted to this function the better this person would perform this function. Because the size of the brain region influences the shape of the skull overlying this area, Gall and his students believed that one should be able to measure a person's abilities to perform different functions by measuring portions of her or his skull.

Unfortunately, Gall's modular hypothesis was temporarily discarded because it led to the pseudoscience of phrenology, with its many unfounded claims about skull shapes and mental abilities. The major problem with phrenology was that no experimental evidence supported the claims made by the practitioners. The major assumption of modularity, however, was not tested until the middle of the 19th century, when Paul Broca, a French physician and anthropologist, listened to a lecture by Auburtin, who was a student of Bouillaud, one of Gall's students. Gall noted that fluent speakers have prominent foreheads and suggested that the facility of speech is mediated by the frontal lobes of the brain. After the lecture, Broca invited Auburtin to the hospital to see a diabetic man who, as a result of a prior stroke, had weakness of his right arm and was unable to speak except for saying the word *tan*. Although Broca's patient was unable to speak, he was able to comprehend. Because of his diabetes he had insufficient circulation to his legs and developed gangrene. In the 19th century there were no antibiotics to treat this infection, and this man died. A postmortem examination of his brain revealed that the stroke injured his left hemisphere. The stroke was predominantly anterior, in the left frontal lobe (see Figure 3.2). Broca subsequently described eight patients who were right handed and who had lost their speech from damage to the left hemisphere. Broca's observations supported Gall's postulate of modularity or localized functions.

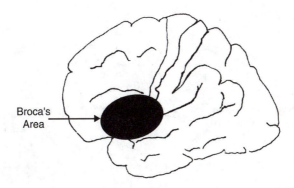

Broca's
Area

Figure 3.2. Diagram of the injury described by Paul Broca in a patient who lost the ability to speak fluently but could comprehend speech. The injury primarily damaged the inferior (bottom) portion of the frontal lobe.

To establish that a system is modular, however, you have to demonstrate not only that brain injury to a focal area causes a specific behavioral disturbance (as Broca demonstrated) but also that injuries to other areas of the brain cause different behavioral disorders. Further support of the modular hypothesis came about 10 years after Broca reported this nonfluent aphasic patient. Then the German neurologist Karl Wernicke reported a patient who was almost the opposite of Broca's patient in that he could speak fluently but could not comprehend speech. This patient had an injury to the posterior portion of the superior temporal lobe (see Figure 3.3). Thus, Wernicke demonstrated a double dissociation, namely, that injury to one part of the brain causes certain signs, but injury to another part of the brain induces different signs.

In addition to demonstrating modularity of the speech-language system, Wernicke initiated the development of information-processing models. His clinical observations suggested that this left posterior area of the brain contains the auditory memories of how words sound and that normally this posterior area is able to send this word-sound information to the anterior area, which Broca had found to be important in programming the movements needed to speak. From this new information-processing model one could make new predictions (see Figure 3.4). For example, if these two regions were intact but disconnected by damage to the pathway that connects these two areas (the arcuate fasciculus), a patient should be fluent and able to comprehend, but when speaking, naming, or repeating, the patient would use the wrong speech sounds because the information from the posterior area that contains the memories of word sounds could not provide the anterior

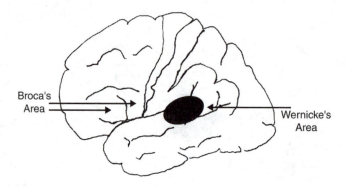

Figure 3.3. Diagram of the injury described by Karl Wernicke of a patient who spoke in jargon and could not comprehend speech. The injury involves the superior posterior portion of the temporal lobe.

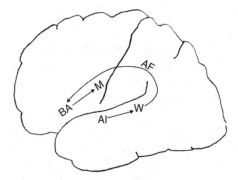

Figure 3.4. Diagram of Karl Wernicke's model of how the left hemisphere mediates speech. A1 = primary auditory cortex, which performs auditory analyses of incoming stimuli; W = Wernicke's area, which stores the memories or representations of the speech sounds (phonemes) that comprise words; AF = arcuate fasciculus, which is a bundle of nerve fibers that carry information from Wernicke's area to Broca's area; BA = Broca's area, which contains the knowledge of how to move the articulatory apparatus to make speech sounds; and M = motor cortex, which sends this information to the brain stem that contains the motor neurons that move the muscles in the tongue, lips, and mouth.

area with this information. Subsequently, as predicted by Wernicke's information-processing model, this type of aphasic disorder was described and was called conduction aphasia.

Broca's and Wernicke's seminal studies led to the golden age of the study of brain-behavior relationships called neuropsychology. This golden age lasted until the First World War, and then there was a shift in position to the mass action or nonlocalization hypothesis. The reason for the decline of the localizationist approach is not fully known, but there were probably two major factors. The first was a change in the political-philosophical zeitgeist. Most of the early localizationist work was done on the European continent, primarily in France and Germany. After the First World War these continental European powers lost much of their power and their influence on Western thought, but the English-speaking countries such as the United States and the United Kingdom flourished. The Anglo-American social and political systems were strongly influenced by the philosophic writings of John Locke, who proposed that the brain was like a "tabula rasa" or a blank wax tablet. Unlike the modularity hypothesis that suggests anatomic specialization, the tabula rasa is uniform and featureless until it receives impressions gained by experience.

The shift toward this antilocalizationist view of brain organization was strongly propelled by the Harvard psychologist Karl Lashley, who removed different parts of rodents' brains to see if there were any specific areas of the brain that, when removed, caused a specific behavioral deficit. Because he found no localized regions where knowledge was stored but rather knowledge seemed to be diffusely represented, he formulated the theory of "mass action." A corollary of this hypothesis is that whatever the location of a brain injury, the more tissue that is damaged, the poorer the animal performs on any task. Unfortunately, during this antilocalizationist period (1920s to 1962), clinical neurologists who presumably should have been interested in localization of function did little to advance knowledge in this field, and many of the British neurologists had a strong negative attitude toward localizationist thinking. Sir Henry Head, one of the leaders of British neurology, wrote inflammatory and derogatory comments about Karl Wernicke's reports. Head (1926) wrote, "No better example could be chosen of the matter in which writers of this period were compelled to lop and twist their cases to fit the Procrustean bed of their hypothetical conceptions." Fortunately, a localizationist and connectistic renaissance began in 1962, when Norman Geschwind, Edith Kaplan, Harold Goodglass, and their students clearly demonstrated brain modularity in patients with brain lesions. The advent of new neuroimaging techniques, such as computer tomography (CT) and magnetic resonance imaging (MRI), began to allow investigators to localize lesions in living patients rather than having to rely on postmortem examination. This technological advance allowed the resurrected science to flourish.

Information-processing models help us understand how the brain works and enable us to ask further questions about brain functions. They presume that the brain stores and processes information in highly interconnected modular systems. These modular systems process information both serially and in parallel. In the past 20 years, we have been able to visualize brain functions by using radioisotopes (e.g., positron-emission tomography or PET scanning) or strong magnets (i.e., functional magnetic resonance imaging or fMRI). When an area of the brain becomes active it uses more energy, and to provide that energy, the active part of the brain receives an increased amount of blood. The PET and fMRI methods can detect the areas of the brain that are active by locating the areas that are receiving increased amounts of blood. These functional imaging studies provided further support to Gall's modularity hypothesis and support the work of localizationists such as Broca and Wernicke. Strong magnets also can be used to detect small brain currents (magneto-encephalography). This technique permits neuroscientists to measure the time between stimulus presentation and cortical processing. As predicted by information-processing models, these studies demonstrate that the brain processes stimuli using both serial and parallel processing.

Modularity and Connectivity

To understand how brains might work when people are performing creative acts, we have to understand the modular organization of the brain, and the modular organization of the brain is at least in part dependent on its anatomy. The cerebral cortex is divided into a left and right hemisphere, and these two hemispheres are connected by a structure called the corpus callosum. The corpus callosum allows information to be transferred from one hemisphere to the other (see Figure 1.1).

Each hemisphere has four major lobes: frontal, temporal, parietal, and occipital (see Figure 1.1). Because most knowledge is stored in the cerebral cortex, it is important to have a large cortex. One way of increasing the relative size of the cortex without increasing the overall size of the brain is to have convolutions, and the human brain is more convoluted than the brain of any other organism. A convoluted brain has mountains called gyri, valleys called sulci, and gorges called fissures. Some of the major gyri of the brain that we will be discussing are diagrammed in Figure 3.5.

Information is carried into the brain from structures such as the eyes, ears, skin, and joints. Before this information reaches the cortex it goes through a relay station in the center of the brain called the thalamus (see Figure 3.8). The visual-sensory information then goes from the optic thalamus to the striate cortex (primary visual area or V1), which is located in the occipital cortex (see Figure 1.1). Joint position and touch information goes from the body to the thalamus and from

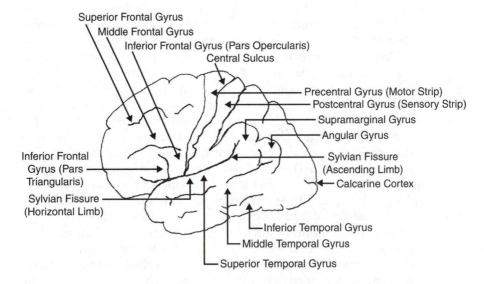

Figure 3.5. Diagram of some of the major gyri and fissures on a lateral view of the brain.

the thalamus to the postcentral gyrus (primary somatosensory area or S1) (see Figure 1.1) and auditory information goes from the ears to the auditory thalamus and then is relayed to an area on the dorsal (top) surface of the temporal lobe, called Heschl's gyrus (primary auditory area or A1) (see Figure 1.1).

The function of these primary areas is to perform analyses of incoming stimuli. For example, the left visual (striate) cortex is important for detecting stimuli that occur on the right side of space (e.g., stimuli that fall on the nasal portion of the retina in the right eye and the temporal portion of the retina in the left eye). The primary cortex analyzes and detects changes in brightness (edges) that are oriented in specific directions and are positioned in specific portions of space. After the primary sensory cortices perform this analysis of the incoming information, this partially processed information is passed to areas called modality-specific association cortices. For the brain to derive meaning when a person sees an object, it must put these lines or edges together to form a percept of the viewed object's shape. Patients with lesions of the brain who can not recognize objects and who can not draw these objects or even match them to other examples of the same object or pictures of the same object have a disorder called apperceptive agnosia. Although these patients are not blind, they cannot develop a percept of the object because they cannot put all the edges they see together to form a shape. These patients often have injury to the visual association areas that surround the primary visual areas. These patients' problems are not with naming or activating concepts since when these same objects are presented in other modalities, such as touch, the patients are able to name the object, describe the object, or show how the object is used.

In the clinic we see patients who cannot recognize objects (or faces) but are able to draw these objects or match them to similar objects. This disorder is called associative agnosia. For example, when shown a picture of a hammer, these patients might be unable to name it, describe its use, or demonstrate how it is used, but they could draw the hammer. There are two mechanisms that can produce this form of agnosia. One reason that these patients may fail to recognize objects is that they have a modality-specific memory failure. Visual association areas, primarily in the posterior (back) ventral (bottom) portions of the brain in the temporal and occipital lobes, can store memories of objects that a person has previously seen (see Figure 1.1). These iconic representations of objects, also called structural descriptions, are stored independently from conceptual-semantic representations, which are important to understanding the meaning of the object. For example, if I showed you an abstract drawing, took away this drawing, and then presented it again to you some time later, together with foils (other similar drawings), you should have little difficulty recognizing the drawing that I originally showed you. If I asked you the meaning of this drawing you might say, "It has no meaning." Thus, modality-specific portions of our cerebral cortex do store modality-specific sensory memories, and if these areas are damaged we may be unable to recognize objects or faces.

There are patients who have associative visual agnosia who cannot name or recognize the meaning of objects or their use, but patients with this form of associative agnosia can form percepts (can draw or match, or both, the sample) and also maintain their visual memories or structural descriptions of objects. The means by which we test their visual memories is to show these patients pictures of objects. Some of these pictures are real objects and others are pseudo-objects. Although these patients can discriminate between the real (which they have seen before) and pseudo-objects, they cannot tell the names of these objects or how to use the real objects. Thus these patients have intact memories of objects (structural descriptions), but these memories cannot successfully access the language and conceptual areas of the brain.

The visual, auditory, and tactile association areas all send projections that meet in the posterior inferior parietal lobe and in the posterior portion of the temporal lobes (see Figure 3.6). Thus, these areas are called

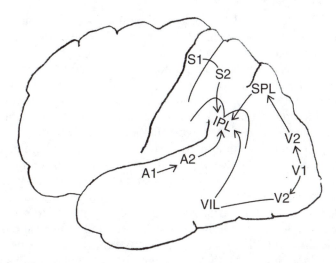

Figure 3.6. Diagram demonstrating that the primary auditory area (A1), the primary visual area (V1), and the primary somatosensory area (S1) all project to their modality-specific association areas (A2, S2) and visual association areas in the ventral temporal lobe (VTL) and the superior parietal lobe (SPL). These modality-specific association areas then all project to or converge in the inferior parietal lobe (IPL).

multimodal or polymodal association areas. Humans' inferior parietal lobe, including the angular gyrus and the supramarginal gyrus (see Figure 3.5), are not present in monkeys' brains. The meeting of all the modality-specific association areas in the posterior parietal and temporal lobe allow humans to perform functions that cannot be performed by monkeys. For example, even in the absence of training, you would have no difficulty pointing to the second array if I, after making three short sounds and then two long sounds and showing you a piece of paper with the following choices, nonverbally indicated that you should point: (1) _ _.. _ (2) ..._ _ (3) _._._. Without extensive training, monkeys would have trouble performing this task. The reason people can easily perform this task is that they can make cross-modal (auditory to visual) associations. Cross-modal associations allow us to develop symbols. Letters are symbols of phonemes. A series of phonemes or words are symbols for actions and objects. Numbers are symbols of quantity.

Hemispheric Asymmetries

Several decades ago Marcel Kinsbourne said to me, "It is a good thing humans have two hemispheres because they love dichotomies."

I replied, "Perhaps humans love dichotomies because they have two hemispheres." Some of the dichotomies that have been used to express the differences in functions between the hemispheres include the following: left linguistic and right nonlinguistic, left categorical and right coordinate, left analytic and right gestalt, left sequential and right simultaneous, left rational and right emotional, and left propositional and right appositional. Many discussions of the lateral asymmetries of hemispheric processing suggest that, depending on the type of cognitive process required, either the right or left hemisphere mediates an activity. I suspect, however, that this either-or proposition is incorrect, and that localization of function or modularity permits parallel processing, and parallel processing confers a processing advantage. For example, when PET first was used to study the brain, investigators injected a glucose radioisotope into the blood of normal participants while they were listening to someone speak. When neurons in an area of the brain are active they use more glucose than areas that are inactive, and with an increase of glucose use, the radioactivity emanating from these active areas increases. These investigators found that not only did a portion of the left hemisphere's language area, called Wernicke's area, show an increase (activation), but also a similar area in the right hemisphere also activated. Because many people in neurology still did not believe in localization of function, and they knew that I was a localizationist, they asked me to discuss the results of one of these studies at an annual meeting of the American Academy of Neurology. I mentioned that we recently reported that patients with right temporal-parietal lesions, unlike those with left hemisphere lesions, can understand *what* is said, or the propositional message, but not *how* it is said, the emotional tone of voice or affective prosody. In contrast, we demonstrated that people with left temporal-parietal lesions might not be able to understand *what* is said but can understand *how* it is being said (emotional prosody). When a normal person listens to another person speak, he or she listens to and processes what is being said not only by the words but also by the tone of voice. Whereas the left hemisphere mediates the comprehension of words, the right hemisphere mediates the understanding of the emotional tone of voice. The ability of each hemisphere to perform a different analysis of the speech (parallel processing) allows normal people to listen simultaneously to both the propositional verbal message and the prosodic emotional message. Thus, when normal participants listen to someone speak, the reason both the left and right hemispheres activate is that these participants are performing simultaneous processing.

Many creative endeavors also probably require parallel processing of the two hemispheres and interactions between the two hemispheres.

Some types of creative acts, however, might depend on the functions or portions of one hemisphere more than the other. Thus, in the next two sections we briefly discuss some of the major functions of the left and right hemispheres. Unfortunately, an exhaustive discussion of all the lateralized functions is beyond the scope of this book, and I suggest that readers who want to learn more details about these lateralized systems read portions of a text edited by Edward Valenstein and me called *Clinical Neuropsychology* (fourth edition, 2003).

The Left Hemisphere

Studies of patients with injuries to the left hemisphere have revealed that these patients have deficits in propositional language. Those with posterior lesions (e.g., Wernicke's area or the posterior portion of the superior temporal lobe) have problems with verbal comprehension (see Figure 3.3). Patients with injuries to regions that are above, behind, or below Wernicke's area often have problems with finding words. People with anterior lesions (i.e., in the region of Broca's area) become nonfluent and have trouble with verbal expression (see Figure 3.2). Patients with lesions in the region of the angular gyrus in the left parietal lobe have trouble with reading and writing (see Figure 3.5). People with injuries to the left angular gyrus also have trouble with calculations—such as adding, subtracting, multiplying, and dividing—and trouble knowing how to perform learned skilled acts and how to solve mechanical problems. The left hemisphere is also important for focused attention and appears to be superior to the right in categorical reasoning.

The Right Hemisphere

Although lesion, behavioral (dichotic listening and visual half field), functional imaging, and electrophysiological studies provide converging evidence that the left hemisphere of right-handed people appears to be dominant for programming skilled movements, calculating, speaking, and understanding speech as well as related functions (such as reading and writing), the right hemisphere appears to be important in spatial cognition. For example, lesion and behavioral studies using a test in which participants have to compute and recognize the spatial relationship of two lines have revealed that the right hemisphere appears to be dominant (Hamsher, Levin, & Benton, 1979). The right hemisphere is also better at determining if pairs of photographic portraits, which are taken at different angles, of people not known to the participants are the same or different people (Benton, 1990). The right hemisphere also plays a dominant role in recognizing photographs of objects that are taken from unusual angles, such as a picture of a bucket taken from directly above.

Although the right hemisphere appears to be dominant at mediating visuospatial skills, studies of patients' ability to draw or copy complex diagrams has revealed that lesions to both the right and left hemisphere impair drawing. This deficit is called constructional apraxia. Some investigators have suggested that constructional apraxia associated with right-hemisphere injury is different from that associated with left-hemisphere injury. For example, when asked to draw a cube, patients with right-hemisphere injuries appear to have trouble drawing the relationships between the lines or angles and the people with the left-hemisphere lesions appear to have problems with organizing the elements of the cube.

In addition to mediating spatial skills, the right hemisphere appears to be important in mediating several forms of nonpropositional speech. I briefly mentioned previously that the right hemisphere mediates the comprehension of emotion prosody, but it is also important for the expression of emotional prosody (Heilman, Nadeau, & Beversdorf, 2003; Ross, 1981; Tucker, Watson, & Heilman, 1977). The comprehension and expression of facial emotions also appear to be mediated primarily by the right hemisphere. In the clinic we have seen patients who have a loss of fluent propositional speech from left frontal lesions, either in Broca's area or above it, but when some of the these patients are asked to perform automatic speech, such as reciting the Pledge of Allegiance or the Lord's Prayer, they can do so fluently. Some of these nonfluent patients can also fluently sing the words to songs and also curse.

One explanation for this preserved automatic speech is that it is being mediated by the uninjured right hemisphere. Support for this postulate came when I was visiting Israel and saw a patient with Lynn Speedie and Eli Wertman (Speedie, Wertman, Tair, & Heilman, 1993). This man was an Orthodox Jew who awoke to find that he could not chant his morning prayers. This man was now about 80 years old and had been chanting these same prayers since he was a boy. When we examined him and asked him to sing, he also had trouble. He was able to tell this entire story, however, using fluent propositional speech. When he received a CT scan it demonstrated that he had a stroke in the right frontal lobe and right basal ganglia. We also reported a woman who had a progressive loss of the ability to express emotions, both by speech prosody and by emotional facial expressions (Ghacibeh & Heilman, 2003). Her MRI showed focal atrophy of her right frontal lobe. Borod and her coworkers (2000) provided evidence that, when compared with nonemotional words processed by the language-dominant left hemisphere, the right hemisphere also processes emotional words.

Brownell and his coworkers (Brownell, Potter, Bihrle, & Gardner, 1986; Brownell, Simpson, Bihrle, Potter, & Gardner, 1990) performed a series of studies that demonstrated that the right hemisphere mediates metalinguistic functions, such as the comprehension of metaphor. For example, if someone with a right-hemisphere lesion was asked to interpret the sentence "He had a heavy heart" and then given two possible interpretations such as, "He was an athlete and because of all the exercise his heart became muscular" or "He was grieving," they might select the former sentence.

Some studies also suggest that the right hemisphere might play a special role in music. Milner (1962) studied a group of patients who had either their left or their right temporal lobes removed because they had medically uncontrollable seizures, and their physicians were attempting to remove the portion of the brain from which these seizures emanated. She assessed these peoples' musical skills with the Seashore Test of Musical Abilities and found that whereas the people who had a removal of the left hemisphere's temporal lobe appeared to have a deficit of ability to recognize and recall rhythm, the people with removal of their right temporal lobe had more problems with melody. Other investigators, however, have not been able to completely replicate these results (Kester, Saykin, Sperling, & O'Conner, 1991).

Patients with right-hemisphere strokes often demonstrate a disorder where they appear to be severely inattentive or even unaware of stimuli that are presented on the left side of space. Although they are more likely to detect stimuli that are presented on the right side of space than those presented on the left side, these patients are also somewhat inattentive to right-side stimuli. To account for this asymmetry, we suggested and provided evidence (Heilman & Van den Abell, 1980) for the postulate that whereas the left hemisphere can attend to stimuli in the right side of space, it cannot attend to left-side stimuli. In contrast, the right hemisphere can attend both to the opposite (left) side of space and to the ipsilateral (right) side. Thus, when the left hemisphere is injured, these patients' right hemisphere can mediate attention in ipsilateral hemispace. When the right hemisphere is injured, however, the left hemisphere can attend somewhat to contralateral right hemispace, but because it is only this injured right hemisphere that can attend to the left-side space, the left side of space goes unattended or neglected.

Based on the above discussion, it appears that overall the right hemisphere appears to be dominant for mediating attention. When presented with a novel or important stimulus, an organism must be alert. When an organism is alert or aroused, its cerebral cortex is physiologically prepared to process incoming stimuli. The right hemisphere not only is dominant for making attentional computations, such as where in space a person needs to direct their attention, as well as determining the significance of a stimulus, but also appears to control the level of arousal (Heilman, Schwartz, & Watson, 1978).

Some tasks require that a person pay attention to details (focused attention), and other tasks require that a person attend to an overall configuration (global attention). For example, look at Figure 3.7, which is called a Navon figure. Now, attempt to find the letter *A* and then find the letter *H*. To find the letter *A* you used focused attention, but when you attempted to find the letter *H* you used global attention. Research has revealed that whereas the left hemisphere appears to be important in mediating focal attention, the right hemisphere appears to mediate global attention (Barrett, Beversdorf, Crucian, & Heilman, 1998; Robertson & Lamb, 1991).

When performing creative acts, one must find the thread that unites, or see the unity in what appears to be diversity. If one looks at the Navon figure (see Figure 3.7), it is apparent that the letter *H* is composed of many smaller letters, but to see the *H* a person needs to see the thread that unites and thus has to use a global strategy. Hence, at the innovative stage of creativity, the right hemisphere–mediated global attentional systems might be more important that than the left hemisphere–mediated focal systems.

During the verification-production stage of creativity, a scientist or artist also has to concentrate on details and thus must use the left hemisphere–mediated, focused system. As I mentioned previously, there are patients with left-side neglect who are unaware of stimuli that are presented on the side of space that is opposite to their right hemispheric lesion. Denny-Brown and Chambers (1958) and Bisiach

```
B        W
C        O
L        M
Q NEJX A
T        D
R        F
Z        X
```

Figure 3.7. Navon figure. To find the letter *H* a person has to use global attention, and to find the letter *D* a person has to use focal attention.

and Luzzati (1978) described patients who not only neglected the left-sided external stimuli but also neglected the left side of internal stimuli or imagery. For example, Bisiach and Luzzati (1978) asked patients primarily who were in a hospital in Milan, Italy, about a famous square in the city of Milan. He told them to image coming out of the front doors of a cathedral situated on one end of this square and to tell him what building on the square they saw in their mind's eye. These patients primarily described the buildings on their right but not on their left. He then asked them to image that they were on the other side of the square looking at the cathedral and to tell him the buildings they now saw. The patients again primarily reported the buildings that would have been on their right, had they been standing across from the church, but these were the same buildings that were initially on their left when they first imagined walking out of the cathedral. The reason I mentioned these reports is that they demonstrate that the brain mechanisms that guide attention to external stimuli might also guide attention to internal stimuli. Thus, when a person images some type of stimulus and uses a global approach, there is a good possibility that this person might be using a right-hemisphere mechanism. If a painter imagines the entire scene before imaging details in the scene and if the scientist images an array of data before he images any specific data, they might be primarily using their right hemisphere.

Size

As I mentioned earlier, Gall thought that if specific anatomic areas mediate specific brain functions then the more brain tissue devoted to this function, the better this function would be performed. Although Gall had posited this about 200 years ago, it was not until about 40 years ago that this hypothesis was scientifically tested. I also mentioned earlier that Wernicke demonstrated that it is the posterior portion of the superior temporal gyrus that contains the memories of how words sound. Thus, if this area of the right hemisphere is injured in people who prefer their right hand, they still will be able to comprehend speech and to speak normally, because the left posterior temporal lobe is intact, but if this region of the brain is injured in the left hemisphere, they will lose their ability to comprehend speech and to speak normally. Geschwind and Levitsky (1968) measured, in the superior portion of the temporal lobe, between the primary auditory area and the end of the Sylvian fissure (planum temporale) on both the right and the left sides of the brain. This area is part of the auditory association cortex. They found that in most people this area, which includes Wernicke's area, was larger on the left side than on the right side (see Figure 3.8). Geschwind and Levitsky's observations supported Gall's hypothesis: Bigger is better. Geschwind and Levitsky, however, did not know the handedness of their participants or if their right hemisphere or left hemisphere was dominant for language. Further support for this anatomic specialization postulate comes from the work of Foundas, Leonard, Gilmore, Fennell, and Heilman (1994), who studied patients who were being considered for epilepsy surgery. Prior to such surgery, patients undergo a procedure called the Wada

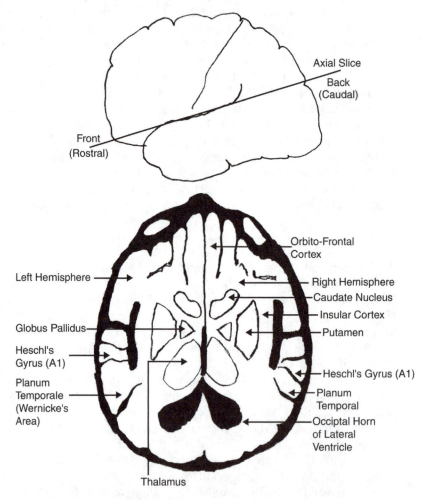

Figure 3.8. Diagram of an axial slice of the brain, demonstrating several anatomic areas and the asymmetry of the planum temporale, the left being larger than the right.

test, in which the physicians induce inactivation of first the left hemisphere and then the right hemisphere by injecting a barbiturate into the left and then right carotid arteries (which are the major arteries that feed blood to most of the cerebral cortex). When the language-dominant hemisphere is put asleep, the patient stops speaking. This procedure allows the doctors to know which hemisphere is dominant for speech so that when they remove epileptic brain tissue they can avoid injuring the parts of the brain that are important for speech and language. Foundas et al. (1994) found that language dominance strongly correlates with the size of Wernicke's area or the planum temporale. As I mentioned earlier, when right-handed patients damage the left inferior frontal lobe (Broca's area) they are unable to speak normally because this area is important in programming the muscles that control the articulatory apparatus (e.g., tongue, lips, palate, vocal cords) when making speech sounds. Foundas, Leonard, Gilmore, Fennell, and Heilman (1996) also found that the Broca's area on the left (language-dominant side) was larger than that on the right. Right-handed people can make faster and more precise movements with the right hand than with the left hand, and Foundas, Hong, Leonard, and Heilman (1998) also found that in right-handed people the region of the left hemisphere's motor cortex that sends signals that control the right hand is also larger on the left side than on the right side.

If bigger is better, than organisms with bigger brains should be more intelligent than those with smaller brains. Elephants, however, have bigger brains than humans do. Although they have special skills that humans do not have, they do not have the intelligence or creativity of humans. As I mentioned, the brain contains many systems, but only a few of these are important for intelligence and creativity. Although the elephant's brain is larger than the human's brain, it does not contain larger areas of cortex critical for higher order cognitive behavior. People have different sized heads, indicative of different brain sizes. In people with very small heads (microcephaly) there is a high probability for subnormal intelligence and restricted creativity, but there is no evidence that people who have large heads are more creative than those with average-sized heads. Overall size may not be as important as is the size of the multimodal areas in the temporal and parietal lobes.

To be creative a person has to have rich stores of knowledge in her or his chosen field. Detailed knowledge allows one to discover the anomalies that lead to new theories. As I mentioned earlier, one of the most important evolutionary changes in the brain of humans is the development of polymodal and supramodal association areas of the parietal and temporal lobes, including the supramarginal gyrus and the angular gyrus (Brodmann's areas 40 and 39) (see Figure 3.5). I also mentioned that lesion and functional imaging studies have revealed that these areas are important in mediating many higher cognitive activities, such as language, mathematics, and spatial computations. In 1907 E. A. Spitzka studied the brains of several well-known scientists and noted that these eminent mathematicians and physicists had large parietal lobes. Since the time of Isaac Newton, there has been no physicist who was more brilliant and creative than Albert Einstein. Einstein was not a neuroscientist, but he was aware that one of the best means to understand the brain mechanisms underlying creativity was to study the brains of creative individuals. Although Einstein wished to be cremated, he wanted his brain to be used for research. When Einstein died on April 18, 1955, at the Princeton (New Jersey) Hospital, the pathologist at this hospital, Thomas S. Harvey, removed Einstein's brain. Rather than keeping the brain intact, however, so that its overall organization could be studied, Harvey sectioned the brain into 240 blocks and sent different blocks to a variety of different people.

Fortunately, Harvey photographed Einstein's brain before it was sectioned into many little pieces (see Figure 3.9). Witelson, Kigar, and Harvey (1999) viewed these pictures of Einstein's brain and, on the basis of these photographs, they attempted to learn if the brain had aberrant morphology. In primates, including humans, the frontal and parietal lobes are separated from the temporal lobe by a large fissure called the Sylvian fissure (see Figure 3.5). In many people the caudal or posterior end of the Sylvian fissure turns upward, and this upward portion of the Sylvian fissure is called the ascending limb (see Figure 3.5). Normally, this ascending limb separates one of the major portions of the parietal lobe, the supramarginal gyrus, into an anterior and posterior division. When Witelson and her coworkers examined this picture of Einstein's brain, they found that, rather than there being an ascending ramus that divided the supramarginal gyrus into anterior (rostral) and posterior (caudal) divisions at the end of the left Sylvian fissure, the Sylvian fissure in Einstein's brain ended at the postcentral sulcus (see Figure 3.5). On the basis of these observations, Witelson and her colleagues suspected that Einstein had a larger inferior parietal lobe than do most other people, and Einstein's parietal lobe, unlike that of most people, was not divided. They suggested that this large and uninterrupted supramodal cortex allowed Einstein to have a functional advantage in performing mathematics and spatial computations.

Witelson's argument about how the morphology of Einstein's brain might have been responsible for his genius, however, is not

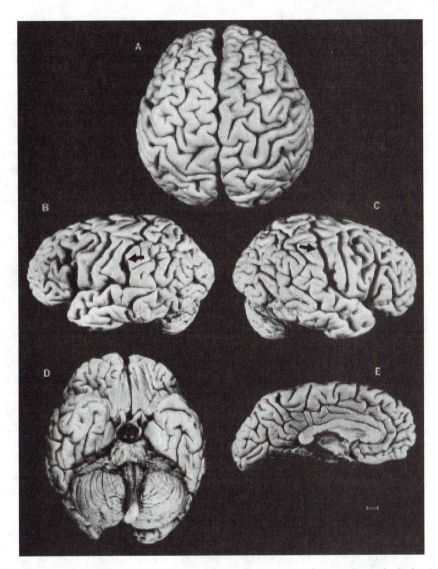

Figure 3.9. Photographs taken in 1955 of five views of Einstein's whole brain (meninges removed): A, superior; B, left lateral; C, right lateral; D, inferior; E, midsagittal view of the left hemisphere. The arrow in each hemisphere (B and C) indicates the posterior ascending branch of the Sylvian fissure as it runs into (is confluent with) the postcentral sulcus. Consequently, there is no parietal operculum in either hemisphere. Scale bar, 1 cm. Reprinted with permission from Elsevier (*The Lancet*, 1999, vol. 353, p. 2150) and the author, Sandra Witelson.

consistent with one of the major postulates of neurology. The brain must fit into the skull, and if the skull becomes too large then its size may disable the person who has to carry this burden. As I briefly mentioned, one way of increasing the cerebral cortex without increasing the size of the brain is by developing hills (or gyri), valleys (or sulci), and gorges (or fissures). This gyrification process allows an increase the amount of cerebral cortex to fit into a fixed volume. In an article that was published before the article about Einstein's brain was published, Witelson and Kigar (1992) suggested that the posterior ascending ramus is the continuation of the main stem of the Sylvian fissure and that, unlike gyri, which are formed by the infolding of cortex, the Sylvian fissure—including the ascending ramus—results from uneven growth of the outer cortex relative to inner structure. That Einstein did not have an ascending ramus, therefore, may suggest that the growth of his inferior parietal cortex was not as great as those who do have such a fissure. In addition, whereas creative people such as Einstein are extremely rare, Foundas and her coworkers noted that the posterior ascending gyrus is not present in 15% to 20% of normal people's brains (personal communication, 2002). Thus, an uninterrupted supramarginal gyrus cannot solely account for Einstein's exceptional creativity.

To learn if the size of the parietal lobe might be a critical element in the brains of geniuses, as suggested by Spitzka, I searched the English literature for articles about brain morphology and genius or creativity. I could find no studies that either supported or refuted Spitzka's postulate, and the hypothesis that creative geniuses in a field might have brain morphology that is different from the general population's morphology has not been tested.

Although highly developed portions of the brain can store specialized knowledge and be responsible for exceptional talents, knowledge and talent alone do not allow one to find the thread that unites. Henri Poincare, the famous mathematician, stated,

> Among the chosen combinations the most fertile will often be those formed from the elements drawn from domains that are far apart. Not that I mean as sufficing for invention the bringing together of objects as disparate as possible; most combinations so formed would be entirely sterile. But certain among them, very rare, are the most fruitful of all.

In an article my colleagues and I recently wrote about the brain mechanisms of creativity (Heilman, Nadeau, & Beversdorf, 2003), we proposed that creativity may be achieved by applying networks representing internal models in one domain of knowledge to other networks that contain domains of knowledge that share some attributes. We also suggested that many different network architectures probably exist within the association cortices of the brain, raising the possibility that creativity by metaphor might involve the recruitment of networks of substantially different architecture in order to escape the constraints of existing (learned) internal models represented in the networks usually used for thinking in a particular domain.

In an influential article, Mednick (1962) suggested that creativity requires the ability to make associations between separate concepts or ideas. This idea is similar to one of the definitions of creativity described earlier: "finding the thread that unites." Mednick's concept is consistent with many of the tests of creativity that judge a person's ability to make remote associations (e.g., name alternative uses of a brick), and Mednick also developed a test called the Remote Associates Test. In this test the participant is presented with a series of words and the goal for the participant is to recognize how these words are associated (e.g., the words might be *blue, American,* and *cottage,* and the correct response might be *cheese*). The Remote Associates Test for creativity has been validated, and many creative people do seem to perform well on this test. This test, however, primarily assesses verbal-semantic associations, and many forms of creativity require the association of very different forms of knowledge. In J. P. Guilford et al.'s (1978) Alternative Uses Test, the responses of the participant can be scored on several dimensions, such as the number of responses in a fixed time or fluency, the number of different categories to which the named items belongs, and—perhaps most important—originality. For example, in the brick test, using the brick as a doorstop or bookends would be less original than using it for chalk or grinding it up and using it as a cosmetic such as rouge. The anatomic bases of the ability to make the associations needed for creative acts is not entirely known, but the brain's associative pathways could be important.

Corpus Callosum and Interhemispheric Communication

I mentioned earlier that the cognitive functions mediated by the two hemispheres are different. The left hemisphere is dominant for mediating speech and other language functions, such as reading and writing, and the right hemisphere is dominant for spatial computations, including the recognition of faces and the recognition and expression of emotions. In addition to these modular and lateralized networks, the two hemispheres might use different forms of attention and reasoning. For example, the left hemisphere uses focused attention and the right hemisphere use global attention. In general the two types of reasoning used to solve problems are deductive-logical and inductive-probabilistic. Parsons and Osherson (2001) studied these two kinds of reasoning using positron-emission tomography. They found that probabilistic reasoning activated mostly areas in the left hemisphere, whereas deductive reasoning activated primarily regions of the right hemisphere. Deductive-logical and inductive-probabilistic reasoning are both important in the creative process, but these forms of reasoning must be interactive. If creative innovation involves the recruitment and association of networks that have different architecture, different forms of stored knowledge, and different means of thinking and solving problems, then interhemispheric communication and coordination seems to be critical for creative innovation and production. Therefore, the corpus callosum would seem to play a critical role in creativity.

One way of treating medically intractable epilepsy is to disconnect the two hemispheres by cutting the corpus callosum. Lewis (1979) administered the Rorschach Inkblot Test to eight patients who had undergone cerebral commissurotomies (sectioning of the corpus callosum) for intractable epilepsy and noted that disconnection of the two cerebral hemispheres tended to destroy creativity as measured by this test. Bogen and Bogen (1988) noted that there is hemispheric specialization and that although the corpus callosum transfers high-level information, normally this transfer of knowledge or interhemispheric communication is incomplete. Bogen and Bogen posited that incomplete interhemispheric communication permits hemispheric independence and lateralized cognition, which is important in the incubation of ideas and perhaps for the storage of independent forms of knowledge (e.g., verbal versus spatial). These authors mentioned Frederic Bremer, who suggested that the corpus callosum serves the highest and most elaborate activities of the brain: in a word, creativity. They also suggest that it is the momentary suspension of this partial independence that accounts for illumination, or what I term *creative innovation*. They did not say, however, what could account for this momentary suspension of partial independence.

To my knowledge no one has compared the structure and function of the corpus callosum in creative versus noncreative people. If there are differences in callosal communication between people who are matched for brain size, these differences might be functional rather than anatomic, but both of these hypotheses need to be tested.

Intrahemispheric Communication

As I mentioned previously, the cerebral neocortex has six layers. The brain cells or neurons that have a triangular shape are called pyramidal cells. These neurons are primarily found in the third and fifth layers of the cerebral cortex. Some of the axons of the pyramidal cells connect with or synapse onto other nerves in the cortex and hence are called association fibers. Most of the association fibers come from the pyramidal neurons in the third layer in the cortex. There are short association fibers, also called *U* fibers, that connect neurons in adjacent cerebral gyri. Deeper in the hemisphere, underneath the cortex, there are longer association fibers (axons) that travel in bundles called fasciculi (e.g., arcuate, superior, and inferior longitudinal fasciculi). It is possible that creative people have a richer net of association neurons in layer three or a greater number and variety of associative white matter pathways. Unfortunately, this too has never been systematically studied, but there has been an interesting report about Einstein's brain that suggests that white matter might be important in creativity.

As I mentioned earlier, when Einstein died, the local pathologist removed Einstein's brain and, rather than keeping the brain intact, he sectioned the brain into 240 blocks and sent it to a variety of people. Marion Diamond and her coworkers were among the people who ended up with a piece of Einstein's brain. Little was reported until about 30 years after Einstein's death, when Diamond and her coworkers (Diamond, Scheibel, Murphy, & Harvey, 1985) performed a histological analysis of Brodmann's area 39 (the angular gyrus), where they observed cell types. They found that, compared with the brains of control participants, area 39 on the left side of Einstein's brain contained a higher ratio of glial cells to neurons. These investigators attempted to explain this result by suggesting that this aberrant ratio was "a response by glial cells to greater neuronal metabolic need." This post hoc hypothesis received much criticism but few alternative explanations. Since the work of Dejerine (1891) it has been repeatedly demonstrated that lesions of Brodmann's area 39 (also called the angular gyrus) induce a reading disturbance (alexia). It has been posited that this region stores memories of the visual or written composition of words, and cognitive neuropsychologists have termed these representations the "visual orthographic lexicon." Because Einstein was dyslexic, it is possible that the changes found by Diamond and her coworkers might not be related to an increase of glial cells but rather a reduction of neurons, and it was this developmental abnormality that led to Einstein's dyslexia.

There is, however, an alternative explanation of Diamond and her coworkers' findings. As I mentioned previously, the corpus callosum is primarily composed of myelinated axons whose cell bodies are in the pyramidal layers of the cerebral cortex. The cerebral connectivity important for creativity, however, might be not only interhemispheric (between the right and left hemispheres) but also intrahemispheric (within the hemisphere). In addition to the myelinated axons that carry information between the hemispheres, the myelinated axons in the subcortical white matter carry information between cortical regions in the same hemisphere. These subcortical white matter connections facilitate both inter- and intrahemispheric communication, and inter-hemispheric and intrahemispheric communication might be important for creative innovation because widespread connectivity allows creative people to combine representation of ideas that have been previously isolated. Thus, Diamond and colleagues' findings might suggest that Einstein's parietal lobe had extremely well-developed subcortical white matter, and this finding might suggest that Einstein's creativity was related to his increased interhemispheric and intrahemispheric connectivity.

Although in this section I speculate that extremely creative people, such as Einstein, might have more extensive intra- and intercerebral connections, to my knowledge there have been no systematic studies that have tested this hypothesis, but there is another observation that might support the relationship between connectivity and creativity. There are people who, when they perceive a stimulus in one modality, can sense this stimulus in another modality. This phenomenon has been called "synesthesia," which comes from two Greek roots: *syn* (together) and *aesthesia* (sensing or perceiving). For example, there are people who, when they hear certain notes or words, see certain colors. This cross-modal sensory excitation can take place between almost any sensory modalities. In addition to cross-modal synesthesia, this phenomenon can also be intramodal such that when people view certain figures in black and white, the figures appear to be in color. If a person without visual intramodal synesthesia were presented with a page that contained the letter *L* distributed over the entire page and with the letter *T* inserted between these *L*s, and this person had to find the *T*, he or she would have to perform a sequential search attempting to decide if each exemplar was an *L* or *T*. If, however, a person has synesthesia, such that when they viewed the letter *T* it looked red and the *L*s looked blue, the letter *T* would pop out and be found sooner than if all the letters were in black. Ramachandran and Hubbard (2001) examined people who had visual intramodal synesthesia using a similar paradigm and found that the people who had synesthesia recognized the target more rapidly than did control participants. The mechanism that accounts for synesthesia is unknown, but one postulate is that people with synesthesia have greater connectivity between the modules that are interactive (e.g., color and shape). Blakemore and Steven (in preparation, quoted by Underwood, 2003) used functional imaging to study an individual with synesthesia and found that when this person was presented with one type of stimulus (e.g., words) the region that mediates color perception was also activated. According to the connectivity postulate of creativity that I described previously, if people with synesthesia have greater connectivity they should also be more creative. This postulate was supported by the observations of Grossenback (quoted by Underwood, 2003), who found that of 84 people who have synesthesia, 26 had careers that required creativity (artists, writers, and musicians).

Procedural Knowledge

In the proceeding section I described how conceptual (including both semantic and spatial) knowledge is stored in the brain. Many skills or special talents, however, are not based on stores of conceptual knowledge. As a child you might have learned to ride a bike. If I asked you how to ride a bike you might be able to tell me that to propel the bike forward, you push the pedals forward and downward alternating between your left and right foot. You might also be able to tell me that if you want to go left you turn the handlebars to the left and vice versa. The most difficult part of learning to ride a bike, however, is learning how to keep your balance, and although after several minutes you might be able to explain to me how you do this, when you ride a bike, even after decades of not having ridden one, you do not keep your balance by using stored conceptual knowledge. Rather you rely on what is called procedural memory.

There are many other examples of procedural memories that we use throughout our life, such as writing letters and typing. Many special talents used in sports and even the playing of musical instruments may be examples of procedural memories. Several experiments, performed in patients who have neurological disease, demonstrated that procedural memories are independent from both the episodic and semantic-conceptual forms of declarative memory. Episodic-declarative memories are important in knowing what, where, and when; for example, recalling when you dined out last week, what you had for dinner, and where you had dinner.

In a classical study, Corkin (1968) studied the episodic and procedural memory of the famous epilepsy patient H. M. This patient had severe seizures that could not be controlled with medications. Studies of his brain waves, the electroencephalogram (EEG), indicated that his seizures were coming from the anterior part of both temporal lobes. To help control these seizures, the neurosurgeons removed his right and left anterior temporal lobes.

The anterior temporal lobes contain several structures that are known to be important in the learning and recall of episodic memories, including a structure called the hippocampus and structures that are closely connected to the hippocampus such as the entorhinal and perirhinal cortex. Although removal of the patient's right and left anterior temporal lobe helped control his seizures, he was left with a profound episodic memory loss. Because this surgery did not alter his stores of conceptual knowledge (semantic memory), his intelligence remained the same, but he had lost the ability to make new episodic memories and hence could not recall when or where he had dinner or what he had for dinner on the prior evening.

To study his ability to form procedural memories, Corkin tested him using rotary pursuit apparatus. This machine has a turntable that rotates like one of the old phonograph turntables. On one side of the turntable there is a small circular disk. The participant is given a metal wand and asked to keep the tip of this metal wand on this metal disk while it is rotating. Each day when H. M. was brought to the laboratory, he did not recognize the investigators performing this experiment and had to be reintroduced. He also did not recall the instructions for using the rotary pursuit apparatus and hence had to be given the instructions each day he was tested. Although he could not recall the laboratory staff or the instructions to use this apparatus, he showed that he could learn this procedure, improving his performance each day and thereby demonstrating that procedural memories or are different from episodic-declarative memories. Other investigators have studied the ability of other people who had severe amnesia (an inability to form new episodic memories) to form new conceptual-semantic memories. New words are always being introduced into our vocabulary (e.g., *Internet*), and in these studies the investigators knew the approximate date when these people developed amnesia and attempted to see if these people had learned new words that had been invented after the onset of their amnesia. They found that these people did learn new words after they suffered a permanent amnesia and hence were able to form new semantic-conceptual memories. One study even examined two people who were born with damage to the structures important for forming episodic memories and found that they had the normal development of semantic-conceptual memories and even performed well on IQ tests (Vargha-Khadem et al., 1997).

Further support for the postulate that the development of procedural memories can be dissociated from episodic and semantic-conceptual memories comes from a study performed in our laboratory. We studied patients with Alzheimer's disease, which affects both episodic and semantic-conceptual memories, by using a rotary pursuit motor-learning paradigm similar to that used by Corkin with H. M., the patient who had both anterior temporal lobes removed. Patients with Alzheimer's disease have amnesia because they have damage to the neurons in the medial temporal lobe (the same area that was surgically removed in H. M.), and they have problems with their semantic-conceptual memories because the neurons in the polymodal cortex are also damaged. When we examined these patients' ability to learn a new motor skill, however, they did as well as matched controls (Jacobs et al., 1999). These results provide further evidence that procedural memory is not mediated by the medial temporal lobe or polymodal-supramodal cerebral cortex.

Deep in each cerebral hemisphere there are clusters of neurons. One of these clusters is called the basal ganglia and the other is called the thalamus (see Figure 3.10). After decades of research that has attempted to determine the function of these basal ganglia, their function is still not entirely clear. One of the diseases, however, that affects these basal ganglia is Parkinson's disease. Normal basal ganglia function is dependent on the neurotransmitter dopamine, and in Parkinson's disease there is insufficient dopamine. Procedural memory was assessed in patients with Parkinson's disease by having them repeatedly use the rotary pursuit apparatus. Unlike H. M., the patients with amnesia from removal of the temporal lobes, and the patients with Alzheimer's disease, the subjects with Parkinson's disease were impaired at improving their skills, indicating a procedural memory deficit. These participants with Parkinson's disease, however, had normal episodic memories and semantic-conceptual knowledge. Thus, it appears that these basal ganglia are important for developing procedural memories. Exactly how they encode procedural memories is unknown, but these basal ganglia appear to be part of a neuronal loop that starts in the cortex (primarily in the frontal lobes), proceeds to the putamen, then to the global pallidus, then to the thalamus, and back to the cortex (Figure 3.10). Different parts of the cortex appear to project to different parts of the basal ganglia, and, although it is not thoroughly investigated, different loops might be important for mediating different forms of procedural memories. Many talented people—including athletes, singers, dancers, musicians, and even artists—depend heavily on these procedural memories.

Unlike episodic or semantic-conceptual memories, which can be learned after one exposure to stimuli, procedural memories require

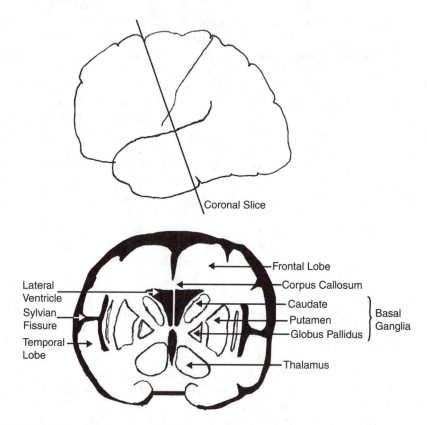

Figure 3.10. Diagram of coronal section through the brain.

practice and feedback. For some reason, procedural memories are best acquired in childhood; thus, the best time to teach skilled behaviors, from learning the violin to playing golf, is in childhood. Most famous golfers like Tiger Woods or tennis players like Pete Sampras started to learn to play their sports when they were children. Most famous musicians also learned to play their instruments in childhood. The reason adults are slower to learn procedural memories is not known, but it might relate to a decrease in the neurotransmitter dopamine that occurs with aging.

Although almost all people who excel in productive arts—such as musicians, singers, and painters—have extraordinary procedural memories in the domain of their talent, there is not a direct relationship between productive talent and creativity. Although many talented musicians might interpret the music they are playing, most performers are playing the music that someone else composed and have not successfully composed their own creative pieces. Similarly, actors interpret the lines written by the playwright, but although interpretation is a form of creativity, it is only a minor form. Thus, although procedural memories are important in the performance or production of creative works, there is little evidence that they are important in creative innovation. In addition, I could not find any studies that demonstrate differences between the brains of extremely talented people and those without special talents. Earlier I mentioned that there are also no studies of the cerebral cortex or white matter connections in extremely creative people. Thus, overall there is no strong evidence for a structural-anatomic basis of genius, but I also think that structural-anatomic hypotheses have not been adequately investigated.

4

Imagery

Imagery is important for two major psychological processes: memory recall and problem solving. Earlier, I described Campbell's (1960) postulate of creativity, which suggests that creative people generate various solutions for problems and then select the best solution. Artists who model with clay or use oil paints can alter their artistic works and see how a variety of solutions look. But a sculptor who works in stone, such as Michelangelo, could not as easily change his stone *Moses* or *David*. Although many great artists try different solutions by making preliminary drawings and then selecting the best solution before they begin to paint or sculpt, many artists have claimed that they use imagery to help them find creative solutions for problems. Imagery allows a creator to form almost an infinite number of variations, to discard those that are inferior, to reshape those that need further work, and to retain those that meet the creator's criteria for excellence.

Many scientists and artists have recognized that imagery is important for creative endeavors, and A. I. Miller summarizes many of these scientists' experiences in his book *Insights of Genius* (2000). For example, Max Planck, the winner of the Nobel Prize in physics in 1918 for his development of quantum theory and the law of radioactivity, suggested that creative scientists must have a vivid imagination because new ideas are generated not by deductive processes but rather by a creative imagination. In regard to creativity, Einstein suggested that imagination is more important than knowledge and that many of his ideas were products of his imagination. In this chapter I describe how the brain generates, views or inspects, and manipulates or alters images. Although I primarily discuss visual imagery, similar processes can occur in other sensory modalities.

Kosslyn (1999) suggested that there is both low- and high-level vision. Whereas low-level vision uses visual input ("bottom up") to localize edges and detect motion, color, and depth, high-level vision, such as object recognition, relies in part on "top-down" processing, including the activation of stored information about the properties of objects. Imagery often aids these higher level processes. In regard to memory, imagery can be used to help store information and can be used to help retrieve information. For example, if I asked you to remember the three words *slippers, elephant,* and *telephone,* you could verbally rehearse these words or you might image an elephant wearing slippers while talking on a telephone. After you were distracted and no longer able to verbally rehearse or to image these three objects, if I asked you to recall these three objects you would be more likely to recall the objects if you imaged an elephant wearing slippers while speaking on a telephone than if you just verbally rehearsed the phonological representations of these three words.

In regard to the retrieval of information, if I asked you whether the distance between New York City and Chicago was greater or less than the distance between Saint Louis and Los Angeles, to answer this question, you might generate in your mind's eye a map of the United States and estimate the relative distances between these cities. Thus, although the information about the relative distance between cities was stored in your brain, the knowledge was implicit and became explicit only after you imaged the map and compared the distance between these cities in your mental image.

In regard to problem solving, imagery can be used to help solve problems that one could not easily solve using verbal reasoning. For example, a salesperson who lives in New York City has to drive to three cities, Washington, DC; Buffalo; and Chicago. If she plans to travel to the cities in that order and then return to New York City, she might not be traveling the shortest route. Hence, she might image a map of the United States and make several virtual trips in her mind's eye. She realizes if she travels to Buffalo after visiting Washington and then after visiting Buffalo travels to Chicago and back to New York, she would be partially retracing her path. She then realizes that after driving to Washington, traveling to Chicago and then to Buffalo before returning to New York City will save her many hours of driving.

Just as this salesperson used imagery to help her solve a practical problem, creative people might also use imagery to solve other types of problems. Imagery might allow creative people to perform virtual experiments. Imagery can also allow creative people to "view" images of objects or processes or combinations of objects that they have never actually seen (e.g., an elephant wearing slippers while speaking on a telephone) or that might not even exist. Perhaps one of the easiest means to create such an image is to combine two or more partial images of real objects. Many of the ancient mythological creatures were created by joining two animals—such as the Chimera, which is a combination of a lion and a serpent—or by fusing a human and animal—such as the centaur, which has the head, arms, and trunk of a man and the body of a horse; the Minotaur, which combines a bull with a man; and the mermaid, which has the head, arms, and trunk of a woman and the tail of a fish. If you want to create an image of a monster for a movie you could use your imagery to join a flying bird with a head of a rabid wild boar whose mouth is foaming and who has the prehensile tail of a new world monkey. Imagery might allow you to morph the relationships of specific objects such that the teeth of this flying rabid boar are razor sharp and contain barbs.

Visual Perception

According to Kosslyn (1999), since the time of Aristotle it has been thought that visual perception and visual imagery share the same underlying mechanisms. Behavioral studies have demonstrated that when a person uses imagery, he or she experiences a deficit in perception and vice versa. That these two activities interfere with each other suggest that they are competing for the same neural apparatus. If both imagery and the perception of objects use the same neural apparatus, then under some circumstances a person should confuse imaged objects with seen objects. Johnson and Raye (1981) demonstrated this confusion in normal college students. Studies of brain-damaged individuals (Levine, Warach, & Farah, 1985) and functional imaging (using positron-emission tomography) provide further support for this hypothesis. For example, when asked to image objects, the individual's calcarine cortex (V1 or primary visual cortex) (see Figure 1.1) will show activation (see Kosslyn, 1999, for a review of this literature). Hence, to understand the brain mechanisms that might account for creative imagery, we might find it helpful to review briefly how stimuli are seen, perceived, comprehended, and stored by the brain.

Visual stimuli come into the eye and fall on the back portion of the eye, where the retina is. The retina contains special nerve cells (ganglion cells) that become activated when light falls on them, and these ganglion cells send electrical messages along the optic nerve until they reach a relay station in the middle of the brain called the geniculate or optic thalamus. There are several classes of ganglion cells, including large cells that are called magnocellular and smaller cells that are called parvocellular. The larger magnocellular cells are able to process information more rapidly and hence are more important in visualizing motion. The parvocellular cells appear to have a higher spatial resolution and are better able to respond to spatial frequencies that define colors. These two types of neurons project to different regions of the optic thalamus. A second series of nerves sends messages from the optic thalamus to the occipital lobes. The part of the occipital cortex that receives these signals from the optic thalamus is called the calcarine or primary visual cortex, also called V1 or Brodmann's area 17 (see Figure 1.1). The cells in this region of the occipital lobe detect changes in brightness that occur in specific spatial locations on the retina. The detection of these brightness changes together with their relative location (spatial array) allows a person to develop what David Marr (1982) called a primal sketch. The edges of a visual stimulus usually have the greatest changes of intensity, and the intensity changes allow the viewer to separate the stimulus from the background.

The primary visual cortex (V1 or Brodmann's area 17) sends the information contained in this primal sketch to the visual association areas that surround the primary cortex. According to Fellerman and Van Essen (1991) there are at least 32 different visual association areas. Each of these areas processes a different aspect of incoming visual information. These areas are highly connected to each other, and Fellerman and Van Essen (1991) estimated that each of these 32 areas is probably connected to as many as 15 other areas. The primary visual cortex is spatially organized such that stimulus position in space is recorded spatially in the primary visual cortex, but as this information is progressively processed by visual association areas there is a loss of this point-to-point topographic mapping because the cells in regions of the visual association cortex are not all spatially organized. These visual association areas are important for the further processing of the visual stimulus.

On the ventral or bottom surface of the occipital lobes, there appears to be a region that is important in the processing of color. About 20 years ago, I was a visiting professor at the University of Iowa. Hanna and Antonio Damasio showed me a patient who had a stroke in the lower portion of his temporal-occipital region on the right side of his brain (see Figure 1.1). I asked this patient to stare at my nose and to tell me what happens to my pen when I move it from his right to his left. When I held the red pen in his right visual field, he said, "I see a red ballpoint pen." When I started to move the pen to the left, he said, "Now it's moving leftward." When the pen crossed his midline (midsagittal plane) into his left visual field, he said, "Now I can still see the pen but it has no color." He told me that everything on his left side was now in black and white. When I asked him to hold the pen, he had no difficulty in reaching and grasping the pen even when I moved it. Therefore, although this patient had an inability to see colors (achromotopsia), he could still see and recognize objects and estimate their size (as determined by how wide he opened his hand when he went to grasp the object), and he knew where in space this pen was located, including its movement. For those who would like to read more about this case and view the actual injury, you can find further details in the report by Damasio, Yamada, Damasio, Corbett, and McKee (1980). Functional imaging studies of the brain during the time normal participants are processing colors have provided converging evidence that this ventral-temporal-occipital region is important for color processing (Zeki et al., 1991).

In contrast to that patient who could not see color but could detect movement, Zihl, von Cramon, and Mai (1983) reported a patient who could see and recognize objects and colors but could not see movement (akinotopsia). Therefore, when this patient looked at something moving, he saw it as being frozen in space or as jumping from one portion of space to another. This patient had bilateral injury to the lateral posterior temporal-occipital areas of the brain, a region called V5 (Figure 4.1). Studies of monkeys and functional imaging studies in humans (Zeki et al., 1991) have provided converging evidence that this portion of the visual association cortex is important in perceiving visual motion.

At the beginning of the 20th century, Balint (1909) described a neurobehavioral syndrome that now bears his name. Patients with this syndrome have three neurological signs: optic ataxia, psychic paralysis of gaze, and simultanagnosia. This last sign, simultanagnosia, I describe later in this chapter. Patients with Balint's syndrome can fully perceive objects and recognize the meaning of objects. They can also see color and detect motion, but when they attempt to touch or grasp an object they have difficulty locating its spatial position and therefore their hands seem to wander through space in search of the object. This deficit in accurate reaching is called optic ataxia, and this disorder is thought to be related to an inability to visually compute where the object is positioned in viewer-centered space. Psychic paralysis of gaze is a similar defect of ocular movement. The most

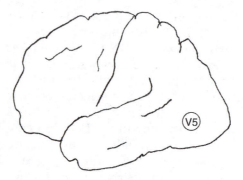

Figure 4.1. Diagram showing area V5, in the lateral posterior temporal-occipital areas of the brain. This visual area is important for motion detection.

sensitive portion of our retina is the fovea. When our attention is drawn to a stimulus, we rapidly move our eyes (saccade) such that the object of interest falls on the fovea. In patients with psychic paralysis of gaze, however, they cannot visually compute the spatial location of this object and they move their eyes to incorrect positions until, almost by chance, the object of interest falls on their fovea. Thus, psychic paralysis of gaze is similar to optic ataxia, except that the latter is a form of misreaching but the former is a form of mislooking. Both disorders, however, are related to a patient's inability to perceive and compute visual-spatial location. Patients with Balint's syndrome, which includes optic ataxia and psychic paralysis, have their lesions in the superior portion of the dorsal lateral parietal-occipital cortex, also called the dorsal stream (see Figure 1.1), and their problem in computing spatial location is related to damage to the parts of the visual association cortex that make these spatial computations.

Visual Recognition

Visual-Object Agnosia

Sigmund Freud (1891) described patients who could see and had normal visual acuity but were unable to recognize common objects. He called this disorder "visual agnosia" (*a* = without; *gnosis* = knowledge). Other neurologists noted that, unlike the patients with Balint's syndrome, some of the patients who lost the ability to recognize objects had maintained their ability to localize objects in space (Potzl, 1928). Mishkin and Ungerleider (1982), working with monkeys, noted the same dorsal ventral dichotomies previously described by these European neurologists. They suggested that after visual stimuli enter the primary visual cortex of monkeys, they are analyzed and processed in the occipital lobe by two visual streams. The dorsal stream goes to the parietal lobes and the ventral stream goes to the ventral temporal lobes (see Figure 1.1). As mentioned, the ventral stream is important in recognizing objects or people and has been called the "what system"; the dorsal stream is important for spatial location and has been called the "where system." As I mentioned previously, people with optic ataxia and psychic paralysis have deficits in this dorsal "where system."

A year before Freud used the term *visual agnosia* to describe patients who could not visually recognize objects, Lissauer (1890) noted there might be two forms of this object-recognition disorder. In one form, which he called "apperceptive agnosia," patients fail to recognize objects because they cannot correctly perceive these objects. This problem with perception is not caused by decreased visual acuity, and many of these patients have normal or near normal visual acuity. When these patients are shown a simple line drawing of an object, they are unable to copy this drawing because they have a perceptual disorder. The borders of the object primarily define the shapes of objects. To perceive an object the primary visual cortex in the occipital lobes must receive visual information from the retina. The primary (calcarine) visual cortex in the occipital lobes detects changes in brightness or edges that are oriented in specific directions and are positioned in specific portions of space. For the brain to perceive an object it must put these lines or edges together to form a percept of the object's shape. If these pieces of usual information are not put together and a percept of the object is not fully formed, a person will not be able to recognize it. A failure of recognition caused by a perceptual deficit is apperceptive agnosia.

After the percept is developed, a person can either copy a picture of the object or recognize a replica of this object from foils, but these processes alone are not sufficient for recognition. There are patients who cannot name objects (or faces) or describe their uses but can correctly draw these same objects. Because they can draw these objects, they appear to be able to form a percept. Lissauer (1890) called this recognition disorder, with its relatively preserved perception, "associative agnosia." Studies of patients with associative agnosia suggest that there might be at least two forms of this disorder. During life, we often see objects that we recognize as having been seen by us previously, but we do not know these objects' names, and we do not know how these objects are used. Thus, our brains also contain perceptual object memories, also called iconic representations or structural descriptions, and these representations can be accessed without knowledge of these objects' attributes, properties, or functions (conceptual-semantic information). At other times we might see an object and not only recall that we have seen it before but also name the object and know its attributes, properties, and functions. If a patient can form a percept of an object but has lost the visual memories or iconic representations of this object, she or he not only will be unable to name it, describe it, or demonstrate its use but also will not know if this object is real or artificial (made up). If a patient has intact object-centered representations (e.g., can tell real objects from artificial ones) and still cannot name or recognize objects in one modality, such as vision, but can recognize objects in other modalities, such as touch, he or she might not be able to recognize these objects because his or her intact object iconic representations cannot access the brain's semantic-conceptual systems.

Simultanagnosia

Earlier I mentioned what has been termed Balint's syndrome, which includes optic ataxia and psychic paralysis of gaze. I also mentioned that these disorders of reaching with the forelimbs (optic ataxia) and directing the position of the eyes (psychic paralysis of gaze) are probably caused by damage to the portions of the visual system that compute the spatial location of a stimulus in the environment to which a person is attempting to view or touch. A third sign associated with the Balint's syndrome is an inability to interpret complex pictures or visual scenes. For example, I showed one of my patients who had this disorder a picture of a Civil War battle and asked her to tell me about this picture. She said that this was a picture of a horse. Although there were horses in this picture, there were many other objects and people. Hence, I asked her to tell me what the entire picture was about. She looked at the picture for a few more seconds and then said, "I also see a tree." This inability to recognize the entire picture but to recognize only components of the scene is called simultanagnosia. Simultanagnosia is the third and final component of Balint's syndrome.

To recognize the meaning of a complex picture or scene, a person has to have the ability to see the objects in the scene and their spatial relationship to each other. Earlier I mentioned that attention can be focused or broadly distributed, local or global. The inability of patients with simultanagnosia to see the big picture might be related to a deficit in global attention. Simultanagnosia could also be related to a deficit in the ability to disengage one's attention from a specific visual object. There is, however, a third explanation for simultanagnosia. Coslett (2002) noted that to be able to comprehend a complex picture or scene that is composed of many objects, a person not only has to see these objects but also has to be aware of the spatial relationships between these objects. As I mentioned earlier, the ventral visual network is important for determining *what* objects are, and it is the dorsal visual system that is important in determining *where* objects are located. To understand a complex picture, these "what" and "where" systems must be able to work together. Watson, Valenstein, Day, and Heilman (1994) suggested that the ventral (what) and dorsal (where) systems both project to the inferior parietal lobes (see Figure 3.6), and Coslett (2002) suggested that a loss of this ability to integrate these "what" and "where" analyses might lead to simultanagnosia.

Visual Imagery

The most important function of the visual system is to process visual input so that we can recognize, localize, and interact with visual stimuli. We can, however, also see things that we are not viewing but rather are in our mind's eye. The ability to see things that are not there is called imagery or hallucination. Hallucinations are defined as false perceptual experiences in the absence of a sensory stimulus (Tekin & Cummings, 2003). This definition of hallucination, however, does not really discriminate between hallucination and imagery because imagery might also be considered to be false (i.e., not real) perceptual experiences. The difference between imagery and hallucinations has to do with intentional awareness. When we imagine something, we are aware that we intended to see something that was not present, but when people have hallucinations they do not intend or desire to see whatever it is they are seeing. Although there are some rare reports of people who have hallucinations and use these hallucinations for creative endeavors such as painting, it is more common for creative people to use imagery intentionally for activities such as writing fiction and painting.

As I describe in chapter 9, the organ of intention is the frontal lobes. Injury to the frontal lobes causes what has been termed "executive disorders." One of the most important jobs of executives is to allocate resources and assign duties. Patients with frontal lobe injuries cannot properly allocate resources or assign duties and thus become stimulus bound. Using functional magnetic imaging, Ishai, Ungerleider, and Haxby (2000) compared the brain activation evoked by perception with that evoked by imagery. They found content-related activation during imagery in extrastriate visual cortex, and this activity was restricted to small subsets of the regions that showed category- related activation during actual perception. Within the ventral temporal cortex, activation during imagery evoked stronger responses in the left hemisphere, whereas perception evoked stronger responses on the right. Visual imagery also evoked activity in the frontal cortex. These results support the postulate that imagery, as opposed to hallucinations, is implemented by top-down mechanisms mediated in part by the frontal cortex. Further support for the postulate that the frontal lobes might be important in either activating or inhibiting representational networks comes from a recent study, using positron-emission tomography, which suggested different roles for medial and lateral rostral prefrontal cortex (Brodmann's area 10). Whereas the lateral prefrontal cortex appears to activate representations stored in posterior neocortex, the medial prefrontal cortex is involved in suppressing internally generated representations (Burgess, Scott, & Frith, 2003).

Some investigators have suggested that the primary visual cortex (V1, the calcarine cortex, or Brodmann's area 17) (see Figure 1.1) is where visual images are displayed and then inspected (Kosslyn, 1999). My colleagues and I studied two patients who had bilateral lesions of the primary visual cortex. They were so severely cortically blind that they could not count fingers or even tell if the room lights were on or off. Both of these patients appeared to have intact visual imagery. In addition, functional imaging studies have suggested that blood flow to the primary visual cortex does not increase during visual imagery (Mellet et al., 2000).

Although the primary visual cortex does not appear important in the production of visual images, other areas of the visual-association cortex do appear to be important. In addition to having shapes, images can have color, spatial positions, and even movement. Support for the postulate that some of the same areas important in perception and recognition of the meaning of seen stimuli are also important in imagery comes from the observation of patients who have brain injury that interferes with specific aspects of stimuli processing and who also often have parallel deficits in imagery (Farah, 1989). For example, I mentioned that injury to the ventral temporal-occipital lobes might be associated with achromotopsia, an impaired ability to see the hues of colors (Damasio et al., 1980). DeRenzi and Spinnler (1967) described a patient who had an acquired achromotopsia on color vision tasks, such as the Ishihara test for color vision, and also had trouble with visual imagery such that the patient could not image the colors of common objects.

Earlier I described the ventral "what" and dorsal "where" systems and explained that patients with injury to the ventral "what" system might have trouble recognizing objects or people, a disorder called visual agnosia. I also noted that patients with injury to the dorsal "where" system might be impaired at finding the location of an object in space, and when they reach for an object they often and repeatedly reach into the wrong area of space, a disorder called optic ataxia. Levine and coworkers (1985) studied a patient who had object agnosia from bilateral ventral temporal lesions and another patient who had impaired object localization from bilateral dorsal lesions. These investigators found that their patients' imagery deficits paralleled their perceptual-recognition deficits. For example, the patient with a dorsal lesion could neither localize visual stimuli nor describe landmarks from memory but could perceive and recognize objects and image objects. The patient with the ventral lesion could localize visual stimuli and recall the position of landmarks but could not recognize seen objects or image objects from memory.

In addition to this dorsal-ventral what-where dichotomy, there are also left-right hemisphere imaging dichotomies. Feinberg, Rothi, and Heilman (1986) reported a patient with a left ventral temporal-occipital lesion who had an object agnosia. Patients with posterior lesions of the right but not left hemisphere can have problems recognizing emotional faces (Bowers, Bauer, Coslett, & Heilman, 1985) but not objects. Bowers, Blonder, Feinberg, and Heilman (1991) demonstrated that although patients with left posterior lesions have impaired object imagery, patients with right-hemisphere lesions have impaired imagery of emotional faces. Thus, activation of the object representations stored on the left hemisphere are important for object imagery, and activation of facial images and facial emotions stored in the right hemisphere are important in facial emotional imagery.

When reading a book or hearing a story, many people note that they experience visual images. The ability of stories to activate visual images suggests that semantic-conceptual representations also have the ability to activate visual images. In the clinic, I have seen patients with dissociations between the visual and the verbal-semantic systems. For example, patients with lesions of the left ventral temporal lobe, in addition to having trouble with reading words, might also have trouble naming colors, called color anomia. Because these patients' perisylvian language systems are intact and connected with the auditory and motor systems, these patients can comprehend speech and speak normally. They can also write normally. Although they can see written words by using their right hemisphere's visual systems, to read aloud or comprehend these written words they have to access to the left hemisphere's language systems. This left ventral (bottom) posterior temporal-occipital lesion not only prevents written words from gaining access to the left hemisphere's visual cortex but also prevents the words seen by the right occipital lobe from reaching the left hemisphere's language systems. When patients with these left ventral temporal lesions are shown colors and asked to name the color, they also might have difficulty performing this task. When they are asked to match colors or to name the typical color of certain objects (e.g., What is the color of a carrot?), they often perform correctly. The visual information has to access the language cortex for the patient to name colors, and a left temporal-occipital lesion prevents this visual information from gaining access to the language cortex. Matching colors can be performed without the patient's having to access language, and thus patients with these lesions can perform this task. When asked questions about the colors associated with concepts (e.g., red hot and green with envy), patients with this disorder do well because the semantic-conceptual systems have already stored this word knowledge and thus there is no reason to access input from the visual system or even visual representations. Beauvois and Saillant (1985) reported a patient who had color anomia and thus could not name visually presented colors but could match colors. When this patient was shown black-and-white pictures of objects, she was able to tell the color of the real object, but when she was asked to tell the color of named objects (e.g., What is the color of a cucumber?), she had trouble. It was thought that she had trouble answering these questions because this task requires visual imagery and there is a disconnection between the areas of the brain that store colored visual images and the parts of the brain that mediate language.

Studies that describe these types of verbal-visual imagery dissociations suggest that there are rich connections between the linguistic semantic-conceptual representations and visual representations. Thus hearing or reading stories might evoke visual imagery, and seeing objects or scenes can also evoke language representations. Similar relationships probably exist between other domains of stored knowledge, and many forms of creativity are probably strongly dependent on these relationships.

One of the major criteria of creativity is novelty. Thus, when one uses imagery in creative acts, he or she often has a need to transform images. Using a transformation process, one can image objects and scenes that have not been seen or heard. In one of the most famous imagery experiments conducted, Shepard and Metzler (1971) showed participants meaningless objects and then had them select the same object that they were shown from several choices, but in these choices the objects had been rotated. These investigators demonstrated that the greater the rotation of the object from its initial position, the longer it took the participants to choose the correct object. On the basis of these results, the authors suggested that finding the correct object (matching to sample) depended on imagining the object being rotated.

Warrington and James (1988) showed participants with right-hemisphere disease pictures of common objects. Some of these pictures showed objects from an unusual view (e.g., steam iron as viewed from the front), and other pictures showed objects from a more traditional view (e.g., a water bucket from the side). To recognize the objects that were presented with unusual views, a person would have to alter the image in the brain and bring it into a more traditional view. These investigators found that patients with right-hemisphere parietal lesions have trouble with this task. Hamsher, Levin, and Benton (1979) showed that patients with right-hemisphere posterior lesions had problems matching faces when these were shown in different views. This task also requires the mental rotation of images. Finally, using the paradigm of Shepard and Metzler (1971), investigators have studied brain-damaged and normal participants to show that posterior portions of the right hemisphere are critical for mental rotation. Thus, although both hemispheres appear important for imagery, the right hemisphere might be more important for spatial imagery transformations than is the left.

In summary, the ability to image and the ability to alter images are often important processes for creative innovation, and creative imagery is used in the arts, such as painting, sculpting, and writing, and in the sciences. Although most of our discussion has dealt with visual imagery, creative people can image in other modalities. For example, composers often imagine musical scores and lyrics. Functional imaging studies have revealed that when participants imagine music without lyrics, their right hemisphere's auditory-association cortex activates (Halpern, 2001), but when they imagine hearing the lyrics, the left hemisphere's language cortex activates (Ducreux, Marsot-Dupuch, Lasjaunias, Oppenheim, & Fredy, 2003). Although imagery appears to be an important ingredient in the creative process, several studies that examined the relationship between creativity and imagery found that the ability to image was not much greater in those who are more creative than those who were less creative (LeBoutillier & Marks, 2003). Thus, imagery, like general intelligence, is a critical ingredient for creativity, but is not sufficient. After a person reaches a threshold of ability, there is not a close relationship between the ability to image and creativity.

5

Handedness

Almost all mammals have a lateral motor preference or paw preference, but in almost all animals, except for humans and great apes, there is not an overall left-right asymmetry. Humans have the greatest motor bias. Approximately 90% of people prefer to use their right hand. The other 10% can either prefer their left hand or have no hand preference. I call the former group left-handers and the latter group ambidextrals or nonright-handers. There are some reports that suggest people who are left handed might be more creative. Leonardo da Vinci, an artist and inventor who had remarkable gifts for creativity in multiple domains, was probably left handed. Although I do not know for certain that da Vinci was left handed, I do know that he wrote in mirror script. Studies performed in our laboratories have revealed that writing in mirror script might be easier or more natural for left-handed than right-handed people (Tankle & Heilman, 1983), and on the basis of the observation that da Vinci wrote in mirror script, researchers have assumed that he was left handed (Schott, 1979). It has also been reported that many of the other great renaissance visual artists, such as Michelangelo and Raphael, also were left handed.

The hand preference for creative people has not been thoroughly studied, but there is some evidence in the literature that in certain disciplines there is a higher prevalence of left-handed creative people than can be accounted for by chance. This appears to particularly true in the arts. For example, Peterson (1979) found that there was a higher proportion of left-handed people who majored in either music or visual arts than those who were science majors. Hassler and Gupta (1993) studied the handedness of accomplished musicians and found that left-handedness was related to musical talent. Newland (1981) studied left- and right-handed young adults who did or did not have a college background by giving them the Torrance Test of Creative Thinking and found that the participants who preferred their left hand scored higher in this test than those who were right handed, and the participants with a college background scored higher than those who did not have a college background. One study examined the creative ability of children who either were in grade school (second grade and fifth grade) or were undergraduates in college by administering the Torrance Test of Creative Thinking and found that at every level the left-handed participants were more creative than those who preferred their right hand (Stewart & Clayson, 1980). Finally, Coren (1995) studied the relationship between handedness and divergent thinking. He found that left-handed people, especially men, had a greater capacity for divergent thinking than did right-handed people, and this ability increased with increasing sinistrality. As I discuss in the chapter on the frontal lobes (chapter 9), divergent thinking has been thought to be a critical element of creativity.

The reason why left-handedness should be associated with enhanced creativity is unknown, but in this chapter I explore some possibilities. I first discuss the possible neurobiological bases of hand preference, because if hand preference is related to creativity than the genesis of the hand preference might help explain the relationship between preference and creativity. Then, I discuss the possible brain mechanisms that might account for differences in creativity between people who have right- and left-hand preferences.

Genesis of Hand Preference

Survival of the Fittest

The reason the majority of people are right handed is still unknown. There are several theories. Darwin's theory of evolution states that the most fit survive, but why would right-handed people be more likely to survive than left-handed people? One theory, called the "sword and shield hypothesis," suggests that right-handed people would fight holding the sword in their right hand and their shield in their left hand. In contrast, left-handed people would hold their swords in their left hand and the shield in their right. When right- and left-handed people were in a battle, the right-handed people would be more likely to survive because, independent of hand preference, the heart is on the left side of the chest and hence more vulnerable when the shield is held in the right hand. The problem with this theory is that there is evidence that even prior to the advent of swords the majority of people had a right-hand preference, and this theory would not help explain why creativity might be linked to handedness.

Fetal Position

Another theory suggests that the fetus in its mother's womb is more likely to be in a position where its left arm and hand are toward the mother's spine and thus have less freedom to move than does the right arm. This gives the right hand–left brain an advantage that increases as the child matures. The problem with this theory is that it cannot account for the observation that the position of the fetus in the womb is not random and again this theory will have little explanatory value for the relationship between hand preference and creativity.

Culture

Many cultures discourage the use of the left hand. Even in the United States and England, countries that are noted for their tolerance of diversity, the scientific term for left-handedness is *sinistral,* which means evil. In many other languages the terms used for left-handedness also have negative connotations. In the United States, children who write with their left hand are no longer trained to switch hands and to write with their nonpreferred right hand, but only a few generations ago this was a widespread practice. Despite the relaxation of cultural pressure in the United States, the percentage of people who are right handed has remained about 90%. Thus, although cultural factors might influence the overall prevalence of hand preference, cultural influences do not appear to play a critical role.

Brain Asymmetries

Although almost all people who study hand preference would agree that hand preference is related to some form of brain asymmetry, the reason why a person prefers one hand or the other is still not entirely understood. I briefly discuss three of the major theories: (a) language dominance, (b) praxis laterality, and (c) deftness.

Language Laterality

Many people think that the hemisphere that is dominant for mediating language determines handedness. When patients get strokes they usually damage either the right or left half of their brain (hemispheres). As I mentioned in chapter 2, more than 130 years ago Paul Broca, a French physician and anthropologist, reported eight patients who were all right handed and all had an impairment of speech-language (aphasia) from a left-hemisphere injury. On the basis of these observations, he proposed that if a person prefers his or her right hand then the left hemisphere mediates speech-language. Subsequent studies have replicated his findings, and there is now overwhelming evidence that more than 95% of right-handed people have their speech-language mediated by their left hemisphere.

Each hemisphere controls the opposite hand, and one of the most important skilled activities we perform with our hands is writing. Writing requires both language and motor skills. Because in right-handed people it is the left hemisphere that mediates language and controls the right hand, people who have language in their left hemisphere might prefer to write with their right hand because this hand has direct access to the systems that mediate language. If a person who has language mediated by the left hemisphere attempts to write with the left hand, he or she must first transfer linguistic information from the left to the right hemisphere, which controls the left hand. The interhemispheric transfer of information is less efficient than direct access. Thus, language laterality has been posited to be an important factor in hand preference.

One of the problems with the language-writing theory of hand preference is that children show evidence for hand preference even before they write. In addition, even more than 90% of people who were never taught to read and write are right handed.

About 10 years after Broca's report, Karl Wernicke, a 19th-century German neurologist, demonstrated that the left hemisphere of right-handed people is also important for the comprehension of language. Many of the actions that we perform with our hands and arms are in response to language commands, both internal and external. Because the same hemisphere that comprehends language controls actions of the right hand, the use of the right hand might be more efficient than the use of the left hand that is controlled by the nonlanguage-dominant right hemisphere.

As I mentioned, the major band of fibers that connects the two hemispheres is called the corpus callosum. Occasionally, strokes injure the corpus callosum and sometimes the corpus callosum is cut by neurosurgeons to prevent the spread of epileptic seizures in patients who cannot be adequately controlled by medications. Right-handed patients who have had callosal injury often find that their left hand acts in a bizarre fashion. For example, one patient I had the privilege of examining told me that once, when she was getting dressed, she wanted to wear a blue dress and thus took a blue dress out of the closet with her right hand. When she went to get the matching blue shoes with her left hand, her left hand picked up red shoes. The type of observation that this patient related to me has led some people to call this left hand an "alien" hand because it appears to be under control by some foreign force.

Stories such as these suggest that our conscious intentions, or goal-directed actions, are mediated by the verbal left hemisphere. People with callosal disconnection, can not communicate these intentions to their nonverbal right hemisphere, which might have different intentions. Because conscious intentions might be mediated by "inner speech," the right hand would have privileged access to these intentions.

It takes several years after a child is born before its corpus callosum becomes entirely myelinated, and unmyelinated nerve fibers inadequately transmit information between the hemispheres. Thus, during the early stages of development, the child's right hand and arm has privileged access to verbal intentions, and this asymmetrical access in children is even greater than that found in normal adults.

Although language laterality might be one of the important factors that determine hand preference, there is one important observation that suggests that it cannot be the entire explanation. Some patients who have epilepsy have an abnormality of the cerebral cortex that becomes electrically irritable and is the source of the epileptic seizures. If medications cannot control these patients' seizures, the surgeon might elect to remove this abnormal part of the cortex. The surgeon, however, does not want to remove any part of the cortex that is important for language. Thus, before a patient undergoes surgery, the neurologist injects a barbiturate into the right and then the left carotid artery (the major artery that feeds blood to each hemisphere). This barbiturate puts the hemisphere that receives this sedative asleep. If when the left hemisphere is put to sleep a person cannot speak, it is the patient's left hemisphere that is dominant for language and vice versa. Using this selective hemispheric anesthesia procedure, investigators (Milner, 1974) have learned that 70% of people who prefer their left hand have left-hemisphere dominance for language, and thus these people who prefer to use their left hand have language dominance that is similar to people who prefer their right hand. Fifteen percent of left-handers, however, do have their language mediated by their right hemisphere, and the final 15% have both hemispheres mediating language. The observation that the majority of left-handed people are left-hemisphere dominant for speech and language provides evidence that language laterality cannot solely account for hand preference. Thus, there might be other factors that determine hand preference.

Praxis Laterality

Throughout our lives we learn to perform skilled acts such as using tools, writing, and drawing. Many of the acts are important for creative endeavors. Watson and Heilman (1981) examined a right-handed patient who had a stroke that damaged her corpus callosum. When we asked her to pantomime using a tool, such as a hammer, she performed flawlessly with her right hand and arm but performed poorly when using her left arm. Because this woman was right handed, her left hemisphere probably mediated language. When we gave her the command to use a hammer, it was the left hemisphere that decoded this linguistic message; perhaps she could not pantomime the use of a hammer with her left hand because her callosal damage prevented the verbal message from reaching the right hemisphere, which controls the left hand. We, therefore, made a hammering pantomime and asked her to copy or imitate this pantomime. Again, she performed flawlessly with her right hand but poorly with her left hand. When we also gave her an actual hammer to use with her right hand then her left hand, she also showed this same hand asymmetry. Imitation and the actual use of tools and objects can be performed in the absence of language. Thus, this woman's failure to correctly use tools and objects with her left hand suggests that some other form of knowledge is stored in her left hemisphere and with callosal disconnection could not be accessed by her right hemisphere.

Liepmann (1920) suggested that in people who prefer their right hand, their left hemisphere not only mediates language but also contains the memories or representation of how to perform skilled acts. He provided support for this hypothesis by demonstrating that in right-handed people the loss of the ability to perform skilled movements (apraxia) was associated with left- but not right-hemisphere strokes. He also suggested that it was the laterality of these learned movement (praxis) representations that accounted for hand preference.

In general there has been strong support for this postulate, but there have been reports of right-handed people who developed apraxia from right-hemisphere injuries. One of these patients whom we examined also was aphasic (Rapcsak, Gonzalez-Rothi, & Heilman, 1987). Thus, this patient's hand preference or handedness could not be entirely explained by either language or praxis laterality, suggesting that another asymmetry might be important in determining hand preference.

Deftness

Deftness is defined as the ability to make fine, precise, and independent finger movements. Although the term *dexterity* is also used for these abilities, this word derives from the word *dextral,* which pertains to the right hand or right side, and many people are more deft with their left hand than with their right. Nonhuman primates, such as old world are very deft, and Lawrence and Kuypers (1968) found that in monkeys, injury to the corticospinal system, which sends movement messages from the cerebral cortex to the motor neurons in the spinal cord, impaired these monkeys' ability to make precise independent finger movements.

Magnetic stimulation can produce electrical currents through the skull and thereby activate the corticospinal motor neurons in the motor cortex. Triggs and coworkers (1994) found in right-handed people that the threshold for activating the motor neurons in the left hemisphere was lower than it was for the right hemisphere, suggesting that right-handed people have larger motor representations in their left hemisphere than in their right hemisphere. Nudo, Milliken, Jenkins, and Merzenich (1996), however, found that the cortical representation of hands could change with practice and therefore it was unclear if the asymmetries of the motor cortex were induced by nurture (practice) or nature. Foundas et al. (1998), using structural magnetic resonance imaging, measured the size of the hand area in the brains of right-handed people and found that the motor cortex on the left side was larger than that on the right. Although the physiological configuration of cortex might change with practice, it is unlikely that the anatomic configuration would change, and the findings of Foundas et al. suggest that there are anatomic asymmetries of the motor system, and these asymmetries might in part account the functional asymmetries found by Triggs et al. as well as account for hand preference.

All right-handed people, however, are not more deft with their right hand than left hand, and although most people have greater arm strength with their preferred arm, there are people who have a non-preferred hand that is stronger that their preferred hand. Thus, deftness, like language and praxis laterality, cannot alone explain hand preference, and hand preference appears to be related to multiple factors. In addition, none of the factors that have been described previously can explain why hand preference would influence creativity. Thus, perhaps handedness might be linked to another factor or factors that influence creativity.

Creativity and Left-Hand Preference

Creativity is heavily dependent on novelty, and in the chapter on intelligence (chapter 2) I wrote about the importance of divergent thinking in creativity. I also discuss divergent thinking in the chapter on the frontal lobes (chapter 9). Coren (1995) studied the relationship between handedness and divergent thinking and found that left-handed people are better at divergent thinking than are right-handed people. The reason for this left handed superiority for divergent thinking is not known. When presented with a problem, however, divergent thinking might depend on the ability to recruit networks that have a substantially different architecture than those usually recruited in response to this problem. This allows a person to escape the constraints of existing internal models, represented in the networks usually used for thinking in a particular domain. Hence, creativity might require the ability to make associations between a variety of different concepts and representations, and, as mentioned, the cortex in the right and left hemispheres, which are connected by the corpus callosum, store very different types of representations.

The corpus callosum mediates communication between the hemispheres, and interhemispheric communication might play a vital role in creative endeavors. Support of this postulate comes from the observation that there is a reduction of creativity associated with damage to the corpus callosum. Witelson (1985) reported that the corpus callosum is larger in left-handed people than in right-handed people, and she suggested that the greater use of bihemispheric cognitive representations in left-handed people might be related to the greater anatomical connection between the two hemispheres. Thus, in people who are left handed, the increased ability of the hemispheres to communicate might provide a greater ability to recruit and associate diverse networks that store different forms of information, a process that might be very important in the creative process: seeing the thread that unites.

In the chapter on neurotransmitters (chapter 8), I describe the relationship between creativity and mood disorders, such as depression. In many creative domains there is a high prevalence of people who have mood disorders. Several studies have also examined the relationship between hand preference and depression. These studies found that the prevalence of depression is higher in people who are left handed than people who are right handed. For example, Elias, Saucier, and Guylee (2001) administered a depression inventory to a large group of college students and found that left-handed men were much more likely to have suffered with depression, but the reason for the association between left-hand preference and depression is not known.

To better understand the relationship between hand preference and creativity, we might find it worthwhile to examine several different domains of creativity. In the following sections I discuss some creative domains.

Musicians

Hassler and Gupta (1993) studied 51 young adult musicians and non-musicians. These participants were tested with Wing's Standardized Tests of Musical Intelligence and a handedness questionnaire. These investigators did find that musical talent was related to left-handedness. In another study, however, Hering, Catarci, and Steiner (1995) investigated professional musicians who were playing in orchestras, and they did not find a higher incidence of left-handedness in these orchestras than found in the general population. In a third study of handedness and musical ability, Jancke, Schlaug, and Steinmetz (1997) examined asymmetries of hand skills on two handedness tasks in consistent right-handed musicians and nonmusicians. These right-handed musicians revealed a lesser degree of hand-skill asymmetry than consistent right-handed nonmusicians, and it was this increase of left-hand skills in musicians that accounted for their reduced asymmetry. These results suggest that even right-handed musicians might be more ambidextrous than nonmusicians. Practicing skilled movements, however, not only can enhance motor performance but can even alter the portions of the brain that mediate these skills. For example, Nudo and his coworkers (1996) trained monkeys to perform skilled motor tasks and noted that the brain areas that control the finger of the hand that learned this task enlarged. Thus it remains unclear if this increased tendency of musicians to be ambidextrous is related to their genetic endowment or if accomplished musicians practice long hours to increase the skill of both hands and this practice alters their motor asymmetry.

Although practice can enhance motor skills, in most hand-preference inventories right-handed people appear to be more biased toward using their preferred right hand than are people who prefer their left hand. Hence, in general left-handed people tend to be more ambidextrous. Playing most musical instruments requires the coordinated use of both hands, and this might give left-handed people an advantage. Christman (1993) noted that although playing some instruments requires temporal integration (e.g., the string instruments), playing other instruments requires independent bimanual motor activity (e.g., the keyboard instruments), and people who had mixed handedness (e.g., ambidextrous) are superior at playing the instruments that require independent bimanual activity.

Schlaug, Jancke, Huang, and Steinmetz (1995); Lee, Chen, and Schlaug (2003); and Ozturk, Tascioglu, Aktekin, Kurtoglu, and Erden (2002) found that musicians had larger corpus callosums than matched control participants. These investigators posited that it was nurture rather than nature that determined these differences, suggesting that the early commencement and continual practice of bimanual training is the "external trigger" that induced this callosal enlargement. As I mentioned earlier, Nudo et al. (1996) demonstrated that functional specialization can be altered with practice and Rosenzweig (1972) demonstrated that animals placed in enriched environments had larger heads than those who were not placed in these environments. To my knowledge, however, there is no direct evidence that practice can alter the size of the corpus callosum. Although talented musicians can be creative in their interpretations, it is primarily the people who write and compose music who are the most creative in this domain. I searched the literature, but unfortunately, I could find no studies that assessed composers' handedness or examined their brains.

Visual Artists

In the introduction of this chapter, I mentioned that some of the greatest artists were left handed. When I searched the literature for systematic studies of visual artists (painters, sculptors, etc.), I could not find many systematic studies of handedness in this group. In one of the few studies I found, Peterson (1979) investigated hand preference in art students and found in this group of art students there was a higher percentage of people who preferred their left hand than there is in the general population. In contrast, in one of the few studies that attempted to learn the hand preference of great painters and to find out what proportion were left handed, Lanthony (1995) studied the portraits of the painters but found that self-portraits were worthless because painters often paint themselves by viewing a mirror image. Thus, an investigator who was attempting to learn if the artist was left or right handed by examining self-portraits could not tell if the artist painted what he or she saw in the mirror (that would have right-left reversed the hand holding the brush) or if he or she corrected for the mirror image. To avoid this confound, Lanthony only studied portraits of painters made by another painter or by photography. Right-handed artists make hatchings (e.g., for shadows) that descend from right to left, and left-handed artists make hatchings that descend from left to right. Thus, Lanthony also studied artists' hatchings. Finally, Lanthony examined the literature that was available about famous artists. Using these methods Lanthony was able to include in this study 500 painters. These painters were divided into two groups: 127 painters studied by portraits and hatchings, and a population of 373 painters studied by hatchings only. In the first population, the proportion of left-handed painters was 4.7%. In the second population, the proportion of left-handed painters was 2.1%.

In the general population, the prevalence of left-handedness is about 7% to 10%. Thus, according to Lanthony's study, left-handed people are underrepresented in a population of highly creative painters. Prospective studies that assess the handedness of painters, however, need to be performed.

We do not know why there is a higher proportion of creative visual artists who are right handed. As I mentioned, studies of brain-damaged people have revealed that damage to the right hemisphere impairs visual-spatial, visual-perceptual, and visual-constructive processes (see Benton & Tranel, 1993, for a review). For example, in a face-matching test, participants are asked to determine if two faces are the same or different. In this test the photographs of the two faces are taken at different angles such that the participant cannot determine if the two pictures are the same or different people by making point-to-point comparisons, but instead, the subject must develop an object-centered or face-centered perceptual representation. Patients with right-hemisphere injury are often impaired on this face-matching test. Patients with right-hemisphere disease are also impaired in a test where they are shown a series of cards with two line segments and are asked to study and recall the relationship (angle) between these two segments.

Patients with either left- or right-hemisphere injury, such as stroke, have problems with drawing and copying drawings, but they make different types of mistakes. Whereas the patients with left-hemisphere disease have problems with planning the drawing, those with right-hemisphere disease cannot accurately represent the spatial relationships between the elements in the drawing. By virtue of using their left hand, visual artists might have more direct access to the hemisphere that is dominant for visual-spatial and visual-perceptual processing, which might give left-handed people an advantage, but this postulate is not in accord with Lanthony's (1995) results.

The hypothesis that the right hemisphere can better mediate the visual-spatial processes that are important in drawing and painting also draws support from studies of patients who have undergone section of the corpus callosum for the control of epilepsy. This procedure disconnects the right and left hemispheres. When patients who have had this procedure are asked to copy or draw pictures with their left hand, which has access primarily to the right hemisphere, they performed much better than when they attempt the same drawing with their right hand. This finding is also inconsistent with Lanthony's (1995) results.

People who teach visual arts attempt to capitalize on this hemispheric dichotomy. For example, Betty Edwards (1999), who wrote *Drawing on the Right Side of the Brain,* claimed that her book is one of the first practical applications of the information reported by Sperry and his colleagues, who demonstrated using the split-brain (callosal disconnection) paradigm that the two hemispheres had different processing strategies and that the right hemisphere had superior spatial abilities. In this book, however, Edwards does not suggest that right-handed people use their left hand to draw and paint as some people have suggested, but she does attempt to teach people the means by which they might activate and predominately use the right-hemisphere processing strategies.

Although when using the left hand, they might have greater access to the right hemisphere that mediates visuospatial skills, left-handed people often have a different brain organization than do people who prefer their right hand. As mentioned, 70% of left-handed people have their language mediated by the left hemisphere, the other 30% can either mediate language with both hemispheres or mediate language with the right hemisphere. Masure and Benton (1983) assessed visuospatial judgment in a population of left- and right-handed people who had injuries of either their left or their right hemisphere. In the right-handed patients, impaired performance on visuospatial tests were found to be almost exclusively associated with right-hemisphere injury. In Masure and Benton's study, the left-handed patients showed the same performance pattern as the right-handed patients. They found that a high proportion of left- and right-handed patients with right-hemisphere lesions performed abnormally, whereas all the patients with left-hemisphere lesions performed normally. On the basis of these results, Masure and Benton concluded that the hemispheric cerebral organization of visuospatial functions do not differ between left- and right-handers. Hence, if there are differences in artist ability between left- and right-handed people, this difference cannot be related to the hemispheric mediation or organization of visuospatial skills.

The left hand, might also have direct access to other representations that are important in artistic production. One of the most important skills that creative artists need is the ability to portray emotions. There are many means by which emotion can be portrayed, but perhaps one of the most common is in the painting of faces. About 30 years ago in our laboratories, We (DeKosky, Heilman, Bowers, and Valenstein, 1980) studied patients with strokes that were limited to either the left or right hemisphere by showing them pictures of emotional faces and asking the patients to name the emotion expressed by the face, or by having the patients point to a face from a series of faces that expressed an emotion named by the examiner. These patients were also asked to tell them if two faces were expressing the same or different emotions. We found that when compared with normal controls and patients with left-hemisphere strokes, the patients with right-hemisphere strokes were impaired at discriminating emotional faces. Because the right hemisphere might be dominant in processing faces (Benton & Tranel, 1993), it is possible that the findings reported by DeKosky et al. were related to a deficit in facial recognition rather than a deficit in the recognition of emotional faces. Subsequent studies not only replicated the DeKosky et al.'s study but also revealed that the deficit in emotional-facial recognition induced by right-hemisphere injury could not be entirely accounted for by a visuospatial defect or a deficit in face processing (Bowers et al., 1985).

Imagery is very important in the creative process and visual imagery is a very important skill for creative visual artists. In chapter 4 I discussed imagery and mentioned the study of Bowers, Blonder, Feinberg, and Heilmann (1991), who studied object versus emotional-facial imagery, and demonstrated that patients with right-hemisphere lesions are impaired at imaging emotional faces but not objects and patients with left-hemisphere lesions are impaired in object but not emotional-facial imagery. Thus, it appear that the right hemisphere contains representations of emotional faces and the left hand might have better access to these representations.

Studies of patients with right- and left-hemisphere lesions have demonstrated that the right hemisphere also appears to be critical for the expression of emotions under natural conditions (Blonder, Bowers, & Heilman, 1991). In concert with Blonder et al.'s findings, Sackeim, Gur, and Saucy (1978) took pictures of normal people who portrayed emotional facial expressions, cut them in half, and created whole faces from the left and right half faces. They showed normal people these composite left and right faces that were expressing emotions and asked these people to judge or rate the intensity of emotion expressed by these composite faces. Sackeim and coworkers found that the composite picture made from the left-side components expressed emotions more strongly than did the composite made from right-side components.

Schirillo (2000) reported that portrait artists have predominantly painted portraits with the model's left cheek facing the viewer. These painters do this even more when women are the models (approximately 68%) than when men are the models (approximately 56%). Schirillo also noted that many of the portraits painted by Rembrandt typify this asymmetry. The reason that artists paint portraits in this manner is not known, and it is also unclear how this asymmetry might be related to handedness, but the finding that the left side of the face is more emotionally expressive might account for why the artists have their models pose in this position.

The visual system is crossed such that when a normal person looks straight ahead and a visual image is shown on the left half of their visual field, this image projects to the right hemisphere. If the image is flashed to the right side it projects to the left hemisphere. When words are flashed to the left versus right visual field, people detect the words better when they are seen on the right than left because the left hemisphere is dominant for language. In contrast, when pictures of faces are flashed to the right or left visual field, normal people see them better when they are flashed to the left than to the right visual field. When the task was to recognize emotional facial expressions, the left-visual-field–right-hemisphere asymmetry was even stronger than detecting nonemotional faces. These studies in normal people provide converging evidence that the right hemisphere is dominant not only in the processing of faces but also in the processing of facial emotions. If emotional faces are seen better in the left than in the right visual field, but the left face is more expressive than the right, when a model directly faces the artist the part of the model's face that best expresses emotions will be observed by the artist's right visual field. This right visual field projects to the left (verbal) hemisphere, which is less proficient at perceiving emotions and performing visuospatial processing. Although the great artists might not have known about these hemispheric asymmetries, they might have had implicit knowledge about these asymmetries of facial expression, and this knowledge might be the reason they had the models turned so that the model's left side of their face would be seen by both sides of the brain.

The use of the left hand to paint or draw might allow direct access or selective activation of the right hemisphere, which is dominant for mediating visuospatial skills, storing the representations of emotional expressions, and performing global processing. All these functions are important for artistic skills, but creativity and artistic skills are not always directly linked. There are many extremely talented painters who are able to accurately represent a face or a scene; however, these artists might not be creative and instead be primarily craftsmen or craftswomen.

Authors-Writers

As I mentioned earlier, since the classic work of Paul Broca it has been known that the left hemisphere is dominant for mediating language. This does not mean, however, that the right hemisphere plays no role in creative verbal communication. Skilled authors often use metaphor and connotative as well as alternative word meanings. Brownell, Simpson, Bihrle, Potter, and Gardner (1990) studied patients with right- and left-hemisphere lesions by using a sorting task in which participants responded on the basis of the alternative meanings of words (adjectives and nouns) that have more than one meaning (polysemous). *Warm,* for example, means having a higher than median temperature but also means loving and affectionate. They found that in spite of having aphasia, the patients with left-hemisphere damage were better at detecting metaphoric meaning than were non-aphasic patients with right-hemisphere damage. On the basis of these results, these authors concluded that in normal people the right hemisphere is dominant for mediating metaphor. In another study Brownell et al. (1986) presented pairs of sentences and had the participant make inferences about the meaning of these two sentences. They demonstrated that compared with those patients with left-hemisphere damage, the patients with right-hemisphere damage were impaired at making inferences. Kaplan, Brownell, Jacobs, and Gardner (1990) studied the ability of right-handed patients who had either left- or right-hemisphere damage to understand the nonliteral interpretation of conversations and found that patients with right-hemisphere damage were more impaired than patients with left-hemisphere damage. The comprehension of nonliteral utterances is important in understanding a character's intentions and his or her internal states.

In creative writing the ability to use techniques such as metaphor and inference is critical, but so is the overall organization of sentences and paragraphs. Delis, Waper, Gardner, and Moses's (1983) study of patients with right- and left-hemisphere damage showed that the patients with right-hemisphere damage were also impaired at organization. In regard to content, creative writers often portray emotional states and write humorous works. Bihrle, Brownell, Powelson, and Gardner (1986) studied the ability of patients with right- and left-hemisphere strokes to comprehend humor by showing them cartoons, and they found that patients with right-hemisphere disease were impaired at detecting humorous cartoons. There are multiple forms of humor, and the role that each hemisphere plays in processing humor still needs to be investigated.

On the basis of this brief review, we can see that creative writing requires the use of both hemispheres. Thus, writing with one hand versus the other would not confer any benefit. In addition, now many writers use keyboards where both hands are used. Because creative writing would require the use of both hemispheres, perhaps people who have better interhemispheric communication by means of the corpus callosum would be more creative. Earlier in this chapter, I mentioned that people who prefer their left hand might have thicker corpus callosums, and if bigger is better, a thicker callosum might allow better interhemispheric communication. If this were the case, then we would expect a higher proportion of left-handed versus right-handed people to be creative writers. I searched the literature to see if there were more creative writers who were left handed, but I could find no studies either to support or to refute this postulate. The only systematic study I could find was by Halpern, Haviland, and Killian (1998), who examined the relationship between handedness and the portions of the Medical College Admission Test that assess verbal reasoning. These investigators found that left-handed people who took this test obtained higher scores on the verbal reasoning test than did right-handed people, but right-handed people scored higher, on average, on writing. Overall, one always has to be cautious about making positive statements in the absence of scientific evidence, but I suspect if a high proportion of writers preferred their left hand, this relationship would have been reported. Thus, like visual artists such as painters, the prevalence of left-handed creative writers is probably no higher than the prevalence of left-handedness in the general population.

6

Gender

Before leaving my training in Boston to join the neurology faculty at the University of Florida, I received several pieces of practical advice from some of my mentors. Once, when I was speaking of seeing certain diseases, primarily in a specific race, one of my mentors told me that as a Caucasian man, I should never discuss racial or sex-gender differences in brain function. I heeded this advice until Anne Foundas asked me to be a discussant in a symposium she was giving at the annual International Neuropsychology Society meeting. As advised, I told her over the phone, "No, thanks." Anne, however, is one of my former fellows, and when my fellows ask me to do something I have trouble saying no. So she persisted and I agreed. I thought I would start my discussion with a joke that perhaps would relieve my tension and put some of the people in the audience in a good mood so that they would not be too critical about what I was going to say about gender differences. I started by telling the following neurology story:

This patient has terrible headaches and the doctor tried every possible medicine. When the doctor found nothing that would work to relieve these headaches, the doctor told the patient that the only thing left to do was to get a brain transplant. The doctor, however, told the patient that the insurance company would not pay for this procedure. The patient asked the doctor the cost, and the doctor told the patient that it depended if you get a man's or woman's brain. The man's brain would cost about $1 million, but the woman's brain would only cost about $25,000.

Before I could finish my story, several women in the audience stood up and looked like they were ready to rush the podium and attack me, so I quickly finished the story: "The patient asked about the big difference in price and the doctor replied, 'Well, unlike men's brains, women's brains are used.'"

I hope this joke also sets a good mood for the women reading this chapter, because although women's brains are well used, in this chapter I discuss the observation that women appear to be less creative than men and that this gender difference might be related to differences in the brains of men and women. I considered heeding my mentor's advice about writing about gender differences, and I thought about not including a chapter on gender. One of my most influential mentors, however, was Norman Geschwind, who together with Albert Galaburda wrote a series of articles in the *Archives of Neurology* in which they discussed the possible differences in the brains of men and women. Because Norman was my primary mentor, I thought I would take the liberty of discussing the issue of gender differences in creativity.

In his book *Genius* (1995), H. L. Eysenck stated, "Creativity, particularly at the highest level, is closely related to gender; almost without exception, genius is found only in males." When I first read this sentence, I said to myself, *What about Madame Curie? She won two Nobel Prizes, one for physics and one for chemistry. How many men have done that?* Then when I started to think about other women who had won the Nobel Prize, I recalled Rita Levi-Montalcini but had trouble coming up with other women's names. Eysenck referred to the Cox (1926) study of geniuses, which listed no women. Eysenck also wrote that one cannot find a woman in a list of the 100 best painters and sculptors. Simonton (1994) did not find a woman in a list of the 120 most famous composers. After reading this I thought about my favorite poet Emily Dickinson and about Virginia Woolf and Gertrude Stein and all the creative women publishing novels today. Eysenck agreed somewhat that women can write, but, he stated, "It's only among poets and novelists that a small percentage of women can be found in the top class."

Although in this chapter I discuss possible brain differences between men and women that might explain the gender differences in creativity, even today there are strong cultural influences that might account for these differences. Today, even in the most literate and tolerant societies, such as the United States, Great Britain, France, Italy, and Israel, boys and girls are raised differently. Whereas girls are brought up to focus on family and interpersonal relationships, boys are brought up to be independent, to compete, and to achieve. Unlike creative men, who are often married with children, creative women often go unmarried (Simonton 1999). In his attempt to explain the gender differences in creativity, Eysenck (1995) stated that marriage and child rearing cannot account for the gender differences because Zuckerman (1977) found that women published less than men but these gender differences had nothing to do with family obligations. Eysenck gave two possible biological reasons for the gender differences in creativity. The first reason deals with psychopathology and the second reason deals with intelligence.

Gender Differences in Psychopathology

Eysenck (1995) suggested that the "dispositional trait underlying schizophrenia" is an important ingredient of creativity and noted that the incidence of schizophrenia is higher in men than women. The *Diagnostic and Statistical Manual of Mental Disorders* (4th ed.) (*DSM-IV*) (American Psychiatric Association, 1994) stated, however, that although men tend to be institutionalized at a greater rate, community-based studies have suggested an equal gender ratio between the men and women who have schizophrenia. As I mention in the chapter on neurotransmitters (chapter 8), enhanced creativity appears to be associated with affective disorders. According to the *DSM-IV,* bipolar disorders are also equally distributed between men and women. Major depressive disorders, however, are reported more frequently with women. Although the higher incidence of depression in women might be related to an ascertainment-reporting bias (e.g., men are less likely to go for professional help), the incidence of mood disorders cannot account for the observation that men are more likely to be more creative than women. The incidence of anxiety disorders is also much higher in women than men. Although the preponderance of anxiety disorders in women might also be related to an ascertainment bias, as I discuss in the neuropharmacology section, anxiety is associated with high levels of norepinephrine, and high levels of this catecholamine might reduce or restrict the size of neuronal networks and bias of the brain toward processing external stimuli versus the activation and manipulation of stored representations. Thus, the bias toward external input that occurs with high norepinephrine level may prevent asking "what if" questions of the networks that store cognitive representations. The suppression of intrinsic excitatory potentials induced by high levels of norepinephrine might also prevent many of the association neurons that do not receive direct afferent input from achieving firing threshold, and the reduced activity of association neurons may lead to relatively sparse, constricted, nonoverlapping associative network conceptual representations. Highly distributed representations allow one to perform inference and generalization, processes that are critical to creativity, and thus anxiety would reduce creative innovation. I discuss the role of norepinephrine and arousal in more detail in chapter 8, which deals with neurotransmitters and creativity.

Intelligence

Eysenck (1995) also suggested that gender differences in IQ might be important in explaining the differences in creativity between men and women. He quoted the work of Lynn (1994), who found that men score on average 2.35 points higher than women on the Wechsler full scale IQ (1981). Eysenck noted that small differences in the mean score become greatly increased at the extremes of the distribution, such that if one assumes a perfectly normal Gaussian curve of distribution the expected probability of a man scoring an IQ of 160 or higher would be 0.0055167, but for a women the probability would be 0.0004743. Hence, if one randomly selects 10,000 people, there would be 55 men with an IQ higher than 160 but only 5 women. Eysenck stated, "A difference of a whole order or magnitude would certainly be of considerable importance in relation to producing works of genius."

There are two major problems with Eysenck's (1995) intelligence thesis of sex differences in creativity. First, measurements like those taken by the Wechsler Adult Intelligence Scale (1981), might not be as well suited to women as to men. For example, in a study of gender differences in tests of visual-spatial abilities, men performed better than women, but when the tests were untimed there were no significant differences (Goldstein, Haldane, & Mitchell, 1990). Many portions of the Wechsler test are timed, and the difference between men and women might be nothing more than a factor of speed. In addition, Stanley (1993), in a study of mathematically precocious youth, found that although the boys did better in math, the girls were superior in literature and composition. IQ tests such as the Wechsler test do not require composition. Second, as mentioned, although there might be an IQ threshold of about 120, there is no direct relationship between IQ scores and creativity.

Laterality and Modularity

One of the reasons why men's and women's creative endeavors might differ is that the modular organization of their brains might differ. Several investigators have provided evidence that, when compared to men, women are more likely to have bilateral hemisphere mediation of language (Gur et al., 2000; McGlone, 1977; Shaywitz et al., 1995). In addition, Gur et al. (2000) demonstrated that it was primarily men who showed right-hemisphere activation with spatial tasks. Other investigators were, however, unable to demonstrate sex differences in the lateralization of language (Frost et al., 1999).

As I noted earlier, Geschwind and Levitsky (1968), Foundas et al. (1994), and many other investigators have reported that there are hemispheric anatomic asymmetries, especially in the perisylvian region, such that the planum temporale is larger in the left hemisphere than in the right hemisphere. Studies have also shown that these asymmetries are more robust in men than women (Good et al., 2001; Kulynych, Vladar, Jones, & Weinberger, 1994). Not all studies, however, showed these sex differences between men and women (e.g., Foundas, Faulhaber, Kulynych, Browning, & Weinberger, 1999). Studies of the size of the major pathway that connects the two hemispheres, the corpus callosum, suggest that there is an inverse relationship such that the greater the asymmetry between the right and left hemispheres, the smaller the size of the corpus callosum and that this inverse relationship seems to be stronger for men than women (Aboitiz, Scheibel, Fisher, Zaidel, 1992). Studies that compared the size of men's and women's corpus callosum found that when corrected for overall brain size, the callosum is relatively larger in women than men, especially in the posterior portions such as the isthmus and splenium (Steinmetz, Staiger, Schlaug, Huang, & Jancke, 1995). Not all studies, however, could replicate these findings, and some have suggested that the smaller the brain the relatively greater the size of the corpus callosum (Jancke, et al., 1997; Pozzilli et al., 1994).

As I also mentioned in the chapter 5 on creativity and hand preference, that the corpus callosum is larger in left-handed people than in right-handed people (Witelson, 1985). A higher percentage of left-handed people have language-speech that is mediated by both hemispheres. Witelson (1985) suggested that the more the hemispheres share cognitive functions, the greater the anatomical connections between the two hemispheres. As also mentioned previously, several studies have suggested that women are more likely to have language bilaterally distributed than are men, and perhaps it is this bilateral distribution that is associated with relatively larger interhemispheric connections.

The corpus callosum contains axons that project from cortical neurons in one hemisphere to neurons in the other hemisphere. Although men have more neurons than do women, the cortex of men and women are equally thick, suggesting that women have a greater number of neuronal connections per neuron. It is this relatively increased connectivity in women that might account for their relatively larger corpus callosum.

Women appear to be more likely to develop degenerative dementia than are men. Women also live longer than men and the older a person is the more likely he or she is to get dementia. When corrected for age, however, the incidence of dementia is higher in woman. In degenerative dementia, such as Alzheimer's disease, there is a loss of cortical neurons, and the higher incidence of Alzheimer's disease in women might be related to a decreased reservoir of cortical neurons (de Courten-Myers, 1999). That men have more neurons than do women might suggest that men's brains might be more modular. As described earlier, the modularity or localizationist hypothesis was first put forth by Franz Gall in the latter part of the 18th century and the early part of the 19th century when he suggested that specific portions of the brain mediate specific functions. He also proposed what might now be termed "anatomically distributed modular cognitive systems." According to this hypothesis, although the different human faculties mediated by the brain are located in different anatomic areas of the cerebral cortex, they are highly interconnected. Thus, if women have a widely distributed language network, it is possible that other modules that mediate other nonlanguage skills would not be as well developed.

Support for this postulate comes from studies that assessed visuospatial abilities in women and men. Visuospatial or spatial abilities are primarily nonverbal. Visuospatial abilities include skills such as navigating and finding routes; reproducing angles; estimating relative magnitude of distance, length, and angles; and having the ability to rotate objects in three dimensions. Two of the tests that might require the least amount of verbal mediation are the spatial rotation test and the Judgment of Line Orientation Test, originally devised by Benton and Tranel (1993). In the former test (block rotation), the participants are shown a picture of an object that is made up of a series of attached square blocks (see Figure 6.1) and they have to select from several choices the picture that depicts this block after it has been rotated in space. In the Judgment of Line Orientation Test, participants are shown two line segments that are unattached (see Figure 6.2). Each of the segments is at a different angle from horizontal. After

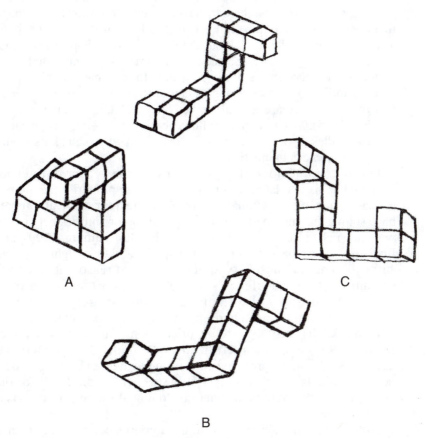

Figure 6.1. Imagery task. The participant is asked to view the top object and then indicate which of the three (A, B, or C) following objects is the same as the top object.

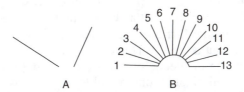

Figure 6.2. Visuospatial task. The participant is first shown the left figure (A), which has two lines at different angles from horizontal. This figure (A) is then removed, and the participant is shown a figure (B) that has lines at angles that vary from 1 to 180 degrees. The participant is asked to name or point to the figure that has the same two lines that she or he just viewed.

viewing these segments, the participants view a protractor-like image that contains multiple line segments that range from 0 to 180 degrees. The participants have to pick out the segments on this protractor that are the same angles as those seen in the target segments. Studies of gender differences in the ability to rotate three-dimensional objects and the ability to reproduce angles demonstrate that men are superior to women in these areas (Collaer & Nelson, 2002; Voyer, Voyer, & Bryden, 1995). What is unclear, however, is why men are superior to women in these types of visuospatial tasks and why such skills would lead to differences in creativity.

One of the teleological explanations for the gender differences in spatial skills is related to survival. Men were primarily the hunter-gatherers, hence navigational skills were critical for survival. Studies have shown that men perform some spatial-motor abilities better than women, such as accurately throwing projectiles (Kimura, 1999), and findings such as these do suggest that spatial abilities might have had survival benefit. But this type of teleological reasoning does not explain what it is about men's brains that makes them superior in these visuospatial skills. Studies of brain-damaged people have revealed that right-hemisphere injury impairs both mental rotation (Ditunno & Mann, 1990) and line orientation (Hamsher, Capruso, & Benton, 1992) more than left-hemisphere injury does. Functional imaging studies have provided converging evidence (Deutsch, Bourbon, Papanicolaou, & Eisenberg, 1988; Harris et al., 2000) for the postulate that the right hemisphere is dominant for performing visuospatial computations.

Although spatial skills are of minor importance in writing poetry and novels, these skills appear to be important in physics, chemistry, and engineering as well. Other disciplines such as painting and sculpting are also are very dependent on spatial skills. Whereas women do better at arithmetic (Kimura, 1999), men in general appear to be superior in higher forms of mathematics (Kegel-Flom & Didion, 1995), and several investigators have found that visuospatial skills are important in higher forms of mathematics (Casey, Nuttall, & Pezaris, 1997; Geary, Saults, Liu, & Hoard, 2000).

Although the influence of culture on gender differences has not been entirely eliminated, one possible reason why men do better on these spatial tasks is that many women have language distributed in both hemispheres, but men's language is mediated almost entirely by their left hemisphere. Support for this gender difference postulate come from morphological and lesion studies and functional imaging. As mentioned, some studies of the planum temporale (see Figure 3.8), an area critical in language processing, have suggested that men have a larger asymmetry than women (Good et al., 2001). If women's right hemisphere had a greater potential to mediate language than do men's right hemisphere, we might expect that right-handed women would have a much higher incidence of crossed aphasia (aphasia in a person who prefers his or her right hand from an injury to the right hemisphere) and a better prognosis for recovering from aphasia after a left-hemisphere injury. Overall, when I looked at this literature, I did not find that it fully supported these predictions. The failure to find support for this gender difference in the hemispheric distribution of language might be related to confounding factors. In contrast to the data from lesion studies, functional imaging studies in normal individuals have demonstrated then when performing language tasks, men primarily activate their left hemisphere, but women are more likely to activate both hemispheres (Jaeger et al., 1998). According to a limited capacity model, if women's right-hemisphere networks are more likely to store language representations and mediate language functions, then the remaining right-hemisphere processing networks that are available to mediate spatial cognition might be limited and thus not be able perform in a manner comparable to men whose right hemisphere is not occupied by language representations.

Dorsal Versus Ventral Systems

There is another possible explanation of the gender differences in spatial abilities and forms of creativity. Collaer and Nelson (2002) found that although men were superior in the Judgement of Line Orientation Test, if they altered the response array such that the base angles were not aligned with the bottom edge of the paper, the men's advantage was no longer present. The authors interpreted this finding as suggesting that men used a more global approach and did not solely focus on the lines but also looked at the position of the array on the page. As I mentioned earlier, the visual system is divided into a ventral "what" system and a dorsal "where" system (see Figure 1.1). Object recognition and recognition of familiar faces is more dependent on the ventral "what" system, and functions such as spatial localization are more dependent on the dorsal "where" system. The retina contains special nerve cells (ganglion cells) that become activated when light falls on them, prompting them to send electrical messages along the optic nerve until they reach a relay station in the middle of the brain called the lateral geniculate or optic thalamus (see Figure 6.3). The optic thalamus has two types of neurons: neurons that are large and send information rapidly, called magnocellular, and neurons that are small and send information more slowly, called parvocellular. The visual

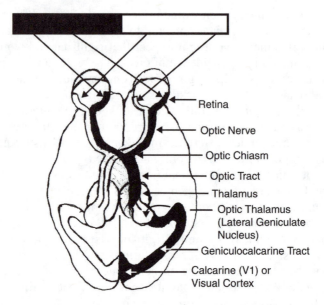

Figure 6.3. Diagram of the visual system, demonstrating that stimuli that fall on the retina are projected back by the optic nerves through the optic chiasma to the lateral geniculate or optic thalamus. From the optic thalamus, this information is then projected by way of the geniculo-calcarine tract to the primary visual cortex (V1).

information sent by the parvocellular system to the occipital lobes has high-contrast sensitivity and hence is well suited for detailed (focused) visual analyses, such as that needed to read letters and words. In contrast, the visual information processed by the magnocellular system has low-contrast sensitivity that is good for analyzing global configurations. A second series of nerves sends visual information from the optic thalamus to the primary visual cortex in the occipital lobes. The part of the occipital cortex that receives this signal from the optic thalamus is called the calcarine cortex or V1. The cells in this region detect changes in brightness that occurred in specific spatial locations on the retina. The V1, or Brodmann's area 17 (see Figure 1.1), sends this information to the visual association cortex where it is distributed to the ventral "what" and dorsal "where" systems. As I mentioned earlier, men appear to be superior to women in performing spatial "where" analyses, but women are superior to men in facial recognition (Lewin & Herlitz, 2002), which requires "what" analyses. Lesion studies suggest that reading is also performed by the ventral system, and men have two to three times a higher rate of developmental dyslexia than do women (Katusic, Colligan, Barbaresi,

Schaid, & Jacobsen, 2001). It is possible that magnocellular neurons are primarily fed into the dorsal "where" system, and the information that comes into the parvocellular neurons are primarily directed to the ventral "what" system. Perhaps men have superior spatial abilities because they have better developed magnocellular systems and women are superior in face recognition and reading because they have better developed parvocellular systems. Alternatively, the differences between men and women might be related to differences in the development of the ventral versus dorsal systems. In the future, women's and men's brains need to be studied to directly test the hypothesis that men and women have different magnocellular versus parvocellular systems or ventral versus dorsal systems.

Brain Size

To explain the greater number of men who have been recognized for their creativity, Lynn (1994) noted that men have larger heads than women, and head size correlates with brain size. It is true that men have larger or heavier brains than women, but it is also true that elephants have larger brains than men, and there is no evidence that elephants are smarter or more creative than men or women. Although men appear to have a greater number of neurons, their cortical thickness is the same as women's, suggesting that there is a reciprocal increase in the neuropil (neuronal connections) in the cerebral cortex of women (Rabinowicz, Dean, Petetot, & de Courten-Myers, 1999). As I mentioned, rather than the number of neurons, or the absolute size and weight of the brain, a measure of connectivity might be a critical factor for the ability to learn and store knowledge, such that the more synapses that can be formed, the greater is the knowledge that might be stored. Even when one controls for species and gender, studies that assessed the relationships of overall head size, forebrain size, total cortical area, or size of the interhemispheric commissures do not reveal a good correlation between these size measurements and intelligence (Tramo et al., 1998). If studies clearly demonstrated that men are more creative than women and this difference in creativity is not related to the cultural and social factors, it might then be possible that brain size accounts for creativity.

One of the major themes of this book has been that creativity or "finding the thread that unites" might be dependent on a person's ability to activate large conceptual networks or to communicate between independent modular systems that store different forms of knowledge. Thus, creativity might be heavily dependent on connectivity. In the cerebral cortex, adjacent neuronal assemblies are connected intracortically. Neurons in adjacent gyri are often connected by *U* fibers that are axons of cortical neurons that dip below the cortex and travel to another cortical area that is nearby. Distant intrahemispheric and interhemispheric communications, however, are mediated by axons that travel well below the cortex in the subcortical white matter. Because men, on average, have larger brains than women and the thickness of the cortex of men is not different from that of women, it is possible that men have more subcortical white matter than do women. Filipek, Richelme, Kennedy, and Caviness (1994) observations supported this postulate. With more subcortical long axons, men might be able to more efficiently carry on long-distance conversations within their brains. It might be this ability to communicate between anatomic and functional distinct modules that allow men to more readily develop creative solutions and find the thread that unites.

As I mentioned earlier, Marion Diamond et al. (1985) found a higher glial cell–to–neuron ratio in Einstein's brain than they did in control individuals. Glial cells perform many functions, but their primary functions are structural and supportive. The axons that travel below the cortex and connect anatomically separate areas of cortex have a coating on them that is called myelin, and it is this coating that gives the subcortical white matter its characteristic color. Glial cells called oligodentrocites produce myelin. Although Einstein's high glial ratio might have been related to Einstein's dyslexia, it is also possible that this increased ratio was evidence of a high level of connectivity.

Bird Brains

One of the art forms most important to people in all cultures is music. G. Miller (2000) compared the recorded output of prominent jazz, rock, and classical musicians and found that men produced 10 times more music than did women. Perhaps even more dramatic is the gender differences in composers. I tried to think of one famous classical composer who was a woman, but I could not think of one. The reason music is so important to people is still unknown, but there are several theories, including music's being a means of social bonding. Perhaps that can explain why music is heard during sexual rites (including dances), during advertising or proselytization, during military parades, and in houses of worship during religious rites (including college football games). Social bonding is important for the survival of people and cultures. Music is also used to control emotions and moods. For example, Thayer (1996) reviewed a series of studies to find out what people did to get out of a bad mood and found that almost 50% of people used music to regulate their moods. Although for military purposes, bonding might be more important to men than women, but most people who listen to music are not in the military.

Many species of birds use song for courtship, and male birds primarily use this courtship display to attract female birds. G. Miller (2000) wondered if music in humans was also a means of courtship and if, like birds, there is a male preponderance. As I mentioned previously, Miller studied gender differences by comparing the recorded output of prominent jazz, rock, and classical musicians and found that men produced 10 times more music than did women. On the basis of this finding, Miller concluded that even in humans music continues to be primarily used by men as a courtship display to attract women.

As in other domains of creativity, women might have been culturally inhibited when it came to music, but today there are many very talented women who compose and perform music. In addition, although there are differences between the brains of men and women, there is nothing known that could account for men's propensity to compose and perform music.

Sex Hormones

Although the biological basis of sex differences in the brain's structure and function has not been entirely elucidated, there are at least two reasons that the brains of men and women might be different, size and laterality of cognitive processes. These two reasons, however, are not entirely independent. As I mentioned earlier, men's brains are larger than women's brains and there are more neurons. Although these differences are at least in part developmental, it is unknown whether these differences between men's and women's brains are induced by differences in hormonal exposure during development, are related to genetic differences independent of the hormonal influence, or are a combination of both. Men's and women's brains from the fetus to old age are exposed to different sex hormones, and hormones might influence thought patterns, moods, and behavior, both during development and after maturation. As mentioned previously, one of the major differences between the brains of men and woman is the lateralization of cognitive functions, and it has been thought by several investigators that sex hormones might influence the laterality of functions (Geschwind & Galaburda, 1985; Witelson, 1991). Grimshaw, Bryden, and Finegan (1995) studied the relations between prenatal testosterone levels in second-trimester amniotic fluid and lateralization of speech, affect, and handedness at age 10. Girls with higher prenatal testosterone levels were more strongly right handed and had stronger left-hemisphere language-speech representations. Boys with higher prenatal testosterone levels had stronger right-hemisphere specialization for the recognition of emotion. This pattern of results is most consistent with the claim that prenatal testosterone leads to greater lateralization of function.

In addition, there is evidence that hormones such as androgens and estrogens might influence cognition, even postnatally. For example, Maki, Rich, and Rosenbaum (2002) studied 16 young women during two different stages of their menstrual cycle. During the follicular stage of the menstrual cycle, both estrogen and progesterone are low, and during the midluteal phase, both are high. These investigators found that whereas explicit memory was unchanged during the high estrogen phase, visuospatial functions were not as well-performed as during the low estrogen phase. Choi and Silverman (2002) studied the relationships between route-learning strategies and circulating testosterone and estrogen in a large population of students by obtaining salivary assays from the students. They found that testosterone levels were positively correlated with the use of route-learning strategies in men, but not in women. In addition, Wisniewski (1998) compared the spatial ability of hypogonadal men to normal men and found that the hypogonadal men had a decreased left-visual-field–right-hemisphere superiority, suggesting that testosterone might have a greater influence on the right hemisphere than left hemisphere, and the right hemisphere appears to be dominant for performing spatial tasks. Keenan, Ezzat, Ginsburg, and Moore (2001) studied frontal-lobe executive functions in postmenopausal women while they were taking or not taking estrogen and found that executive functions improved with estrogen. Although divergent thinking, so important in creativity, is, at least in part, mediated by the frontal lobes, I could not find any studies that examined women's creativity while they were on and off estrogen.

On the basis of some of the studies I reviewed earlier, Kimura (2002) concluded that gender differences in the cognitive abilities are a product of not only current but also early hormonal environments. Thus, it is possible that men have a better chance of being recognized as creative because they have better spatial abilities and that this difference might reflect genetic and hormonal influences both early and late. Independent of spatial abilities, however, we still do not know if a person's gender influences creativity.

7

Neurological Disorders

Studying patients with discrete brain lesions has allowed neurologists, neuropsychologists, and cognitive neuroscientists to learn that the brain is organized in a modular fashion such that there are specific areas of the brain that mediate specific functions. In the past 20 years, the ability of investigators to perform functional imaging has brought converging evidence for the concept of modularity or localization of function. In addition, many behaviors exhibited by people are complex, and studies of the behavioral changes associated with lesions of the brain have allowed scientists to fractionate many of these complex functions into their component parts. In this chapter I review how some neurological disorders might influence creativity.

Focal Lesions (Stroke)

Studies of patients with strokes have taught us much about how different areas of the cerebral cortex mediate specific behaviors, and, as I mentioned, creativity is heavily dependent on a number of cognitive skills. Thus, damage to specific areas of the cortex can result in a loss of the skills that depend on the portion of the cortex that is injured.

Alajouanine (1948), a French neurologist, reported several famous creative people who developed aphasia (a language–speech disorder) from a stroke. One was an author and another was a fine artist. Not surprisingly, after suffering with aphasia the author was no longer artistically productive, and even though, according to Alajouanine, his aesthetic sense and judgment remained intact, his agrammatic aphasia (Broca's aphasia) had impaired his artistic realization. Not so for the artist, who even after he developed Wernicke's aphasia (in which a patient has a loss of verbal comprehension), maintained his artistic skill and creativity. According to Alajouanine, "He expressed the poetry of the Normandy coast, the glowing beauty of flowers or marine life and the richness of feminine flesh." Furthermore, Alajouanine wrote, "His pictorial art is far from being only a purely sensorial expression; it contained numerous intellectual and affective components, which, however, are untouched by aphasia." Alajouanine also suggested that this artist's painting might have improved after his stroke: "His always sharp affectivity is still sharper. . . . According to connoisseurs, he has perhaps gained a more intense and acute expression," but he did not explain what might account for this improvement.

Epilepsy

According to Simonton (1999), Cesare Lombroso—in his classic book, *The Man of Genius,* which was published in 1891—claimed that genius was often associated with epilepsy. There have been many creative writers who have been presumed to be epileptic, including Machado de Assis (1839–1908), who is considered one of Brazil's most important writers, and Gustave Flaubert (1821–1880), the famous French novelist who is perhaps best known for his *Madame Bovary.* Flaubert, like other authors with epilepsy, was thought to have left temporal lobe epilepsy. Edgar Allen Poe wrote about episodes of unconsciousness and confusion. Although most people thought that these episodes were induced by substance abuse, including alcohol and drugs, Bazil (1999) suggested that Poe might have suffered with complex partial seizures, a form of localized epilepsy.

In our hospital, we had a patient who was epileptic but who was mistaken as a person who abused drugs. This patient had a partial complex seizure disorder that was difficult to control and thus was being evaluated at our medical center. After he had anticonvulsant blood levels drawn, and before he had a chance to see his physician, he went to the bathroom. Another patient who was being seen by the cardiologists also walked into this bathroom after our patient entered. He noticed that this epileptic man appeared to be confused and disoriented. After the cardiology patient left the bathroom, he called the police. The police came to the bathroom and noticed that not only was the patient confused but he also had several puncture wounds in his arms. Not knowing that he just had blood drawn for hydantoin (Dilantin) levels and that the intern who attempted to draw his blood had a difficult time entering a vein to get his blood, the police thought that he had just injected himself with a narcotic and, therefore, arrested him. His wife was in the doctor's office waiting for him to return from the bathroom. When he did not return in about 15 or 20 minutes, she decided that something was wrong and thought that he either had had a seizure or was lost. She went to the bathroom, opened the door, and called inside. There was no response, and so she asked a man in the hallway to look in the bathroom for her husband. This man looked in the bathroom but reported to the wife that the bathroom was empty. She then walked around the halls looking for him. Finally, she went down to see the health center police and asked them if they knew anything about the whereabouts of her husband. When she described him and told them why he was here, the police realized they had made a terrible mistake and retrieved him from the Gainesville police head-quarters. This episode occurred just a few years ago, but Bazil (1999) noted that at the time Poe lived, little was known about complex par-tial seizures, and with the knowledge that these types of mistakes are made now in modern hospitals, by trained police, there is a good pos-sibility that episodes of unconsciousness and confusion experienced by Poe might have been related to seizures rather than drugs.

Another well-known creative writer who was thought to have epilepsy is Fyodor Dostoevsky. His epileptic seizures appeared to begin in childhood and lasted his entire life (Kiloh, 1986). Because he had aura followed by convulsions, he possibly also had complex partial seizures with secondary generalization. In addition to having bouts of depression, which might have been related to his epilepsy (see below), he also had many other mental disorders. For example, he was very compulsive and also had severe hypochondriasis, which gave the psychoanalysts such as Sigmund Freud an opportunity to explain Dostoevsky's creativity by using psychodynamic mecha-nisms. Dostoevsky, however, had a progressive memory impairment, and it is unclear how psychodynamic mechanisms can account for this progressive disorder. The medial part of the temporal lobe, which contains structures such as the hippocampus (see Figure 7.1), is very important for storing verbal memories. One of the most common areas of the brain for seizures to occur, is in the medial and anterior temporal lobe. These seizures can cause cell (neuronal) death and scarring. Hence, patients with epilepsy who have seizures that start in the left medial temporal lobe often have an impairment of verbal memory.

105

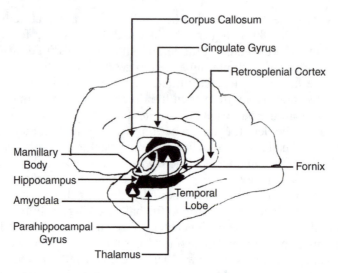

Figure 7.1. Diagram of the medial temporal lobe, which includes the hippocampus critical for forming new declarative memories (what, when, and who).

Trimble (2000) wrote about the epileptic poet Charles Lloyd and noted that Lloyd also had bipolar disorder. Trimble suggested that the epilepsy was probably destructive to the creative writing process. Thus, although the observation that several creative writers had epilepsy might suggest that there is a relationship between epilepsy and creative writing, epilepsy is a common disorder and to my knowledge no one has formally attempted to learn if there is a significant relationship between this disorder and creativity.

Intelligence is not directly related to creativity, but as mentioned previously, there is a threshold, and a person has to be relatively intelligent to be a successful author. Many people who have chronic complex partial seizures have IQs that are below average, and if investigators performed a study that compared the percentage of successful writers who are epileptic versus the percentage of successful writers who are not epileptic, the success rate might very well be lower in the epileptics. Thus, this study would have to be adjusted for intelligence, and this adjustment would make the study very difficult to perform. If we assume, however, that there is a relationship between epilepsy (i.e., complex partial seizures) and creative writing, how could the presence of this neurological disorder account for this relationship?

Many of the creative epileptics such as Dostoevsky had bouts of depression. Devinsky and Vazquez (1993) studied mood disorders in epileptic patients and found that depression was commonly associated with this disorder. Paradiso and coworkers (2001) found that 34% of patients with temporal lobe epilepsy were depressed, and those with seizures that start in their left temporal lobe, which several of these famous authors appeared to have, were more likely to be depressed than those with right temporal lobe epilepsy. As I mentioned, and will further mention, people with affective disorders have a propensity for creativity. There is, however, another possible relationship. Norman Geschwind (1979) noted that many of his patients with complex partial seizures and especially those that started in the left temporal lobe often wrote copious notes. On the basis of his clinical impression, he wondered if patients with seizures that emanate from the left temporal lobe had what he termed "hypergraphia." Sachdev and Waxman (1981) studied the writing habits of people who had temporal lobe epilepsy (complex partial seizures) and compared them to matched controls. These investigators found a much higher incidence of hypergraphia in the epileptic population. Geschwind (1979) also noted that patients with complex partial seizures and especially those that emanate from the left temporal lobe appeared to have a "deepening" of cognitive and emotional responses. The combination of an increased propensity to write, mood disorders, and a deepening of emotional experience might lead to an increase in the probability that an intelligent person with complex partial seizures (temporal lobe epilepsy) might turn out to be a creative writer. The reason that temporal lobe epilepsy induces hypergraphia, a deepening of emotions, and an increased incidence of depression, is unknown. It is possible that any chronic affliction that has a continuing social stigma, is intermittent as well as unpredictable and is a major cause of disability that can cause or produce symptoms such as depression and a deepening of emotions. This explanation, however, cannot account for the observation that these changes are associated only with some forms of epilepsy. This explanation also does not account for the hypergraphia. Thus, until further hypothesis-driven research is performed, these relationships remain unexplained.

Dementia

Bruce Miller and his coworkers (Miller et al., 1998; Miller, Boone, Cummings, Read, & Mishkin, 2000) wrote a series of papers on the emergence of artistic talents in a form of degenerative dementia called frontotemporal dementia, or frontal temporal lobar atrophy. The two most common forms of degenerative dementia that are seen in the clinic are Alzheimer's disease and frontotemporal dementia. Most patients with Alzheimer's disease start off with a memory loss and then develop other cognitive deficits, such as problems with naming, route finding, drawing, copying, and even performing learned skilled movements (ideomotor apraxia). The signs and symptoms associated with frontotemporal dementia are often different from those seen with Alzheimer's disease. In one form, patients lose their social skills and perform antisocial acts. Some patients may also become abulic and sit around all day doing nothing useful. Other patients with frontotemporal dementia might have a language deficit that causes their speech to become progressively less fluent or they might have trouble with naming and comprehension; unlike patients with Alzheimer's disease, their visual-spatial memory might remain intact. When we obtain brain images (MRI) from patients with Alzheimer's disease, we often see atrophy in the medial temporal lobes and in the parietal lobes, but patients with frontotemporal dementia may have atrophy of the frontal lobes or anterior temporal lobes or both. In addition, frontotemporal dementia might be asymmetric and primarily involve only one side of the brain. Unlike patients with Alzheimer's disease who on microscopic examination of the brain have deposits of amyloid (plaques) and tangled fibrils in their neurons (neurofibrillary tangles), patients with frontotemporal dementia have a variety of different microscopic changes, including intraneuronal inclusions called Pick bodies (after the neurologist who first described this syndrome), ballooned neurons that stain poorly, or even no specific pathological markers.

It is often difficult to know, in retrospect, when a dementing disease has started. Several of the artists described by Miller and his coworkers (1998 and 2000), however, appeared to have started drawing or painting prior to the time they had the symptoms and signs of a frontotemporal dementia or at the time their dementia was just beginning. What was remarkable about these patients is that in spite of their dementia they continued to paint and some even improved their artistic skills. As I described earlier, the left hemisphere primarily mediates verbal activities and the right hemisphere appears to be more important for the type of spatial skills important in painting. Miller and his coworkers noted that most of these artistic people had degeneration that was limited to the left temporal lobe, sparing the frontal and parietal lobes, and that their creative skills were nonverbal. According to Sergent (1993), composers such as Ravel, who had a focal degeneration of his left hemisphere, could continue to be productive, but from Miller et al.'s reports we cannot learn if these people's talents existed before the onset of the dementia. Miller et al.'s reports do seem to indicate, however, that some patients increased their artistic skills during the time they had their dementing illness.

The reason stroke and degenerative diseases of the left hemisphere might enhance artistic skills is not entirely known. Patients with right-hemisphere injuries often demonstrate a syndrome called unilateral spatial neglect (Heilman, Watson, Valenstein, 2003). When these participants are presented with a long horizontal line and asked to mark the middle or bisect the line, they displace their bisection mark to the right of actual midline. To explain this deficit, Kinsbourne (1970) suggested that normally, to move one's eyes or direct one's attention to either the right or the left side of space in response to a lateral stimulus, the hemisphere opposite the stimulus would have to become activated and this activated hemisphere would also have to inhibit the opposite hemisphere. If the opposite hemisphere was not inhibited and both hemispheres were activated, the person or animal would not be able to move his or her eyes and attention to one side of space. Furthermore, when events such as stroke injure the right hemisphere, this damaged hemisphere is unable to inhibit the uninjured hemisphere, whereas the uninjured hemisphere continues to inhibit the damaged hemisphere. This activation imbalance between the two hemispheres induces an attentional-spatial bias such that the patient's attention is biased toward the right, and this rightward attentional bias leads patients to misplace their bisection mark to the right of actual midline. To help explain why brain injury can induce the emergence of a new or improved skill, Kapur (1996) suggested an explanation similar to that used by Kinsbourne to explain neglect. Kapur used the term "paradoxical functional facilitation" for the facilitation of a function induced by a lesion that destroys an inhibitory circuit. Miller and his coworkers (1998 and 2000) suggested that perhaps a similar phenomenon was occurring in their patients and that left anterior temporal lobe degeneration "contributed to the unexpected emergence of talent in our patients."

If a person has a focal injury to the brain, it does not preclude the possibility that other uninjured portions of the brain can develop new skills and enhance already acquired skills. We even demonstrated that, with practice, patients with dementia can reconstitute a skill that was previously impaired. For example, we demonstrated that three patients with probable dementia of the Alzheimer's type who were suffering with a name-finding disability were able to regain the ability to use words that they had lost (Leon et al., 2003). Thus, the finding that patients with focal left-hemisphere degeneration are able to acquire visual-spatial or musical skills does not mean that this degenerative process lead to the development of creativity. Unfortunately, there is no means by which Miller and his coworkers (1998 and 2000) could test this disinhibition postulate in their participants. There is, however, another model of brain injury that could be used to test this postulate. In patients with uncontrollable epilepsy, often the seizure focus is in either the left or the right temporal lobe. Although antiepileptic medications are used to control these patients' seizures, some patients cannot be controlled by medications and must have the epileptic focus removed. Surgeons do this by removing the anterior temporal lobe. These operations are performed often in medical centers around the country. Whereas some investigators have reported a decline of musical abilities with right temporal lobectomy and trouble with word finding following left temporal lobectomy, to our knowledge no one has reported an increase in verbal creativity with right temporal lobectomy or an increase of musical or artistic creativity with removal of the left temporal lobe. Before we can reject this "release" hypothesis, however, it needs to be experimentally tested, and this has not been done.

Finally, Miller and his coauthors (1998) used the term *talent*, and talent might refer to skill rather than creativity. Hence, it is not clear that these demented patients are truly creative as defined in this book. An increase of skills is not the same as an increase of creativity, and although Miller et al. provided evidence for the development of artistic skills, they did not provide evidence that with frontotemporal dementia there is an increase in creativity.

Developmental Learning Disability

About three decades ago, I was listening to Norman Geschwind speak about dyslexia to members of the Orton (dyslexia) Society. Norman liked to say things that would shock his audience, and during his talk he said, "Dyslexia is a social disease." At that time when someone spoke about social diseases, they were usually speaking about sexually transmitted diseases, such as gonorrhea and syphilis. There were many dyslexic people and parents of dyslexic children in the audience who appeared to be angry when he made this comment. He, however, held up his hand and said, "Wait, let me explain." He mentioned that in the history of humans, it is only recently that reading has become so critical for success. He asked who would be our leader if we lived in a hunter-gatherer society: the person who could read and write the best or the person who could get us back to camp after the hunt? He also mentioned that he would not be surprised if the people with the best visual-spatial abilities have a higher incidence of dyslexia.

Earlier I mentioned that Diamond et al. (1985) studied Einstein's left inferior parietal lobe, including Brodmann's area 39 or the angular gyrus (see Figure 3.5). When Diamond and coworkers performed a histological analysis of this area, they found that, compared with the brains of control participants, the angular gyrus (Brodmann's area 39) on the left side of Einstein's brain contained a higher glial cell–to–neuron ratio. These investigators attempted to explain this result by suggesting that this aberrant ratio was "a response by glial cells to greater neuronal metabolic need." They also suggested that this increased metabolic need might be related to Einstein's unusual conceptual powers. The report of Diamond et al. (1985) was severely criticized because with aging there is a loss of cortical neurons, and their control participants were younger than Einstein (Hines, 1998). These investigators provided no information about the control participants' socio-economic status, their cause of death, or their premorbid health. Even if one assumes that methodological errors did not account for the results reported by Diamond et al., it is not apparent how a relative reduction of neurons could account for Einstein's creativity.

Einstein had developmental language disorders. Hoffman and Dukas (1972) quoted a part of a letter he wrote in 1954 where he explained, "My parents were worried because I started to talk comparatively late, and they consulted a doctor because of it. I cannot tell how old I was at that time, but certainly not younger than three." Like many children with delayed speech, Einstein also had developmental dyslexia (Kantha, 1992). Dejerine (1891) demonstrated that lesions of the left angular gyrus (Brodmann's area 39) induce acquired alexia, and it is possible that people with developmental dyslexia may also have abnormalities in this region. Kantha (1992) suggested that the abnormalities reported by Diamond et al. might have been related to Einstein's dyslexia rather than his genius. Geschwind and Galaburda (1985) suggested that the delay in development of the left hemisphere might allow the right hemisphere, which mediates spatial computations, to become highly specialized.

Einstein was perhaps the greatest scientist of the 20th century, and Picasso was one of the greatest artists. Picasso also appears to have had a language learning disability. Both of these individuals' creativity, in part, depended on spatial skills. Is this just a chance relationship or is there a significant relationship between developmental language disorders and the types of creativity that depend on visual-spatial skills? Unfortunately, there are still not many studies that have systematically examined this relationship. Wolff and Lundberg (2002) assessed art students at very a competitive university and compared them with other students at the university who were not art students. They found that the reported incidence of dyslexia was greater in the art students than in those who were not art students. Many developmentally dyslexic people have as their underlying deficit impaired phonological skills such that they have trouble converting letters or combinations of letters, such as the *th* (graphemes), into their associated speech sounds or phonemes. These investigators also assessed the art and nonart students' phonological skills and found that the art students' skills were significantly poorer than were those of the nonart students. Similarly, Eisen (1989) assessed the creative ability of children with and without learning disabilities. Eisen found that the children with learning disabilities performed better than the children without learning disabilities on the nonverbal task, but not on the verbal task. Winner and coworkers (2001), however, could not replicate these findings. Children with dyslexia often have other behavioral disorders, such as attention deficit disorder with or without hyperactivity, and although these disorders might have influenced the results of these types of experiments, the authors attempted to correct for these comorbid disorders, but still did not find that the dyslexic group had superior spatial skills. Hence, the relationship between developmental language disorders and spatial skills remains unresolved.

If we assume that people with developmental language disorders have greater spatial skills, what could be the explanation? As I mentioned earlier, in primates, including people, visual stimuli that come from the retina go to the occipital (visual) cortex by way of a relay station in the middle of the brain called either the optic thalamus or the lateral (visual) geniculate nucleus (see Figure 6.3). Visual information carried to the visual cortex may travel over a rapid transport system that has large cells in the optic thalamus and is thus called the magnocellular division. Alternatively, visual information might be transported by a slow transport system that has smaller neurons in the thalamus and is called the parvocellular division. Galaburda and Livingstone (1993) found that when they measured the speed of visual signals in dyslexic people, the dyslexic people's signals appeared to be slower than control subjects' signals, suggesting that visual information in these dyslexic people's brains was carried primarily by the slow or parvocellular system. When they studied the brains of people who were dyslexic and had died, they found abnormalities in the magnocellular system. The fast magnocellular system carries low-contrast information and the slow parvocellular system carries the high-contrast information. Reading letters and words would seem to depend more heavily on the high-contrast (parvocellular) system, and thus this finding in the visual system can easily explain dyslexia. The auditory systems, however, also have two parallel systems (parvocellular and magnocellular), and to be able to detect individual phonemes that make up words, a person has to perform a rapid auditory analysis. When children learn to read, they primarily use a grapheme (letter or letters) to phoneme (letter sound) conversion strategy to sound out words, and people who are unaware of the phonological composition of words often suffer with developmental dyslexia. Thus, a deficit in the magnocellular auditory system might preclude people from fully decoding the phonemic structure of words, and this might lead to developmental language disorders. In the visual system, whereas the parvocellular visual system is important in detecting what, the magnocellular division primarily is important in spatial processing. The findings that spatial skills are more dependent on the low-contrast, rapid transmission magnocellular system and that developmental dyslexic people have impairment in the magnocellular system would appear contradictory. Therefore, the observation that dyslexic people have superior spatial skills cannot be explained by this magnocellular deficit. If it is true that developmentally dyslexic people do have enhanced spatial skills, there would have to be another explanation, but I do not know what it is, unless developmental dyslexia in unrelated deficits in the magnocellular division and the disinhibition postulate I previously mentioned also accounts for these observations such that delayed development of the left-hemisphere reading-writing systems allowed the right-hemisphere visual-spatial and global-attentional systems to better develop.

Autism

In the preceding section I described the concept that certain cognitive functions appear to be mediated by specific portions of the brain (i.e., modular organization). By modular, I do not mean that these modules are encapsulated to the extent that modules cannot influence each other. The normal person's cerebral cortex is highly connected, and it is the connectivity between these modules that might be important in creative innovation. I also mentioned the postulate that although many creative people have highly developed talents, outstanding talent alone does not ensure creativity.

People who have autistic spectrum syndromes (pervasive developmental disorder, Asperger's syndrome) are characterized by the abnormal development of social skills, impairments of communication, and a severely restricted repertoire of interests and stereotypic behaviors. Some people with autistic syndromes develop extraordinary skills in one domain. In spite of these extraordinary skills in one domain, they might have little or no skills in other domains. Benjamin Rush, who many consider one of the fathers of American medicine, in 1789 reported the case of Thomas Fuller. This man had the special ability to perform calendar computations. For example, Benjamin Rush asked him how many seconds a man, who was 70 years, 17 days, and

12 hours old, had lived. Fuller thought about this problem for about a minute and 30 seconds and responded, "2,210,500,800 seconds." This response was correct and even included 17 leap years. Although Fuller was able to perform these amazing computations, he understood little about math other than counting and calendar computations (Treffert & Wallace, 2002).

Subsequently, in 1887, J. Langdon Down, who worked in the Earlswood Asylum in London and was the person who first described Down's syndrome, reported 10 patients who overall had low intelligence, but like Fuller, in specific domains they had very special talents. He called these people "idiot" (low IQ) "savants" (from the French root *savoir,* to know). Almost all of Down's idiot savants were men, and men appear primarily to constitute most other reports of this rare condition.

The special talents of these idiot savants have been reported to occur in several domains. In addition to the calendar skill demonstrated by Fuller, there have musical savants like Thomas Bethune, who had a vocabulary of less than 100 words but could play, without written musical scores, 4,000 different pieces on the piano (Treffert & Wallace, 2002). Although different idiot savants can have different types of skills, almost all these skills appear to depend on an extraordinary memory. Down also described a boy who could recite each word of *The Decline and Fall of the Roman Empire,* by Edward Gibbon. Hou et al. (2000) studied six artistic savants, and in spite of their great artistic skill, all six demonstrated a strong preference for a single art medium and showed a restricted variation in artistic themes. The finding that in spite of great talent there was a paucity of creativity also comes from a study by Craig and Baron-Cohen (1999), who used the Torrence test and other means of assessing creativity and found improvised creativity in people with autism. A. R. Luria (1968) in his *The Mind of a Mnemonist* wrote about a man with a remarkable memory, but unlike the idiot savants I mentioned earlier, he was not severely intellectually disabled. With his excellent memory he did very well in school, and many people had high expectations for his having a successful career after he completed school, but he was a failure in almost every occupation he attempted. The only thing in which he succeeded was displaying his extraordinary memory in shows. Luria suggested that in spite of this man's outstanding memory and academic record, he was a failure because his ability to manipulate knowledge was poor. Success in many endeavors depends on creativity, and although one needs a good memory to be creative, creativity does not solely depend on memory or learned skills but requires the manipulation of stored knowledge.

The reason why savants have these remarkable memories and skills is unknown. Treffert and Wallace (2002) suggested that the savants' skills are mediated by the right hemisphere and are related to the left hemisphere's dysfunction that disinhibits or releases the right hemisphere from the left hemisphere's control. There is little or no evidence to support this postulate in people with autism. Many savants, as I mentioned, do have exceptional number and math skills. Studies of brain-damaged individuals appear to indicate that it is the left hemisphere that is important for number skills and calculations. In addition, some savants recall every word from entire texts, and in most people it is the left hemisphere that is important for mediating language and speech. Furthermore, children with early or congenital damage to the right hemisphere, as well as those who have their left hemisphere removed or the callosum cut, are not typically savants.

I think that there are several possible explanations for savants' extraordinary domain-specific skills and their difficulty with manipulating knowledge or thinking creatively. One possibility is that the savant's brain is organized such that they have all their eggs in one basket. Thus, unlike normal people who have multiple representational modules that are highly connected, savants have primarily one or two extremely well-developed systems at the expense of the normal development of other systems. It is also possible that the anatomic modules in the brains of savants are poorly connected. During normal development connectivity might, in part, allow specialization by exerting inhibitory control. Thus, when one is learning language, not only does the left hemisphere develop language-based representations but the left hemisphere also prevents or inhibits the right hemisphere from developing these same representations and thus allows the right hemisphere to develop different representations. After these different representational modules are developed, connections between these modules might allow communication between these representational systems, which is so important in creative efforts. Perhaps savants have impovished connections between modules, and this deficient connectivity induces constriction of cognitive processes. Support for this connection hypothesis comes from the observation that the size of the corpus callosum in people with autism is smaller than in the control participants (Egaas, Courchesne, & Saitoh, 1995). In chapter 9 I discuss the importance of the frontal lobe in divergent thinking. People with autism have limited divergent thinking suggesting that their frontal lobe functions might be impaired.

Catecholamines might influence the size of semantic networks such that with increased brain catecholamines, cognitive networks can become constricted. In addition, giving high doses of catecholamine agonists (e.g., apomorphine) to animals can induce many of the signs of autism, such as stereotypic behaviors. There is also some evidence that people with autism might have increased levels of catecholamines and that medications that reduce the influence of catecholamines might help people with autism. In the next chapter I discuss the role of neurotransmitters on creativity.

8

Neurotransmitters

Relaxation and Sleep

One of the best means of developing a neuropsychological hypothesis about a specific behavior is to study groups of people who can or cannot produce this behavior and learn what common factor or factors distinguish these groups (finding the thread that unites). Several scientists have reported that they were able to solve a difficult scientific problem during sleep or when they were either falling asleep or awakening from sleep. One of the most famous examples of this phenomenon is August Kekule, who in 1865, while attempting to learn the structure of benzene, went to sleep and dreamed of a snake chasing its tail. This dream provided Kekule with the idea that benzene is a ringlike structure. Recently, Kekule's recounting of this episode has undergone scrutiny, with the suggestion that he never had this dream (Strunz, 1993). Before and after sleep, however, people are often in a state of relaxed wakefulness. Creative people who are actively working on a problem describe moments of insight when they were able to solve previously insoluble problems. Often these moments of insight come at a time when the person is relaxed and at rest. In 1898 Ramón y Cajal (1898/1999) wrote a book titled *Advice for a Young Investigator*, in which he suggested,

If a solution fails to appear after all of this, and yet we feel success is just around the corner, try resting for a while. Several weeks of relaxation and quiet in the countryside brings calmness and clarity of the mind. Like the early morning frost, this intellectual refreshment withers the parasitic and nasty vegetation that smothers the good seed. Bursting forth at last is the flower of truth, whose calyx usually opens after a long and profound sleep at dawn in those placid hours of the morning that Goethe and so many others consider especially favorable for discovery.

There are several examples of this principle that famous creators have written about. For example, Henri Poincare, the famous mathematician, was working on a mathematical problem that he could not solve. He wrote, "Disgusted with my failure, I went to spend a few days at the seaside and thought of something else. One morning walking on the bluff, the idea came to me" (quoted in Eysenck, 1995). When there was a plague at Cambridge University, where Isaac Newton taught, he went home to his mother's farm and was relaxing on the farm when he got the ideas for developing calculus. Easterbrook (1959) suggested that emotions reduce the use of cues, and Eysenck (1995) suggested that during conscious problem solving, cortical arousal is high and this high level of cortical arousal narrows the associative field and suppresses the ability to make remote associations, but lowered arousal might allow these remote associations to emerge. These investigators did not, however, discuss how arousal might influence associations.

Support for the postulate that the level of arousal might determine the size of neural networks comes from some recent research by Contreras and Llinas (2001). With high-speed optical imaging, these investigators used voltage-sensitive dyes together with intracellular recording in slices of brain taken from a guinea pig to record the portions of the neocortex activated by subcortical stimulation. In general, during high arousal states there is rapid cortical activity as determined by an electroencephalogram (EEG), but with decreased arousal EEG activity slows. They found that low-frequency electrical stimulation of the subcortical white matter activated discrete cortical sites, but over the next few milliseconds this activation spread to other cortical areas. In contrast, during high-frequency stimulation, the excitation remained fixed to a small column of neurons that were directly above the stimulating electrode. Intracellular recording from the neurons around the excited column during rapid stimulation revealed increased inhibitory synaptic activity that probably stopped the spread of activation.

Psychopathology

According to Eysenck (1995), Aristotle claimed, "No great genius has ever been without some madness." According to Simonton (1999), Aristotle also wrote, "Those who have become eminent in philosophy, politics, poetry and the arts all had tendencies toward melancholia." John Adams said, "Genius is sorrow's child." In his book, Eysenck tried to make the argument that there is a strong relationship between creativity, psychosis, and schizophreniform thinking, but then quoted Eisenman's studies that demonstrate that schizophrenics are even less creative than normal hospital employees, who Eysenck noted are not "particularly creative." Kraepelin in 1921 noted that manic-depressive psychosis was often associated with enhanced creativity (Weisberg, 1994). Post (1996) studied the biographies of a large group of world-famous creative people, such as composers, scientists, artists, and writers. To classify these people, Post used the diagnostic criteria found in the *Diagnostic and Statistical Manual of Mental Disorders* (3rd ed.) (*DSM-III*) (American Psychiatric Association, 1980). He found that scientists had the lowest percentage of psychopathology and writers had the most, but in all these groups the percentage of people classified as having psychopathology was relatively high. For example, he found that 18% of the scientists, 38% of artists, and 46% of writers had severe psychopathology. He also found, however, that actual psychosis was very low in this group (1.7%), and there was an almost complete absence of schizophrenia. Andreasen (1987) studied a group of 30 creative writers and compared them with 30 matched controls who were not creative writers. She also examined their families. The writers had a very high rate of mental illness, especially affective disorders such as bipolar disease and depression. In addition, she found that there was a high rate of affective disorders in these people's relatives. Jamison (1989) studied British writers and found that 38% of his experimental participants had been treated for affective disorders and that about three quarters of these writers had received either antidepressants or lithium (used to treat bipolar or manic-depressive disorder). Other investigators have also reported that many of our most creative writers, composers, painters, and scientists have suffered with mood disorders, either bipolar or monopolar (Andreasen & Glick, 1988; Poldinger, 1986; Post, 1996; Richards, Kinney, Lunde, Benet, & Merzel, 1988; Slaby, 1992).

Scientists who perform research with human participants must have their research approved by an institutional review board (IRB). These boards are so concerned with government regulations and government threats that some board members do everything they can to prevent an investigator's research from being approved. For the most part, the

119

research that we do in our laboratories is behavioral. For example, we test the ability of people who have suffered with a stroke to learn if they might have more trouble naming objects than actions (nouns versus verbs). There is not even a remote possibility that we could harm these people by this type of testing, but to get protocols for research such as this approved by the IRB might take months to a year, with requests for multiple revisions. Most of these requests for revisions are trivial. For example, the IRB has asked us, "What will you do if someone gets anxious because they cannot find the correct name of an object?" Anybody who has to deal with bureaucrats such as those found on the IRB or has to work with granting agencies such as the National Institutes of Health might argue that it is dealing with these organizations while attempting to be creative that induces psychopathology. Most scientists who work at universities at least get paid (but for many it is not much and when they do invent something that might bring them financial reward, this invention is usually the property of the government or the university). But although scientists usually get paid, the life for the artist or writer is usually much more difficult. After writing novels, biographies, and other types of books, many authors cannot find anyone who will publish their work. There are only a limited number of galleries and only a few people who buy nondecorative art. In addition, museums show the works of well-known artists only. Thus, artists have difficulty getting their works shown. When a small but fortunate few do get their works published or shown, they must then deal with harsh critics who seem only to know who became great after they died.

Newton's law of inertia (bodies at rest tend to remain at rest) appears to also be true for science and art. People and society are resistant to change, and because the creative person is attempting to implement change, he or she often comes up against resistance, and, usually, the greater the change the greater the resistance. In the 35 years that I have been performing research and publishing papers, I have found that there appears to be a negative correlation between the degree of creativity of a research project or report and the difficulty I have either receiving funding to support this research or getting this research published.

Disappointment and frustration can lead to mood changes, and it is possible that the attempt to implement and gain recognition of creative acts leads to the mood disorders observed in creative people. Many creative acts also require solitude and introspection, and these conditions can also lead to mood disorders. Thus, although there is little question that creative people subject themselves to conditions that might induce mood changes, most investigators and theorists believe that the mood disorders experienced by creative people are not reactive but are endogenous, and it is the psychopathology that leads to creativity.

Sigmund Freud (1908/1959) suggested one of the first theories that attempted to account for the relationship between psychopathology and creativity. Freud suggested that as adults we learn that libidinal energy must be expressed by socially acceptable means and that creative expression might be one means of sublimating this energy. Unfortunately, like many psychodynamic theories, these hypotheses are difficult to test and do not explain the brain mechanisms that account for creativity. In addition, as I wrote in the introduction, an explanation of the brain mechanisms underlying creativity should be ideally reductionistic such that one theory should account for a myriad observations that appear to be independent, but are not finding the thread that unites.

In contrast to the psychodynamic theories of Freud, one thread that might unite those states that lead to creativity—including resting, relaxing, dreaming, and depression—are alterations of the brain's neurotransmitter systems, primarily a reduction of catecholamines, including norepinephrine (McCarley, 1982). Brain levels of norepinephrine might influence creativity because they moderate the size of neuronal networks.

Behavioral support for the postulate that catecholamines modulate the size of neuronal networks comes from the priming studies of Kischka and coworkers (1996). These investigators used a lexical priming task in which either real words or pseudowords are flashed on a screen and the participants are asked to press a computer key, as rapidly as possible, when they determine that the word on the screen is a real word, but they are not to press a key if a pseudoword is seen. Sometimes these real words and pseudowords are preceded by another word that is called a prime. The preceding word is called a prime because if this preceding word is related to the real target word, the prime word will help the participant recognize the real target word and thus reduce the response time. The more highly associated the prime word is to the target word (e.g., *doctor* and *nurse*), the more efficient the word recognition and the more rapid the response time or key press. In contrast, the less the two real words are related, the less influence the prime word has on word recognition or response time. In our brains we have neuronal networks that store knowledge about words and their meaning (lexical-semantic representations). When these lexical-semantic networks are activated or excited by the prime, if the representation of the target word is also stored in this activated network, recognition will be more efficient than if the word is unrelated to the prime because with related words, the lexical-semantic networks that are needed for recognition are already activated. When a prime is unrelated to the target, however, the prime activates a network, but because the target word is not part of this activated network, recognition of the target word requires that a new network be activated before the person can recognize that the target word is a real word.

When Kischka et al. (1996) administered L-dopa to normal participants and tested priming, they found that direct semantic priming (e.g., winter-summer) was only marginally influenced by this medicine. The administration of L-dopa, however, significantly reduced the effects of indirect priming (summer-snow). On the basis of these results, Kischka et al. suggested that dopamine increases the signal-to-noise ratio in semantic networks by reducing the spread of semantic activation. Although Kischka et al. attributed this effect to the dopaminergic system, L-dopa is a precursor of both dopamine and norepinephrine, and the administration of L-dopa to these individuals may have also increased the level of norepinephrine.

In the Remote Associates Test, participants are presented with a series of word triads (e.g., *blue, American,* and *goat*) and are requested to find a word that is associated with all three words (e.g., *cheese*). Like the priming task, this test might assess the size or breadth of lexical-semantic networks. During stress, performance on this test deteriorates (Martindale & Greenough, 1973). One of the reasons why stress can reduce performance on this task is that stress is associated with increased activity of the noradrenergic system. Further support for this postulate comes from the results of a study in which students with test anxiety dramatically improved their scores on the Scholastic Aptitude Test when they took the beta-adrenergic blocker propranolol (Faigel, 1991). The Scholastic Aptitude Test tests crystallized intelligence (knowing facts, such as that Albany is the capital of New York State) and fluid intelligence (e.g., How are a zebra and a tree similar?). Perhaps the beta-blockade reduced the influence of norepinephrine on neuronal networks, allowing for activation of larger networks, and the activation of large networks enhances cognitive flexibility.

The basal forebrain (including the nucleus of Meynert, diagonal band of Broca, and the medial septum) sends neurons that contain the neurotransmitter acetylcholine to almost the entire cerebral cortex (see Figure 8.1). There are several lines of evidence that these cholinergic neurons in the basal forebrain modulate cortical activation or the degree of cortical arousal. Cape and Jones (1998) injected the neurotransmitter norepinephrine into the basal forebrain. When recording brain activity, by using an EEG, they found that these injections induced high-frequency EEG activity at between 30 and 60 Hz

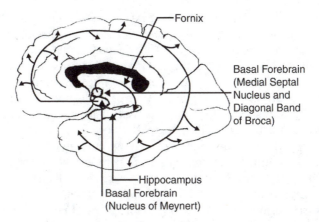

Fornix

Basal Forebrain
(Medial Septal
Nucleus and
Diagonal Band
of Broca)

Hippocampus
Basal Forebrain
(Nucleus of Meynert)

Figure 8.1. Diagram of the basal forebrain, which contains cholinergic neurons that project to the cerebral cortex (from the nucleus of Meynert) and parts of the limbic system, such as the hippocampus (from the medial septum and the diagonal band of Broca).

(gamma activity) and reduced the amount of slower EEG activity. This gamma frequency is found during states of high vigilance or arousal (e.g., when an animal orients or alerts to a novel or highly significant stimulus). Thus, they concluded that norepinephrine regulates the activity of the basal forebrain, which in turn influences the activity or arousal of the cerebral cortex.

Subconscious Incubation

Many creative people have related that after discovering an unresolved problem, they are unable to immediately to solve this problem. After multiple attempts, they might become frustrated, give up trying to solve the problem, and then move on to other problems. Sometimes, after a few days, weeks, or months, suddenly the solution of this problem might come to them. As I mentioned, this experience has been termed "illumination," or the "aha" experience, by Wallas (1926). The ability to suddenly understand the solution of a problem suggests that the brain has been actively manipulating stored knowledge. Wallas called this process of subconscious knowledge manipulation "incubation." In his book *Origins of Genius,* Simonton (1999) quoted the famous French mathematician Poincare. As I mentioned in the relaxation section, Poincare wrote how he could not solve a mathematical problem and got his mind off this problem and then came up with the solution (i.e., "I went to spend a few days at the seaside and thought of something else. One morning walking on the bluff, the idea came to me."). On reflecting on this aha experience, Poincare posited that his sudden inspiration was "a manifest sign of long unconscious work."

During the latter part of the 19th century Freud wrote much about how unconscious activities influence our thoughts and actions. In the mid-20th century many academic psychology departments were immersed in Skinnerian behaviorism, and during this time, the construct that unconscious mental activity had an influence on human behavior was disregarded. In the past 20 or 30 years, however, neuropsychologists have provided convincing evidence that the brain can mediate cognitive activity while the person who is performing this activity might not be consciously aware that this activity is taking place. For example, Bauer (1984) studied one of my patients who had prosopagnosia (failure to recognize the faces of people who were previously known to this man) from bilateral traumatic hematomas (blood clots) of the ventral (bottom) temporal and occipital lobes. These hematomas impaired the visual "what" system I previously described. In his hand, Bauer recorded the electrical resistance which changes when the hand sweats and the hand sweats when someone becomes alerted or aroused. Bauer (1984) showed pictures of some famous people to the patient and asked him either to name this person or to describe what made this person famous. This man was unable to recognize any of these faces, but when he was asked relevant questions about these faces, as opposed to irrelevant questions, this patient had an electrodermal response suggesting that he had unconscious or covert knowledge of these faces. For example, when shown a face of Richard Nixon and asked if this man was a famous athlete, the patient said that he did not recognize the face, and no electrodermal response was recorded. In contrast, when asked if this picture was former President Nixon, the patient again said that he did not recognize the face, but this time he did show an electrodermal response, suggesting that somewhere in his brain he had maintained a representation or image of Nixon's face. Although his visual system was able to access this representation, this stored face knowledge did not reach his conscious awareness.

Another example of unawareness in the presence of knowledge is a study performed by Marshall and Halligan (1988). There is a disorder called hemispatial neglect that causes patients to be unaware of stimuli presented in the half of space that is contralateral to a hemispheric injury (e.g., right hemisphere) (Heilman, Watson, & Valenstein, 2003). These investigators showed the participants who had left-sided unawareness a sheet of paper that contained pictures of two houses, one drawn above the other. The houses were identical except that the left side of one house was on fire. When participants with hemispatial neglect were asked in which house they would rather live, they said there were no differences between the houses, but when the examiner asked them still to point to the house in which they would rather live, they usually pointed to the house without flames. These results suggest that although these patients were not consciously aware of the flames coming from the left side of the house, some part of their brain did see the flames and reasoned that a house with flames would not be an ideal place to live.

Neuroscientists do not entirely know why we are aware of some things and unaware of others. However, recently, Meador, Ray, Echauz, Loring, and Vachtsevanos (2002) studied patients who were undergoing neurosurgery for epilepsy and thus had their cerebral cortex exposed and accessible. It had been posited that high-frequency (e.g., gamma of 30 to 50 Hz, as measured on the EEG) coherent neural activity integrates processing across distributed neuronal networks to achieve a unified conscious experience. Thus, to test this hypothesis, digital intracranial electrocorticographic recordings from implanted electrodes were obtained in six patients who were undergoing surgery for medically intractable epilepsy. These patients were stimulated in the hand opposite to these recording electrodes with simple near-threshold somatosensory (touch) stimuli. The patients were aware of some of these low-intensity stimuli and unaware of others. For those stimuli that were consciously perceived, there was gamma coherence in the primary somatosensory cortex that occurred approximately 150 to 300 milliseconds after these perceived contralateral hand stimuli were applied. For the stimuli that were not perceived stimuli, this gamma activity was not observed. These results suggest that conscious perception is dependent on coherent rapid cortical electrical activity.

The work of Contreras and Llinas (2001) together with the observations of Meador and coworkers (2002) suggest that although conscious perception of threshold stimuli might be related to high-frequency neural activity, during this high-frequency activity neural networks that are not directly involved in the detection of these stimuli are actively inhibited. Thus, high-frequency activity appears to focus neuronal processing, thereby enhancing the signal-to-noise ratio and facilitating conscious awareness. As I mentioned, finding a creative solution to a problem often depends on the simultaneous activation of widely distributed modular networks that store diverse sets of representations, and high-frequency activity of the cerebral cortex might restrict the distribution of activated networks.

The electrical activity of the cerebral cortex can be influenced by neurotransmitters and neuromodulators. Norepinephrine has been proposed to influence the signal-to-noise ratio in the cerebral cortex. Studies have revealed that norepinephrine decreases spontaneous firing of neurons and augments neuronal activity evoked by an external stimulus (Waterhouse & Woodward, 1980). Such relative enhancement of responses to strong inputs relative to low-level or basal activity has been found in the cerebral cortex and is consistent with recent neural modeling work that posits norepinephrine acts to enhance signal-to-noise ratios in target systems (Servan-Schreiber, Printz, & Cohen, 1990). Hasselmo, Linster, Patil, Ma, and Cekic (1997) also demonstrated that norepinephrine changes the signal-to-noise ratio by suppressing intrinsic excitatory synaptic potentials relative to the potentials elicited by direct afferent input. The bias toward external input that occurs with high norepinephrine states may prevent asking "what if" questions of the networks that store cognitive representations. In addition, connectionist modeling has also suggested that a moderate amount of noise allows networks to settle into optimal solutions. Suppressing intrinsic excitatory potentials may prevent many association neurons that do not receive direct afferent input from achieving a firing threshold. The reduced activity of association neurons may lead to activation of relatively sparse, constricted, and nonoverlapping associative networks. As I mentioned, the activation of highly distributed representations might allow one to perform inference and generalization, processes that are critical to creativity.

Further support for this norepinephrine postulate comes from a study of the role of the locus coeruleus and norepinephrine system in the regulation of cognitive functions. Locus coeruleus–norepinephrine neurons in the brain stem give rise to an extensive set of projections to the cerebral cortex, limbic system, and thalamus. The locus coeruleus is a small brain stem nucleus, but probably enervates a greater variety of brain areas than any other single nucleus. Many of the strongest projections of the locus coeruleus–norepinephrine system are to the areas of the brain that are most important in attentional processing, such as the inferior parietal lobes (Morrison & Foote, 1986). Investigators have concluded that high levels of tonic locus coeruleus activity that induces increased levels of norepinephrine in the cortex favored "bottom-up" processing, which is important for sampling new stimuli and increasing behavioral responsiveness to unexpected or novel stimuli (Aston-Jones, Chiang, & Alexinsky, 1991). Although low levels of locus coeruleus activity have not been tested, we suggest they might be associated with "top-down" processing, which is critical for the innovation stage of creativity.

Aston-Jones and coworkers (1991) studied monkeys performing a visual discrimination task that requires focused attention. Their results suggest that locus coeruleus–norepinephrine neurons exhibit phasic or tonic modes of activity that closely correspond to good or poor performance on this task, respectively. On the basis of their studies, they developed a model that predicts alterations in electronic coupling among locus coeruleus cells that may produce the different modes of activity. According to this model there are two modes of locus coeruleus firing: The phasic mode of locus coeruleus activity may promote focused or selective attention, and the tonic mode may produce a state of high behavioral flexibility or scanning attentiveness. According to our hypotheses it would be this latter mode that would be important in creative innovation.

To directly test the hypothesis that norepinephrine modulates cognitive flexibility, we performed a study in our laboratories where we (Beversdorf, Hughes, Steinberg, Lewis, & Heilman, 1999) tested normal participants' ability to solve problems when treated with placebo, ephedrine, or propranolol. Ephedrine increases the levels of norepinephrine and propranolol a beta-noradrenergic blocker interferes with norepinephrine's influence on the brain. We used a test that relies heavily on cognitive flexibility: solving anagrams. In this task, normal participants are presented with a series of words in which the letter order has been scrambled and their task in each trial is to recognize the word that uses these letters. We found that this anagram task was performed better after participants took propranolol than after they took ephedrine. To learn if the increase in cognitive flexibility induced by propranolol was produced by central or peripheral nervous system blockade, Broome, Cheever, Hughes, and Beversdorf (2000) tested another group of normal participants' performance on an anagram task and compared the effects of propranolol, which enters the central nervous system, with nadolol, a purely peripheral adrenergic beta-blocker. Participants' solution times on the anagram test were more rapid with propranolol than with nadolol, suggesting that it is primarily the central nervous system beta-adrenergic blockade (i.e., blocking the ability of norepinephrine from influencing neuronal networks) that increases cognitive flexibility. These studies of the beta-blocker propranolol provide evidence that the process of finding innovative solutions (finding the thread that unites) is enhanced by reducing the effect of norepinephrine on the brain.

Foote, Berridge, Adams, and Pineda (1991) reviewed the evidence that the locus coeruleus, by way of its massively divergent efferent noradrenergic projections to the cerebral cortex, participates in arousal and can convert the EEG from nonalert to alert or aroused states. Further support for the adverse influence of catecholamine-induced arousal on creative innovation comes from EEG studies. Martindale and Hasenfus (1978) performed a series of experiments to investigate the relationship between arousal and creativity. To measure arousal these investigators used the electroencephalogram. Since the work of Berger, it has been known that with higher levels of arousal there is faster electrical brain activity as recorded by the EEG. In contrast, with relaxed wakefulness there is the slower, well-developed 8-to-12 cycles–per–second alpha activity. On the basis of participants' ability to write creative stories, Martindale and Hasenfus (1978) placed participants into either the creative group or the uncreative group. In the resting state there were no differences in the EEGs of these two groups, but during the time they were developing their stories (innovation stage) the creative participants demonstrated better-developed alpha activity than did the uncreative participants, who had more rapid activity, suggesting that the creative participants were operating at a lower level of arousal than were the less creative participants.

Unlike the many creative people who have mood disorders, people with autism have been shown to have a severe deficit of cognitive flexibility and impoverished creativity (Craig & Baron-Cohen, 1999). Studies of autism such as those that use "theory of mind" suggest that autism is associated with a deficit in top-down processing (Happe & Frith, 1996). For example, to test theory of mind, investigators might show relatively high-functioning people with autism a series of pictures or a video. In one such picture there are two women (a mother and her friend) walking, with the mother pushing a baby carriage that has an infant inside. This carriage has a hood so that a person has to look inside to see if the baby is in the carriage. They stop walking and the mother's friend goes inside her house to get something. While she is inside her house, the infant's grandmother comes out of another house, takes the infant out of the carriage, and brings the infant into her house. If asked, "When the mother's friend comes out of her house, will she think that the baby is still in the carriage?" normal people would say that without her looking into the carriage she will think the baby is still inside. People with autism, however, are likely to say, "No, the grandmother took the baby inside." Happe and Frith suspected that people with autism, when observing people's behavior, have trouble understanding these people's thought process, a deficit in top-down processing.

We wanted to learn whether people with autistic spectrum disorder have a loss of cognitive flexibility and impoverished creativity because they have a reduction in the breadth of their conceptual networks or decreased ability to activate large and highly distributed semantic-conceptual networks (conceptual constriction). To test this conceptual constriction hypothesis, we used a false-memory paradigm (Schacter,

Verfaellie, & Anes, 1997). When we test normal people's memory by having them recognize previously presented words that come from the same semantic class or overlapping categories (e.g., *sweets, M&M's, caramel, Milky Way, Snickers, chocolate*), many normal people will have false memories and think they were told to recall closely related words (e.g., *candy*) (Schacter et al., 1997). According to associative theory, the distributed representations of the concepts of the words to be remembered substantially overlap the distributed representations of concepts that represent the falsely recognized words. When we tested high-functioning autistic patients (Beversdorf et al., 2000) with this false-memory paradigm, these autistic participants recalled fewer false memories and discriminated true memories from false memories better than did the normal control participants. These results suggest that people with autism have constricted their semantic representations (i.e., relatively sparse and nonoverlapping). The reason for this constriction is unknown, but it might be related to a decrease in connectivity in these people's brains, and there is some evidence to support this connectivity hypothesis. For example, a Golgi analysis allows neuroscientists to examine the neuronal connectivity in brains. Upon examining the brains of people who were diagnosed with autism, using this Golgi analysis, Raymond, Bauman, and Kemper (1996) reported that there was a reduction of dendritic arborizations in the hippocampus. Defective dendritic arborizations could impair the formation of associative networks and can account for many of the signs of autism, such as diminished creativity, poor concept acquisition, impaired generalization, and a lack of cognitive flexibility, but as I mentioned earlier in this chapter, increased levels of norepinephrine can also restrict cognitive networks.

Some, but not all, studies have suggested that autism is associated with an increase of central nervous system monoamines, including norepinephrine (Gillberg & Svennerholm, 1987), and as I mentioned earlier, this increase can account for a constriction of associative networks and conceptual representations. People suffering with autism frequently manifest behaviors that suggest that these people might be hyperaroused (Fankhauser, Karumanchi, German, Yates, & Karumanchi, 1992). For example, they exhibit stereotyped body movements, self-stimulation, hypervigilance, and hyperactivity. Arousal is, in part, mediated by the neurotransmitter norepinephrine. Whereas direct examination of brain norepinephrine has not yet been performed in autism, treating autistic patients with either clonidine (an alpha 2 adrenergic receptor agonist), which reduces the excretion of norepinephrine (Fankhauser et al., 1992), or beta-blockers, which block the effect of norepinephrine on the brain, may improve the symptoms associated with autism (Rately et al., 1987).

129

EEG studies of autistic patients also suggest that some of these people might be in chronically high states of physiological arousal (Hutt, Hutt, Lee, & Ounsted, 1965). In contrast, studies of physiological arousal in depression, as determined by EEG power analysis, have revealed that depressed patients have reduced arousal that is altered with treatment (Knott, Mahoney, & Evans, 2000; Nieber & Schlegel, 1992). If, as I suggested previously, lower levels of physiological arousal allow people to increase the extent of their concept representations and increase their cognitive flexibility, then it would follow that people with depression might have a propensity to be creative and patients with autistic spectrum disorder would tend to have limited creativity.

As mentioned, increased locus coeruleus activity is associated with increased levels of cerebral norepinephrine and this increased norepinephrine induces physiological arousal as determined by changes in the EEG. Neurophysiological studies have revealed that stimulation of only certain parts of the cerebral cortex induces these arousal changes in the EEG. These areas include the frontal cortex and the anterior cingulate gyrus (Segundo, Naguet, & Buser, 1955), which are strongly interconnected.

Functional imaging studies of patients with depression can provide some insight into the mechanisms by which depression might provide the basis for creative inspiration. Many such studies have shown that depression is associated with reduced cerebral blood flow (i.e., reduced synaptic activity) in the dorsolateral prefrontal cortex and the anterior cingulate gyrus (Liotti & Mayberg, 2001). The observed reductions in dorsolateral prefrontal blood flow might be related to the relative failure of depressed patients to spontaneously engage the environment (attend to and develop thoughts or plans about environmental interactions) either because they are pathologically disengaged or because they are engaged in internally defined plans (e.g., introspection, rumination). The reduced activity in the dorsolateral prefrontal cortex and the anterior cingulate cortex that occurs in depressed patients might be important for creative innovation because, as I mentioned earlier, the frontal lobes and anterior cingulate gyrus are the primary cortical areas controlling the locus coeruleus. Reduced activity in these frontal and cingulate regions, by virtue of the reduced input to locus coeruleus, could provide the basis for reductions of cortical norepinephrine, associated reductions in signal-to-noise ratio, and the recruitment of widely distributed networks that contain a rich variety of representations.

Whereas depression might facilitate creative innovation, the verification and production portions of creative endeavors are often associated with high arousal. Thus, these stages of creativity often must await the resolution of depression. In addition to the frontal lobe's crucial role in modulating the activity of the locus coeruleus, the frontal lobes play an important role in many other aspects of creative endeavors. In the next chapter I discuss some of the important functions that the frontal lobes play in many other aspects of creative endeavors.

9

The Frontal Lobes

When I read the biographies of creative people, I am struck by these people's strong creative drive and their ability to persist performing their work, even though many of them never receive any type of external reward, such as money or recognition. Why then do people decide to become artists or scientists? What motivates them and what allows them to persist even in the absence of rewards?

Ramón y Cajal (1898/1999), the creative giants of neuroscience who proved that our brains are made up of interconnected but separate nerve cells or neurons, was also puzzled about creative drive when he wrote,

> The scholar [investigator] struggles for the benefit of all humanity, sometimes to reduce physical effort, sometimes to reduce pain and sometimes to postpone death or at least render it more bearable. In contrast the patriot sacrifices a rather substantial part of humanity for the sake of his own prestige. His statue is always erected on a pedestal of ruins and corpses; his triumphs are celebrated exclusively by a tribe, a party or nation; and he leaves behind a wake of hatred and bloody waste in the conquered territory.

I was struck by Ramón y Cajal's comment because, ever since my 13th birthday when my father took me to Washington, DC, I have noticed that in the United States almost all public buildings, roads, airports, and monuments are named after politicians and generals. When I first visited Paris I was delighted to learn that the French do not follow this tradition. There are statues, monuments, and streets named after famous scientists and artists, but still the largest monument I saw in Paris was Les Invalids, where Napoleon is entombed. Perhaps Ramón y Cajal was correct when he said, "People live in a world of sentiment, and it is asking too much of them to provide warmth and support for heroes of reason."

I remember thinking as a college student that if society celebrated artists and scientists as much as it celebrated politicians and generals, perhaps more people would enter these noble professions. When during my neurology residency training I became interested in performing research, I began to realize that although altruism and a desire to be appreciated and loved are important factors in the motivation of many scientists and artists, the desire for creativity comes from within. Poincare, more than 100 years ago, best summarized this principle when he wrote in his book, *La Science et la Methode,* "Intellectual beauty is sufficient unto itself and only for it rather than for the future good of humanity does the scholar condemn himself to arduous and painful labors."

After generating a hypothesis about the function of a certain part of the brain, testing this hypothesis, and learning something new about the brain, I had a feeling of euphoria come over me. I recall expressing this to my good friend Bob Watson, who said, "Wow, you are weird." Bob Watson was a coinvestigator in many exciting research projects with me when we were attempting to understand how the brain mediates attention, and I suspected he was feeling the same as I was, but I could never get him to admit to it. I was, therefore, pleased to read in Ramón y Cajal's (1898/1999) book *Advice for a Young Investigator* that one of the motives for performing research is "a desire to experience the incomparable gratification associated with the act of discovery itself." He also wrote,

Recall the happiness and emotion displayed by Newton when his genius-inspired conjecture about universal attraction was confirmed by calculation and by Picard's measurements of the terrestrial meridian. . . . This indescribable pleasure which pales the rest of life's joys is abundant compensation for the investigator who endures the painful and persevering analytical work that proceeds the appearance of a new truth, like the pain of childbirth. It is true to say that nothing for the scientific scholar is comparable to the things that he has discovered. Indeed, it would be difficult to find an investigator willing to exchange the paternity of a scientific conquest for all the gold on earth. And if there are some who look to science as a way of acquiring gold instead of . . . the personal satisfaction associated with the very act of discovery, they have chosen the wrong profession! They should wholeheartedly dedicate themselves to the exercise of industry or commerce instead. In fact, beyond the stimulation of a variety and interest, the supreme joy of the intellect lies in seeing the divine harmony of the universe and in knowing the truth—as beautiful and virginal as the flower opening its calyx to the caresses of the early morning sun.

Unfortunately, we still do not entirely know how the brain motivates us to create. As I mentioned earlier, Sigmund Freud, one of the first to advance a theory of creativity, proposed a psychodynamic theory of creativity based on sexuality. He thought that creative people sublimate much of their libidinal energies into creative activities, such as writing, painting, composing, and making scientific discoveries. Although it is difficult to entirely refute Freud's theories, it is clear that certain artists, such a Picasso, do not have much of a need to sublimate their libidinal activity.

Behaviorists such as B. F. Skinner suggest that people create because they have previously been rewarded for their creations (e.g., positive reinforcement). Many of the most creative artists, authors, and scientists, however, never receive recognition or rewards for the work during their life, but most continue to work until they become ill or die. What drives these people to create and to persist even in the absence of any form of external reward is unknown, but I discuss some of the possible brain mechanisms that might induce the euphoria associated with scientific or artistic discovery.

Risk Taking and Substance Abuse

If the creative act brings satisfaction and fulfillment, why do creative people often have affective disorders such as depression? In addition to having a high prevalence of affective disorders, creative people, especially writers, composer-musicians, and fine artists, have a very high rate of substance abuse, such as alcoholism (Post, 1994, 1996). As I mentioned in the chapter on neurotransmitters (chapter 8), although creative people often go through many trials and tribulations to accomplish creative endeavors, creativity itself probably does not induce affective disorders, but rather the people who are creative probably have some of the anatomic, physiological, or neurotransmitter abnormalities that

135

induce affective disorders. Although people who have affective disorders might use drugs as a form of chemical self-treatment, independent of this possible relationship between drugs and affective disorders, the same brain anomaly that makes people susceptible to drug abuse might serve to enhance curiosity, risk taking, and creativity. For example, studies of large cohorts of college students found that the students who use marijuana tend to be novelty seeking and more creative than the students who did not use this drug (Eisenman, Grossman, & Goldstein, 1980).

The mechanism underlying the relationships between substance abuse, novelty seeking, risk taking, and creativity has not been determined. One hypothesis, however, is that drugs enhance creative performance, but studies of creativity under normal states versus intoxicated states do not reveal that drugs enhance the production of creative works (Lang, Verret, & Watt, 1984). As I mentioned, depression might not enhance creative production, but it might be important in creative inspiration and innovation. A second possible relationship between drug abuse and creativity is that creative inspiration often takes place when people have reduced arousal, and some drugs such as alcohol and marijuana reduce arousal. Hence, although these central nervous system depressants probably do not help creative production, these depressant drugs might help creative innovation. There is, however, a third possibility. Independent of these drugs' effects on arousal, it is possible that creative people are prone to addiction and that the same brain mechanisms that make some creative people prone to addiction also enhance their curiosity and propensity to take risks, both important in the creative process.

Drug addiction often interferes with the external rewards that life and work bring to people. Thus, the use of drugs is not an externally driven behavior (exo-incentive), but is an extreme example of internally driven behavior (endo-incentive). Cloninger, Svrakic, and Przybeck (1993) presented a psychobiological model of personality that includes three temperaments or character dimensions. One of these dimensions is novelty seeking, and creative people would have to be considered novelty seekers. Several investigators have found that people who have a strong desire for novelty (high novelty seekers) are at increased risk for drug abuse when compared with low novelty seekers. There is some evidence that exposure to novelty activates, at least in part, the same neural substrates that mediate the rewarding effects of drugs of abuse (e.g., alcohol). The system that has been thought to be important in mediating reward is the mesolimbic dopamine system (Bardo, Donohew, & Harrington, 1996). A portion of the mesolimbic dopaminergic system (see Figure 9.1) projects from

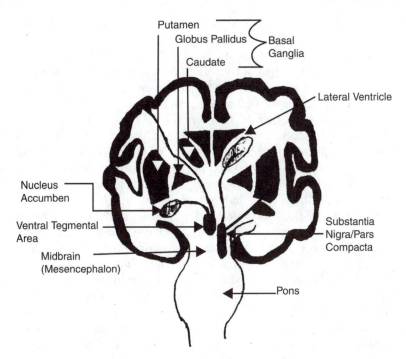

Figure 9.1. Diagram of the dopaminergic-basal ganglia systems. The substantia nigra sends dopaminergic neurons to the putamen and caudate. The ventral tegmental area sends dopaminergic neurons to the ventral striatum and to the cortex.

the midbrain to the nucleus accumbens, and this nucleus is a portion of the ventral striatum, which I describe in more detail later. The ventral striatum and its connections to the limbic system (e.g., amygdala) have been posited to be critical for alcohol addiction. Tupala and coworkers (2001) evaluated the densities of dopamine receptors and transporters in the nucleus accumbens of postmortem human brains of people who had a history of alcohol abuse, and they compared these brains with those of healthy controls. These investigators found in the brains of the alcoholic individuals that the mean number of dopamine receptor sites in this portion of the ventral striatum and in the amygdala was lower than that in the brains of the control individuals. These results indicate that dopaminergic functions in the ventral striatum may be abnormal among people who abuse drugs, such as alcohol. Novelty has been shown to enhance the firing of these dopaminergic neurons (Saigusa, Tuinstra, Koshikawa, & Cools, 1999), and curiosity is the search for novelty. These results suggest that people with alcohol or drug addiction might also use novelty as a means of stimulating the dopaminergic neurons because they find this stimulation is highly rewarding.

Dulawa, Grandy, Low, Paulus, and Geyer (1999) reviewed and summarized the reports that demonstrated reward is related to an increase in the activity of the neurotransmitter dopamine. They also reviewed the evidence that in animals, dopamine modulates the degree of exploratory behaviors. Patients with Parkinson's disease have reduced production of dopamine, and patients with Parkinson's disease report diminished responses to novelty. Some, but not all, studies have even reported that polymorphisms of the human dopamine D4 receptor (D4R) gene are associated with personality inventory measures of the trait called "novelty-seeking" (Schinka, Letsch, & Crawford, 2002). To explore a potential role for the D4R in behavioral responses to novelty, Dulawa et al. (1999) evaluated D4R-knockout (D4R$-/-$) and found that these mice were significantly less behaviorally responsive to novelty than D4R$+/+$ mice, with the largest phenotypic differences being observed in the novel object test.

Although there is a high incidence of substance abuse among some creative disciplines, there is a relatively low incidence in other disciplines. In addition, in every discipline there are people who have no problems with addiction. The reason why certain disciplines have a higher rate than other disciplines might have to do with the demands of the discipline rather the relationship between drug addiction and creativity. For example, if a writer takes several days or weeks off from writing or is sober just 4 hours a day and writes during that time, he or she still might be a productive novelist. In contrast, in medical research, where there are many physicians who perform research, the excessive use of alcohol or other drugs of addiction would interfere with job performance, and when physicians have substance abuse they often must undergo treatment before they are allowed to continue their professional duties. This explanation, however, cannot explain why there are many creative and productive authors who do not have problems with substance abuse. Although the reason for this is not entirely known, it is possible that to some degree there is a reciprocal relationship between the systems that mediate endo-incentive and the exo-incentive drives. Many of the people who have wealth and fame but are not extremely creative might be primarily motivated by the exo-incentive systems. In contrast, those who are very creative but have trouble with addiction might be primarily motivated by the endo-incentive system. Finally, those who are creative but do not have a problem with addiction might have a balance between these systems.

Creative individuals are explorers who discover new ideas, but explorers must take high risks. Following in the footsteps of people who are already successful is generally a low-risk behavior that can provide a sense of security and a feeling of contentment. In contrast, exploring new territories and ideas carries the risks of rejection and failure, but a successful exploration or creation brings euphoria and joy.

Sternberg and Lubert (1995) studied the relationship between risk taking and creativity. They studied risk taking in people by having them engage in a game in which the participants selected from activities: They could perform an operation that, if successful, had high payoff but also had high risks for failure or an operation that had a lower payoff but also had a much lower risk. These investigators found that, in general, creative people would engage in the high-risk, potentially high-reward operations and less creative people would select the low-risk operation.

In my book *Matter of Mind*, I tell the story of young woman whom I had the opportunity to examine during one of my visiting professorships. This young woman was raised in an urban ghetto in a large northeastern city. Throughout elementary, middle, and high school she was an excellent student who was admitted to a highly selective college and was awarded a full scholarship. She did well in college, with a high grade-point average, and she had a steady boyfriend whom she was planning to marry after she graduated. She engaged in no high-risk behaviors, including drug abuse. In the second semester of her junior year of college, she started to engage in high-risk behaviors, including using drugs such as cocaine and engaging in sexual promiscuity. She developed pneumonia and, when she was admitted to a hospital, she was found to have AIDS. She also had amenorrhea and, when this was evaluated, she was found to have a very large pituitary tumor that was compressing the orbitofrontal cortex and the ventral portions of her medial prefrontal cortex (see Figure 9.2).

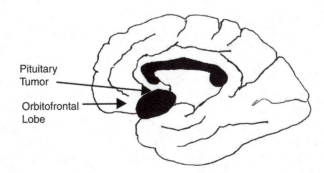

Pituitary Tumor

Orbitofrontal Lobe

Figure 9.2. Diagram of a patient's pituitary tumor that is encroaching on the orbitofrontal and medial frontal regions.

Bechara and coworkers (Bechara, Tranel, Damasio, & Damasio, 1996; Bechara et al., 1997) used a gambling card game to study patients with ventromedial prefrontal injuries. This game is in some ways similar to the game, used by Sternberg and Lubert (1995), that I mentioned previously. The participants picked cards from different stacks and, depending on the card they selected, they either won or lost money. There were stacks of cards that had small or moderate rewards with very small risks, versus a stack that had larger rewards but also very heavy risks that outweighed the potential to earn more. If the participants avoided this latter stack, they would have earned more money when the game was completed. These investigators reported that patients with orbital and medial prefrontal lesions, unlike the normal individuals, continued to select cards from the high-risk deck.

The reason injury to the orbital and medial prefrontal cortex (OMPC) increases the propensity to engage in risky behavior is unclear, but an understanding of the connections of these areas might help. For those who would like details about the anatomy of these areas, I recommend a review of the article by Ongur, Ferry, and Price (2003). The orbital and medical aspects of the OMPC receive different projections, but these two areas are strongly interconnected. The orbitofrontal cortex receives input from almost all areas of the posterior sensory association cortex. Both portions of the OMPC receive input from portions of the limbic system, such as the amygdala, that are known to play a special role in mediating emotions. Thus, in the OMPC there is a convergence and integration of sensory-cognitive information with limbic-emotional information. Olfactory and gustatory inputs also converge in the orbitofrontal cortex together with input from the parts of the brain that monitor the internal milieu of a person's body (visceral afferents).

The convergence of information from the sensory association cortex with visceral afferent stimuli (seeing food and learning that ingesting this food can induce satiation) allows an organism to code the identity of stimuli that have rewarding properties. Thus, Schultz Tremblay, and Hollerman (1998) suggested that the OMPC is part of a circuit that includes both the ventral striatum and the mesolimbic dopamine system, and that this circuit is important in reward. The nucleus accumbens, which is part of the ventral striatum, receives projections from portions of the OMPC and sends projections to the ventral pallidum. The ventral pallidum projects to the medial part of the medial dorsal thalamus, which in turn projects back to the OMPC. The ventral striatum also receives dopaminergic projections from the mesolimbic dopamine system. The cell bodies of this ascending dopaminergic system are in the ventral tegumental area of the mesencephalon. Animals will continually perform behaviors that are associated with stimulation of this dopaminergic-ventral striatal system, demonstrating the importance of this system in reward-guided behavior.

Portions of the OMPC are also closely connected with the hypothalamus, which controls the autonomic nervous system and portions of the endocrine system. Bechara et al. (2000) measured changes in skin conductance induced by sweating (galvanic skin responses) while participants played the card game that measures risk-taking behaviors. These investigators found that before normal participants made a decision to perform a high-risk move, their palms sweated, suggesting that the participants activated their autonomic nervous system. In contrast, their patients with OMPC injury, who repeatedly performed high-risk behaviors in this card game, did not develop a robust skin response before they performed a high-risk behavior.

These results are consistent with what Damasio (1996) called the "somatic marker hypothesis," and this somatic marker hypothesis is, in some respects, similar to James' (1890) visceral feedback theory and Schacter and Singer's (1962) attribution theory. These theories suggest that normally when a person is considering performing a high-risk behavior, the brain induces alterations of the internal milieu of the body, including activation of the sympathetic nervous system. It is the recognition of these changes that influences a person's decisions.

On the basis of the information I reviewed earlier, we can see that people, even in the absence of known brain lesions, who have a propensity to take risks, including extremely creative people, might have a OMPC-ventral striatal system that is different from people who are not risk takers. I previously mentioned the relationship between creativity and substance abuse, and I mentioned that people with a propensity for substance abuse might have aberrant functioning of their ventral striatum, including the nucleus accumbens. I also mentioned that creative people also have a propensity to be depressed. Functional imaging studies of depressed people have revealed abnormalities in portions of the orbital-medial prefrontal-ventral striatal circuit (Drevets et al., 1992). Drevets and coworkers also showed that a portion of the ventral medial prefrontal cortex is 40% smaller in depressed patients than in controls.

Taken together, these finding suggest that the relationship between depression, drug addiction, and risk taking, which is so important in creative endeavors, might all be related to an altered function of this orbital-medial prefrontal-ventral striatal-dorsomedial thalamic circuit.

Creative people receive much joy from their creative endeavors, but it not entirely known how the brain mediates positive affective responses to the created stimuli. Recently, Berridge (2003) wrote a review article about the brain systems that might allow stimuli to induce pleasure. The critical system that Berridge discussed in this review is again the ventral striatal circuit, including the shell of the nucleus accumbens. The shell of the nucleus accumbens is connected to the OMPC, which then projects back to the ventral pallidum, the dorsomedial thalamus, and then back to the frontal lobes. In addition to increasing risky behaviors, lesions in this ventral striatal circuit also appear to induce anhedonia (the loss of the ability to enjoy), and it is this ventral striatal circuit's projections back to the cerebral cortex that might allow people to consciously enjoy novelty and creativity. As I also mentioned previously, like other basal ganglia circuits, this ventral striatal circuit is also heavily dependent on dopamine. The dopaminergic system, and in particular the dopamine D2 receptor, has been implicated in reward mechanisms. This ventral striatal system induces a "reward" when dopamine is released from the neurons at the nucleus accumbens and activates the dopamine receptors.

Motivation and Persistence

To be successful, creative people need to have perseverance and persistence. According to Beals (1996), Thomas Edison said that being a creative genius required "ninety nine percent perspiration and one percent inspiration." The biographies of almost all creative people reveal that, independent of the domain in which they create, they persevere and persist.

Goal-oriented behavior or volition permeates almost all aspects of creativity, and the major organ of volition appears to be the frontal lobes. One mean by which neuroscientists learn the parts of the brain that perform certain functions is to study patients who have injuries to a specific portion of the brain. In the clinic we see people who have lost their initiative and drive, and this loss is called "abulia" (a = without, bulia = will or power). Harlow, in 1868, reported the famous case of Phineas Gage, one of the best-known descriptions of a person who developed abulia from a brain injury.

According to this report, Gage was a hardworking foreman of a railroad crew who had an accident. While using a tamping bar to place explosives, an explosion occurred and this iron bar flew upward and into his head. The rod struck him in the left cheek and went through his left maxillary sinus, and from the maxillary sinus, the rod impaled the frontal lobes of his brain. The iron rod then exited the top of the skull. These types of accidents can cause brain swelling, hemorrhage, and infection, but he miraculously survived this accident. The frontal lobes are important for the expression of speech and the control of movements. Thus, it was also remarkable that he did not suffer with weakness or a loss of speech. His personality, however, did undergo a dramatic change. According to Harlow (1868), before the accident Gage had "a well balanced mind. And was looked upon by those who knew him as a shrewd, smart businessman, very energetic and persistent in executing all his plans." After the accident he lost these skills. According to Harlow (1868), "His mind was radically changed, so decidedly that his friends and acquaintances said he was no longer Gage."

Even after Harlow's dramatic description of the effects of frontal lobe injury, not much research was performed on the functions of the frontal lobes until 1934, when Kleist had the opportunity to examine many of the soldiers who injured their frontal lobes during the First World War. He noted that these veterans also were apathetic and abulic, with a loss of drive and initiative. We still do not fully understand why the frontal lobes are so important for goal-oriented behavior; however, Nauta (1971) a Dutch neuroanatomist who worked at MIT, provided us with one of the best explanations. He noted that information from the outside world is first transmitted to the primary sensory areas. As I mentioned, the auditory system projects to the superior portion of the temporal lobes, touch projects to the anterior portions of the parietal lobes, and vision projects to the occipital lobes (see Figure 3.6). These primary sensory areas perform elementary sensory analyses. Each of these primary sensory areas sends information to modality-specific sensory association cortices. Hence the visual cortex sends information to visual association areas in the occipital, temporal, and parietal lobes; the auditory cortex sends its information to auditory association areas in the temporal lobes; and the tactile primary sensory areas send information to the tactile association areas in the superior parietal lobes (see Figure 3.6). These modality-specific sensory areas synthesize sensory information within a modality, which is important in the development of percepts. These areas also store modality-specific representations of previously perceived stimuli. For example, for a person's brain to derive meaning when the individual views an object, it must put together the lines or edges detected by the primary cortex to form a percept of object's shape, then these percepts activate the stores of iconic representation of previously seen objects, letters, or faces. Subsequently, all these sensory association areas send these activated iconic, echoic, or somesthetic (touch) representations to multimodal areas of the temporal and parietal lobes (see Figure 3.6). These multimodal areas have rich neuronal networks that store memories of the meaning of these stimuli and how these stimuli are related to other stimulus and concepts.

In people with damage restricted to the frontal lobe, such as Phineas Gage, these sensory-perceptual–semantic-conceptual systems are intact, and because these systems are working, people with frontal lobe injuries are aware of their environment, can interpret the meaning of stimuli, and have the knowledge needed to accomplish goals. To succeed in using this knowledge to achieve goals, however, one needs motivation or drive. Knowledge together with motivation leads to goal-oriented behavior. Biological drives are present in almost all creatures. In almost all vertebrates, these biological drives are mediated by the phylogenetically primitive limbic system, including the hypothalamus (see Figure 9.3). Unlike the temporal, occipital, and parietal cortices that monitor the outside world, the hypothalamus and limbic system monitor the inside world of an animal's body. When these internal monitors note a deficiency, they initiate a drive state that motivates behavior. For example, when the sugar (glucose) in the blood drops too low, the animal gets hungry and searches for food. If it finds food, it eats. When the salt in the blood becomes too high, the animal becomes thirsty and thus, looks for and drinks water.

Because patients with frontal lobe injuries have an intact hypothalamus and limbic system, they attempt to satisfy a need such as hunger by looking for and eating food. Although they have the knowledge that they need to have food accessible for the next time they get hungry, they often fail to make the necessary preparations (goal-oriented behavior). The systems important in developing drive states, such as the hypothalamus and limbic system, are strongly connected with the neuronal assemblies in the frontal lobes. The knowledge of how to satisfy these drive states is stored in the posterior (temporal-parietal) multimodal sensory association, areas which are also strongly connected with the frontal lobes. According to Nauta (1971), as the frontal-lobe networks

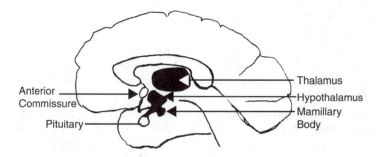

Figure 9.3. Diagram of hypothalamus, including the mammillary body.

develop, they fuse the information about biological drives with the knowledge of how to satisfy these drives. This knowledge fusion leads to the development of goal-oriented behavior or conation.

One of the founders of modern neurology was the 19th-century British neurologist John Hughlings Jackson. Hughlings Jackson was strongly influenced by Charles Darwin's writings on evolution, and he formulated the idea that human's central nervous system was organized phylogenetically such that "lower" or phylogenetically more primitive parts of our nervous system contain the neural apparatus of more primitive animals and the "higher" parts consist of more recently evolved neural systems. In general, the behavioral repertoire of these lower portions is limited, and the behaviors programmed by these more primitive structures are often stereotypic. Throughout evolution, as we developed new parts of our brains, such as the cerebral neocortex, these new areas allowed us to perform a richer repertoire of behaviors. For people to be able to perform these more specific or complex behaviors, we had to have a means by which we could suppress the more primitive stereotypic behaviors that are mediated by more primitive parts of the central nervous system. Thus, the frontal lobes not only allow us to plan and implement goal-oriented behaviors but also inhibit or control the more phylogenetically primitive systems, such as the limbic system. The inhibition of behaviors mediated by more primitive systems, such as the limbic system, allows us to control these more primitive biological drives and emotions, permitting a person to carry out goal-oriented behavior. When the frontal lobes are injured, a person has not only a loss of goal-oriented behaviors but also an inability to inhibit more primitive drives and behaviors.

Because the frontal lobes are important for long-term goals they allow us to perform activities that might not always make us immediately happy but might provide long-term rewards. In his book, *Creativity,* Mihaly Csikszentmihalyi (1996) called these behaviors "exotelic." In the beginning of this chapter, however, I wrote that while some creative artists, writers, composers, and scientists do obtain fortune and fame, very few of these people get wealthy or famous by performing creative acts. Some, when they started their creative careers, might have thought that their creativity would bring them fame and fortune, but after several years many creative people realize that these aspirations will never be fulfilled. This knowledge, however, often does not stop them from continuing their creative activities. Creative people often continue to create because performing this act brings them enjoyment and fulfillment. This self-motivated behavior, which is not performed for any future or immediate rewards, Csikszentmihalyi called "autotelic." For the fortunate few, their creative behaviors are both exotelic and autotelic. Although I agree with Csikszentmihalyi's concepts, perhaps the term *endo-incentive,* introduced earlier, should be used to replace the term *autotelic,* and the term *exotelic* should be replaced with the term *exo-incentive.*

Several years ago I had the opportunity to examine in our Memory and Cognitive Disorder Clinic a famous neurosurgeon who developed a decrement in this endo-incentive system. This surgeon was the Chair of the Department of Neurosurgery at a prestigious university and hospital. In addition to being a superb technical surgeon, he ran a very productive research laboratory and was a leading educator, training many excellent neurosurgeons. Much of his research was supported by grants from the National Institutes of Health. Until about 5 years prior to the time I saw him in our clinic, he had almost continual funding from this agency. The last proposal that he submitted for a renewal of funding was, however, disapproved. The reviewers thought that this proposal contained no new or interesting hypotheses, but rather was just a rehash of his prior work. Because he did not receive funding, he decided to close his laboratory. He did, however, continue to perform surgery and still had excellent surgical techniques. During surgery he was never very kind to the surgical nurses, his residents, or even the anesthesiologists, but it was clear something was wrong when he took to throwing instruments and cursing at people with whom he worked. The dean spoke with him about controlling his temper, but he had problems controlling this aberrant behavior. Several months after he spoke with the dean, he started coming to the operating room late and sometimes leaving early, asking his residents to complete the surgery. For more than 30 years he had always started his clinical ward rounds at 6:00 A.M. and then made rounds again before he left the hospital at about 7:30 P.M. The residents noted, however, that he started to be tardy and sometimes he did not show up until they paged him. Rounds had always been all business, but now he started going over to the nurses and ward secretaries, touching them and asking for sexual favors. The dean spoke with him again, and during this conversation the dean noticed that he had inappropriate laughter and did not seem concerned that he was being accused of sexual harassment.

The dean temporarily withdrew the surgeon's clinical and teaching privileges and requested him to be evaluated. The surgeon and his wife thought it best that he be evaluated at a different institution, and so they flew to Gainesville to be seen in our clinic.

When I evaluated him, he was 63 years old. In addition to the history I just outlined, his wife related to me that she noticed some other changes in his personality. He was always compulsively clean and took a shower both before he left to go to the hospital and when he returned from the hospital. She noticed that now, unless she said something, he rarely bathed. Often, unless she reminded him, he did not change his underwear for several days. Almost his entire adult life, until recently, he would read journals, review papers, or write papers when at home. Now he spent hours just sitting in front of the television. I could not obtain any history of what sounded like depression, and the remainder of his history was not informative.

My neurological examination determined that he had several abnormalities. To see if his visual fields were full, I asked him to look at my nose, and I extended my arms so that one was across from his left shoulder and the other across from his right shoulder. I then told him when I moved either my right or my left hand he was to tell me which hand I moved. Although I repeatedly reminded him to stare at my nose, whenever I moved either my right or my left hand he moved his eyes and looked directly at the hand I moved. When I asked him to relax his muscles and then tried to move his arm, he always seemed to be helping me (facilitory paratonia). When I lightly stroked his palm with my forefinger and middle finger, he grasped my fingers even though I asked him not to hold my fingers. His propensity to grasp my hand when told not to is called the grasp reflex. It is one of those primitive reflexes that allow infant nonhuman primates to hold on to their mothers when they are on the move. Normal human infants have this reflex, but as we mature and increase our repertoire of skilled hand movements, we inhibit this phylogenetically primitive reflex. The surgeon's eyes were also grasping. Although I instructed him to look straight ahead at my nose, his eyes grasped on to my hand movements. We know that there are at least two systems that control the eyes: a phylogenetically advanced system that is controlled by the frontal lobes and is important in goal-oriented behavior, and a more primitive system that is controlled by the colliculus, a structure in the midbrain. When one loses frontal cortical control of eye movements, the subcortical colliculus takes control, as it did in this surgeon.

When I tested his mental status, I found that his language, including his naming, was normal. For example, when given the Boston Naming Test, he was able to name all 60 items. His visual-spatial and visual-constructive skills were also excellent. For example, he could draw intersecting pentagons flawlessly. He was fully oriented and knew the day, month, year, and his current location, but when I further tested his memory with the Hopkins Verbal Learning Test by presenting to him and asking him to recall a series of 12 words (e.g., *tent, tiger, opal, pearl, cave, lion, hotel, sapphire, cow, horse, emerald, hut*) three times,

I found that his memory was impaired. Normally people his age are able to recall more that 20 items in three trails, and he was able to recall only 16. After about a delay of 30 minutes, all he could recall was the word *tiger,* and most normal people his age can recall more than 8 of these items. After 30 minutes I asked him if he could again draw the picture I asked him to copy, and he drew two diamonds rather than the intersecting pentagons.

I noticed that during my examination he often told me inappropriate jokes. This inappropriate jocularity is often associated with right-frontal dysfunction. The behavior of patients with frontal lobe dysfunction is often very dependent on environmental stimuli. This phenomenon is called "environmental dependency" (Lhermitte, 1986). There are several tests we use to see if patients are environmentally dependent. I placed a pencil and paper on a table in front of him (so that he could copy intersecting pentagons), but before I showed him the picture I wanted him to copy or gave him any instructions, he picked up the pen and started writing his name. I then placed a comb in front of him and he started to comb his hair. François Lhermitte (1986), a Parisian neurologist, described several patients with similar behaviors. For example, in a journal article, Lhermitte wrote about a nurse with frontal lobe dysfunction. He placed a syringe with a needle on a table in front of her and she proceeded to give him an injection in one of his buttocks. This form of environmental dependency is also called "utilization behavior." Another simple test of environmental dependency is the 2-1 test devised by the Russian neurologist A. R. Luria (1969). I made a fist and told the surgeon to also make a fist. Then I instructed him to put up two fingers when I put up one finger and when I put up two fingers he was to put up one. On almost every trial this surgeon showed echopraxia, such that when I put up two fingers he initially put up two and then put one finger down. When I put up one finger he would initially put up one finger and then raise the second finger. These tests demonstrate that it is the environment rather than self-generated goals that determined his behavior.

Because the desire to achieve long-term goals allows people to persist, I wanted to test his persistence. I asked him to give me as many different words as he could that began with the letter *A* in 1 minute but not to give me proper names. He gave me 6 items in the first 10 seconds, and then remained silent for the remaining 50 seconds. Two of the items were proper names (*Alice* and *Alabama*), and two were derivatives (*add, addition, additive*). Most people of his age and intelligence are able to name at least 12 items in 1 minute. He performance was abnormal because he did not persist and he got stuck in a set. To further test his persistence, I asked him to close his eyes and to keep them closed for 20 seconds. He was able to keep his eyes closed for only about 10 seconds.

This surgeon's history of a loss of initiative, goal-oriented behavior, and persistence together with an inability to inhibit more primitive drives and emotions is typical of patients with frontal lobe dysfunction. In corporations, it is the executive's job to make long-term plans for the company and to allocate resources so that these plans can be fulfilled. Because patients with frontal lobe dysfunction often are impaired at developing and implementing long-term goals and allocating resources, some people call the deficits demonstrated by this surgeon "executive dysfunction."

To learn what may be causing this surgeon's executive dysfunction, I ordered a series of tests. All tests were normal except for the magnetic resonance images of his brain, which revealed he had severe atrophy of both frontal lobes. Because all his other tests were normal and he had this frontal lobe atrophy, we diagnosed his symptoms as a frontal-temporal lobar degeneration or frontotemporal dementia. Many of the patients with this disorder have abnormal deposits in their nerves cells, and this is called Pick's disease. Others just show swollen cells that do not take up the chemical stains used to perform histological analyses, but most of these patients' brains just show cell loss without any specific form of pathology. He requested and we considered taking a brain biopsy, but unfortunately currently there is little we can do to either reverse or treat any of these forms of dementia and knowing the histological subtype would not alter our treatment, thus we decided not to biopsy his brain. Studies of patients with frontal lobe dysfunction, such as this surgeon, do inform us that people who are creative must have well-functioning frontal lobes.

The ability to have long-term goals and to suppress biological drives when they interfere with long-term goals as well as the ability to persist and not be distracted is what I call "frontal intelligence." Frontal intelligence is one of the major factors underlying success in any profession, including those that require creativity. The frontal lobe networks, however, have another function that appears to be important for creativity: divergent thinking.

Divergent Thinking

Psychologists divide thinking into two forms: convergent and divergent. The type of thinking performed by most problem solvers is convergent. In medical school we primarily teach our students and residents convergent thinking. For example, medical students are taught that if they see a person who has a fever, he or she may have an infection or heat stroke. In addition to the fever, if the patient is unconscious, the physician might still have trouble distinguishing between these two diagnostic possibilities. If, however, the patient has a stiff neck, the patient's fever and unconsciousness are most likely related to an infection of the central nervous system, such as meningitis. To obtain further converging evidence, the doctor can perform a spinal tap, and if the spinal fluid has white blood cells and bacteria, there is now sufficient converging evidence to make a diagnosis of meningitis and to start antibiotic therapy.

Creative people must be able to perform convergent thinking, but this form of thinking often uses standard algorithms and when confronted with anomalies convergent thinking may not lead to the development of new ideas, as does divergent thinking. Convergent thinkers look for signs that they have learned to help them complete the puzzle (fitting the mold). People might need to use divergent thinking because the algorithm they were previously taught cannot entirely explain their observations. That is, divergent thinkers might see an anomaly and recognize that there is no mold into which these observations would fit and hence they start developing new molds. Scientists often observe anomalies. The scientist who restricts his or her thought process to convergent thinking will often dismiss anomalous observations, but the divergent thinker will often use this anomaly to embark on a new adventure of discovery.

I defined *creativity* as the ability to understand, develop, and express in a systematic fashion novel orderly relationships. A critical part of this definition is that to be creative, the work has to be novel or new. Almost all psychologists who have studied creative people or developed tests to measure creative potential have noted the importance of divergent thinking. Divergent thinking is the ability to take a different direction from the prevailing modes of thought or expression.

The concept of divergent thinking was first put forth by William James in 1890, who stated,

Instead of thoughts of concrete things patiently following one another in a beaten track of habitual suggestion, we have the most abrupt cross-cuts and transitions from one idea to another . . . unheard of combination of elements, the subtlest associations of analogy . . . we seem suddenly introduced into a seething caldron of ideas . . . where partnerships can be joined or loosened . . . treadmill routine is unknown and the unexpected is the only law (quoted in Albert & Runco 1999).

Zangwell (1966) suggested that frontal lobe damage or dysfunction would disrupt divergent thinking. Berg (1948) developed a test (the Wisconsin Card Sorting Test) in which participants are required to sort a deck of cards according to the various dimensions illustrated on these cards (e.g., shape, color, number). The participant is not informed of the sorting principle (e.g., shape) but must deduce this from the responses of the examiner after each sort. The ability to reach the first sorting criterion might be an example of convergent reasoning. Throughout this test, however, the sorting principles change (e.g., from shape to color), and the participant must switch her or his strategy based on the responses of the examiner. The ability to switch strategies might be an example of divergent thinking as defined by James: "Instead of thoughts of concrete things patiently following one another in a beaten track of habitual suggestion, we have the most abrupt cross-cuts and transitions from one idea to another" (quoted in Albert & Runco, 1999). Milner (1984) demonstrated that patients who had frontal lobectomies for the surgical treatment of medically intractable epilepsy were impaired at this test, suggesting that the frontal lobe might be critical for divergent thinking.

Perseveration is the inability to switch to a new set or change the form of an activity (divergence). This behavioral disorder is often observed in brain-damaged individuals who have frontal lobe injuries, especially in the right hemisphere. Denny-Brown and Chambers (1958) proposed that whereas the frontal lobes mediate avoidance behaviors, the temporal-parietal lobes mediate approach behaviors. Converging evidence for the postulate that the frontal lobes might be critical for divergent thinking comes from studies of regional blood flow in normal individuals who are performing the Wisconsin Card Sorting Test (Weinberger, Berman, & Zee, 1986) or are performing a divergent thinking test similar to those described by Guilford (1967) and Torrance (1988) in which participants have to give alternative uses of a brick. When normal individuals were performing the Wisconsin Card Sorting Test, they demonstrated an increase in frontal activity, and when creative individuals provided alternative uses of bricks, their frontal lobes also showed more activation than those who were less creative (Carlsson, Wendt, & Risberg, 2000).

Although both studies of patients with frontal lesions and the use of functional imaging with normal participants during the time they are using divergent thinking suggest that the frontal lobes are important for divergent thinking, the means by which the frontal lobes accomplish this remains unknown. The frontal lobes, however, have strong connections to the polymodal and supramodal regions of the temporal and parietal lobes, and the temporal and parietal lobes store conceptual-semantic representations. Perhaps these frontal-parietal and frontal-temporal connections are responsible for activating the semantic-conceptual networks that are critical in developing the alternative solutions and is the basis of divergent thinking.

Support for the postulate that the frontal lobe might be important in either activating or inhibiting semantic networks comes from a recent study using positron-emission tomography. This study suggests different roles for medial and lateral prefrontal cortex (Brodmann's area 10). Whereas the medial frontal lobe is important for suppressing internally generated thoughts, the lateral frontal lobe is important in generating and maintaining these thoughts (Burgess et al., 2003).

Creative-divergent thinking requires the activation of a large variety of conceptual networks, and, as I mentioned earlier, catecholamines influence the breadth of activated networks. Although the neurons that provide the cerebral cortex with catecholamine such as norepinephrine are located in the pons (locus coeruleus), a portion of the brain stem, the activity of the catecholaminergic systems are modulated by the frontal lobes and the frontal lobe is the primary cortical area to project to the locus coeruleus (Arnsten & Goldman-Rakic, 1984). Thus, because of its connections to the temporal and parietal cortex and its control of the locus coeruleus–norepinephrine system, the frontal lobes appear to be a critical element in creative-divergent thinking.

10

Aging

Changes in Creativity With Aging

Simonton (1999) demonstrated that creative productivity is a function of age. In general, there is a sharp increase in productivity between the ages of 20 and 30 years. Productivity appears to reach a peak between the ages of 30 and 50 and then declines over the next several decades. This peak, however, changes somewhat with disciplines. In some disciplines, such as pure mathematics and theoretical physics, most of the important creative work is performed when these people are in their 20s and 30s and then there is a rapid fall off, but in biology and medicine many of the most important creative works are often performed by people in their 30s, 40s, and 50s. In other disciplines, such as art and music, people remain very creative even into old age. For example, Giuseppe Verdi wrote his first opera, *Nabucco*, at the age of 29 and wrote *Falstaff* at the age of 80. Although this division at first appears to relate to the domain of creativity, aesthetic (e.g., art and music) versus data driven (e.g., chemistry and physics), Simonton (1999) mentions that poets flourish when they are young and geologists might have long creative careers. Simonton also suggested that it appears to be career age (the number of years that a person has been creative in a domain) rather than purely chronological age that predicts the downturn.

The reason people are seldom creative until they reach their 20s and 30s is probably dependent on two major factors. The first factor deals with brain maturation. One of the major theses of this book is that creativity depends on a high degree on connectivity within the brain, and I have already described the role of the subcortical white matter and the frontal lobes in creativity. The frontal lobes and other regions of the brain do not fully mature until people reach their 20s. The second factor has to do with the acquisition of skills needed for creative inspiration and production. A person might not fully acquire these skills until that person reaches his or her 20s or 30s. What remains unclear, however, is why with aging there is a decrease of creativity. Simonton (1999) stated, "There have been numerous attempts to offer theoretical explanations of these empirical results, most of which fail because they can not accommodate the facts."

Simonton's model of creativity is primarily based on Darwinian principles of random variation followed by selection. Simonton attempted to develop a multifactorial mathematical model that has as its first major determinant "initial creative potential." Simonton suggested that this potential constrains the number of ideational variants a person is able to generate during his or her lifetime. A second major factor is the age at which creative people start their careers. Two other factors are related to the discipline. According to Simonton's model, the reason creativity decreases with aging is that people run out of variants or new ideas.

The Darwinian model of evolution suggests that genetic changes are random and although most of those changes reduce the ability of an organism to survive, rarely does a genetic alteration induce a phenotypic change that increases this mutant ability to survive and procreate. Creative ideas have many sources, and chance and random variation often can play an important role in creativity. A good example of such a chance occurrence is Alexander Fleming's leaving his petri dishes open and on a counter and leaving the window open window so that the mold could be blown into the laboratory, land in the petri dishes, and kill the bacteria. Thus, observing chance anomalies might lead to the awakening of creative new ideas at any age. New ideas, however, are not always dependent on chance occurrences or the observations of anomalies. Earlier we defined creativity as the ability to understand, develop, and express in a systematic fashion novel orderly relationships. Michelangelo's ability to sculpt *David* from a piece of marble cannot be explained by ideational variation and selective retention. He was able to see *David* in the marble block, even before he lifted his hammer, and he "released" this beautiful masterpiece from this stone. Perhaps the creativity that does not rely on seeing an anomaly, but rather comes from within, is more likely to run out after years of creative production. In medicine, creativity often stems from seeing an anomaly. Prepared minds can detect anomalies at almost any age, which is perhaps why biologists, who repeatedly observe anomalies, have longer creative careers than do theoretical physicists.

Although creative people's decreased productivity with aging might be related to the exhaustion of new ideas, there also might be biological factors. In the next sections I discuss some of these possible biological factors.

Changes in Intelligence

In an earlier discussion of intelligence and creativity, I mentioned that Cattell (1963) posted two forms of intelligence: crystallized and fluid. Crystallized intelligence is primarily stored knowledge. For example, the subtests of the Wechsler Adult Intelligence Scale (1981) that test crystallized intelligence would include those that access vocabulary and information. Fluid intelligence is primarily the ability to manipulate knowledge. On the Wechsler Adult Intelligence Scale most of the fluid intelligence tests are in the performance section (e.g., picture completion and picture arrangement).

With aging there is a decrease in the performance IQ, suggesting that fluid intelligence might decrease with aging, and, as I mentioned, fluid intelligence might be more important in developing creative ideas than is crystallized intelligence. Many of the tests in the performance IQ are timed, and as people get older they get slower. This slowing is both electrophysiological (e.g., evoked potentials) and behavioral. Thus, some investigators have asked whether the lower scores on performance IQ associated with aging were related to slowing. Investigators, however, tested older versus younger individuals on tests from the performance IQ without timing the tests. Although allowing older individuals more time did improve their performance, even without using time to determine scores, older individuals did less well than did the younger individuals (Storandt, 1977). Thus, with advancing age there appears to be a continual increase in crystallized intelligence but a decrease of fluid intelligence (Ryan, Sattler, & Lopez, 2000). Although, as mentioned, there is not a direct relationship between intelligence and creativity, fluid intelligence is probably more related creativity than is crystallized intelligence. The decrease of fluid intelligence as a function of age appears to mirror the changes in creativity seen with aging, but this relationship is correlative, not explanatory.

The Aging Brain

There are many biological changes in the brain that occur with aging. The brain decreases in size and weight with aging (Berg, 1948). These involutional changes usually start at the age of 50 and there is about a 2% decrease for each decade. Quantitative anatomical studies using neurostereology of the aging brain in nondemented people (Pakkenberg et al., 2003) have revealed that the difference in total number of neurons between individuals ranging from 20 to 90 years old is, however, less than 10%. This result suggests that the loss of brain substance is not entirely caused by the loss of neurons. Although there is only a small percentage of neurons lost as a function of aging, many of the neurons that are lost are located in brain areas that might be critical to creativity, including the dorsolateral frontal lobe (e.g., Brodmann's area 10) and the inferior parietal lobe, including Brodmann's areas 40 and 39. With aging even in the absence of a clinical diagnosis of dementia, the histological changes that are often associated with Alzheimer's disease might be observed. These include the deposition of amyloid in the cortex; changes in the neurons, including neurofibrillary tangles; and a loss of dendritic branching or arborizations. Thus, some neurons that are not lost might be sick and not properly functioning. With a loss of dendritic arborizations these neurons are less connected to other neurons. Other changes include granulovacular degeneration (little vesicles or holes in the neurons' cytoplasm) and the deposit of lipofuscin (a form of pigmented fat).

Some physiological research assessing blood flow with positron-emission tomography (PET) has suggested that with aging there might be metabolic changes indicating a reduction in the overall activity of the brain. When patients with medical problems (e.g., hypertension, diabetes) were not used as study participants, however, several studies showed no major difference in blood flow (Duara et al., 1984) or brain activity, as measured by EEG frequency (Duffy, Albert, McAnulty, & Garvey, 1984), as a function of aging. Hence, it is unlikely that the decreased creativity associated with aging is caused by metabolic abnormalities.

Many of the intra- and interhemispheric connections that I wrote about earlier are mediated by myelinated axons, and studies that have compared the loss of gray matter (primarily composed of neurons and their dendritic processes) versus white matter (primarily composed of myelinated axons and supporting structures) have revealed that most of the brain volume and brain weight that is lost with aging is related to loss of white matter (Sullivan, Pfefferbaum, Adalsteinsson, Swan, & Carmelli, 2002; Tang, Whitman, Lopez, & Baloh, 2001). The areas that show the greatest loss are those that myelinate late in development. The loss of subcortical white matter also increases the size of the lateral ventricles (see Figure 3.8). When old people obtain magnetic resonance imaging (MRI) or computer tomography (CT) of their brain, there is often evidence of deep white matter injury. Although neuroradiologists often call these changes "ischemic demyelination" or "leukoariaosis," the cause of the loss and damage to the white matter is not entirely known.

Earlier I wrote about the important role of the major connection between the left hemisphere and right hemisphere—the corpus callosum—in creativity. The corpus callosum is made of myelinated neurons that travel from one hemisphere to the other, and with the loss of the white matter, associated with aging, there is also a thinning of the corpus callosum (Hopper, Patel, Cann, Wilcox, & Schaeffer, 1994; Sullivan et al., 2002). In addition to the anatomic alterations with aging, there is also evidence of a decrease in interhemisphere callosally mediated communication (Reuter-Lorenz & Stanczak, 2000).

The Frontal Lobes and Aging

Injury to the frontal lobes or interruptions of subcortical connections with the frontal lobe impair the functions of the frontal lobes, and some of these deficits of frontal lobe function are called executive deficits. Several studies suggest that frontal lobe dysfunction is often associated with aging. For example, Mittenberg, Seidenberg, O'Leary, and DiGiulio (1989) compared older and younger individuals on tests that assessed frontal, parietal, and temporal lobe functions. These investigators found that it was frontal lobe function that best correlated with age.

Some of the most common executive deficits associated with frontal lobe dysfunction are forms of perseverative behavior. One of the tests that patients with frontal lobe perform poorly is the Wisconsin Card Sorting Test. In this test there are a series of cards that have different geometric designs, and these geometric designs have different colors and a different number of designs on each card. The participants are asked to sort the cards into stacks, but the examiner does not explicitly provide the means (shape, color, or number) by which they are to be sorted. Thus, participants might put all the cards that have the same design in the same pile, independent of their colors or numbers. After several successful sorts, however, the examiner indicates that this sort is no longer correct and the participants normally change their sorting strategy, now sorting by color or number. After several correct sorts, the examiner again indicates that this sort is no longer correct, and the person being tested needs to again change their sorting strategy. The patients with frontal injuries after developing a sorting strategy such as sorting by form continue sorting by this strategy even when the examiner indicates that this strategy is no longer the correct one. This form of perseveration where a person does not develop new strategies is called being "stuck in set." Creative innovation requires that a creative person attempt a new strategy, and if this strategy is unsuccessful or only partially successful he or she needs to attempt another strategy. If a creative person gets stuck in set, then his or her creative career will come to an end. Ridderinkhof, Span, and van der Molen (2002) tested a population of older individuals and found that they are more likely to get stuck in set than are younger people. Hence, the problem the older individuals were having on this task was not related to their inability to induce rules of sorting but rather rigidity, or their reluctance to shift once they found a sorting strategy.

The reason why older people have a propensity to get stuck in set or be mentally rigid is unclear, but there at least two possibilities. As I mentioned earlier, neurons communicate by giving off chemicals called neurotransmitters. One of the major neurotransmitters that appears to decrease with aging is dopamine. For example, Volkow et al. (2000) who with functional imaging (PET) found that with aging there was a decrease of dopamine and a decrease of frontal lobe activation. The cells that give off dopamine are found in the midbrain and from the midbrain travel to both the basal ganglia and the cerebral cortex (see Figure 9.1). Patients with Parkinson's disease have a reduced level of dopamine, and they also have evidence for frontal lobe dysfunction (Green et al., 2002). For example, patients with Parkinson's disease often perform poorly on tests such as the Wisconsin Card Sorting Test, frequently getting stuck in set, and thus the reduced creativity seen with aging might be related to cognitive rigidity and this cognitive rigidity might be related to the loss of dopaminergic neurons associated with aging.

I also mentioned earlier that with aging there is a loss of subcortical white matter. Patients who have diseases that injure their white matter, such as multiple sclerosis or multiple small strokes of the white matter, frequently show evidence of frontal lobe dysfunction and do poorly on tests such as the Wisconsin Card Sorting Test because they get stuck in set.

Right-Hemisphere Deterioration

In chapter 3 I described the role of the right hemisphere in creativity. In summary, the right hemisphere appears to be more important in global than local processing, and global processing is often important in finding the thread that unites. I also mentioned how the right hemisphere is important in visual-spatial functions and how many extremely creative people used visual-spatial strategies to help find creative solutions. Thus, another hypothesis as to why creativity decreases with aging suggests that right hemisphere–mediated functions deteriorate more than those of the left hemisphere (Dolcos, Rice, & Cabeza, 2002). The right hemisphere–deterioration hypothesis of reduced creativity with aging is supported by studies that gave older and younger participants the Wechsler Adult Intelligence Scale. The visual-spatial tasks (e.g., block construction) on the Wechsler Adult Intelligence Scale are part of the performance IQ, and the language tests (e.g., vocabulary) are part of the verbal IQ. As I mentioned, investigators have found that with aging there is greater deterioration of the performance IQ than there is of the verbal IQ. Because the right hemisphere appears to be dominant for visual-spatial functions, one could interpret this decrease to a loss of right-hemisphere function with aging. There are, however, several confounds to this interpretation. For example, many of the spatial tests that are part of the performance IQ are timed and with aging there is slowing of response times independent of task. In addition, the performance IQ is also more of a test of fluid intelligence than crystallized intelligence, and, as I mentioned earlier, with aging there might be a greater decrement of fluid intelligence.

Many visual-spatial functions have been shown to deteriorate with aging, even when using untimed tests (Koss, Haxby, DeCarli, & Schapiro, 1991). For example, when shown incomplete drawing of objects, older participants have more trouble recognizing these objects (Read, 1988), or when older individuals have to find figures that are imbedded in larger figures, they perform more poorly than the younger individuals. Using incomplete information to recognize objects or finding a meaningful stimulus in a noisy background is similar to finding the thread that unites. In contrast to the deterioration of spatial skills, as a function of age, the verbal IQ appears to remain stable, and some studies even showed an improvement of verbal skills with aging. Whereas vocabulary seems to remain unchanged with aging, there are some suggestions that knowledge of grammar and syntax appears to improve. Perhaps this is why novelists are more likely to remain creative to an older age than are mathematicians and theoretical physicists.

Although the assessment of the right hemisphere's versus the left hemisphere's cognitive function as a function of aging remains to be fully determined, Gur and associates (1980) studied the ratio of gray matter to white matter in the left hemisphere versus right hemisphere and found that there is more gray matter relative to white matter in the left hemisphere than in the right hemisphere. This observation suggests that the left hemisphere primarily transfers information within or between contiguous regions and the right hemisphere transfers information across regions. Because with aging there is a greater loss of white than gray matter, the right hemisphere should be more affected by aging than the left hemisphere and the decrease of creativity with aging might be related to a decrease in right-hemisphere function. Gur and coworkers (1991), however, also measured gray-matter atrophy as a function of age and found that there was more gray-matter atrophy of the left hemisphere than right hemisphere, especially in men: a finding that would be in conflict with the right-hemisphere hypothesis for reduced creativity with aging.

Depth of Processing

Objects can have functional and associative relationships or they might have conceptual relationships. Finding the unity in what appears to be diversity is critical for creativity, and when Denney (1974) asked individuals to group objects, elderly people were more likely than younger individuals to group by associative relationships than by semantic categories. For example, whereas a bow and an arrow have an associative relationship, a bow and rifle have a semantic-conceptual relationship (weapons). The means by which the brain develops associative relationships versus conceptual relationships is unknown; however, grouping by associative relationships can be done based on the physical properties. Hence, if a person is asked to group the word *bow* with either *arrow* or *rifle,* one could imagine a bow together with an arrow easier than one could imagine a bow together with a rifle unless one activated the "deeper" concept of weapons. Thus, grouping at the conceptual level is more abstract than grouping at an associative level. The term *abstract* comes from the Latin term *abstractus,* which means to draw away. Abstract nouns, unlike concrete nouns, cannot be defined by their physical characteristics. In chapter 3 I described how the different senses project to different parts of the brain, with visual stimuli going to the occipital lobes, auditory stimuli going to the temporal lobes, and the tactile stimuli going to the anterior portion of the parietal lobes (see Figure 3.6). As I mentioned, each of these primary sensory areas send information to their own modality-specific sensory association cortices. Within a modality these sensory association areas synthesize the sensory input and develop percepts. These modality-specific cortical sensory association areas also contain modal-specific representations (memory) of previously perceived stimuli. Thus, these areas are very important in stimulus recognition. These visual, auditory, and tactile association areas all send projections that meet in neuronal assemblies in the posterior inferior parietal lobe and in the posterior portion of the temporal lobes (see Figure 3.6). These posterior parietal and temporal areas are called multimodal or polymodal association areas. The meeting of all these modality-specific association areas in the posterior parietal and temporal lobe allows humans to perform cross-modal associations and develop supramodal representations. Cross-modal associations allow us to develop symbols (e.g., written or heard words, which are symbols of actions or objects; numbers and mathematical signs, which are symbols of quantity and the relationships between quantities; or musical notes, which are the symbols for the frequency and duration of sounds). These supramodal representations allow us to understand, develop, and store abstract concepts.

The finding that older individuals are more likely to group items by using associative rather than semantic strategies (Denney & Denney, 1982) is compatible with the idea that aging is associated with a loss of the long association fibers, and it is these connections that might be important in the functions of supramodal association areas, which involve understanding how that which appears to be diverse might be related.

Hormones and Aging: Hope Springs Eternal

Serum levels of total and bioavailable testosterone gradually decrease with age in men and are associated with changes in cognition. Cherrier and coinvestigators (2001) examined the relationship between exogenous testosterone administration and cognitive abilities in a population of healthy older men. The investigators raised the circulating total testosterone in the treatment group an average of 130% from baseline at week 3 and 116% at week 6. Because of aromatization of testosterone, estradiol increased an average of 77% at week 3 and 73% at week 6 in the treatment group. Significant improvements in cognition were observed for spatial memory (recall of a walking route), spatial ability (block construction), and verbal memory (recall of a short story) in older men treated with testosterone compared with their baseline evaluation and the performance of the placebo group. Although no one has investigated if hormonal treatment with testosterone can restore the age-related decrease of creativity, it can increase the sex drive, which is not a bad side effect.

11

Nurture

The Archimedes Misconception

One of the most famous stories about the "aha" experience is that of Archimedes, who, while taking a bath, discovered the laws of buoyancy, jumped out of the bathtub, and yelled, "Eureka!" On the basis of this well-known story, many people believe that creative innovation is something that automatically happens, like some form of divine inspiration. Other people believe that creative innovation is a talent that is limited to only a few special people who have special brains and are called geniuses. The postdoctoral fellowship that I have directed for years is primarily directed to train physicians, psychologists, and speech pathologists who have completed their clinical training how to perform research. When I first interview candidates for these fellowship positions, they express the desire to perform research but are often concerned because they have never experienced an "aha" experience and they fear that they might be wasting my time and their time by taking a fellowship that strongly focuses on research. They think perhaps instead they should just go into practice. Typically, I try to reassure them and tell them that the reason they have not been innovative is that in medical school and during their internship and residency they first had to learn a huge amount of information and then had to

163

learn to use convergent thinking to make diagnoses. I explain to them that one of the purposes of their fellowship training is to learn divergent thinking. I explain that if one studies and acquires detailed knowledge in a clinical domain and then sees patients and carefully examines them, it is not unusual for them to see that anomalies are common. After seeing an anomaly, they then have to learn how to generate possible hypotheses to account for this anomaly and learn the techniques for testing these hypotheses. Although some of my former fellows have been more creative than others, all our former fellows have been creative to some extent.

Nietzsche, the late-19th century philosopher, wrote much about creativity, and I enjoyed reading his comments because several of his ideas are very similar to those expressed in this book. For example, he also felt that creativity could be trained. He was especially interested in the writing of fiction. He wrote,

> The recipe for becoming a good novelist . . . is easy to give, but to carry it out presupposes qualities one is accustomed to over-look when one says, "I do not have enough talent." One has only to make a hundred or so sketches for novels, none longer than two pages, but of such distinctness that every word in them is necessary; one should write down anecdotes everyday until one has learnt how to give them the most pregnant and effective form; one should be tireless in collecting and describing human types and characters; one should above all relate things to others and listen to others relate, keeping one's eyes and ears open for the effect produced on those present; one should travel like a landscape painter . . . one should finally reflect on the motives of human actions, disdain no signpost for instruction about them and get a collector of these things by day and night. One should continue in this many sided exercise for some ten years; what is then created in the workshop . . . will be fit to go out into the word. (quoted in de Botton, 2001)

Thomas Kuhn (1996) suggested that in science there are two types of creative acts: the major discoveries like those of Einstein, Mendel, Fleming, Darwin, and Newton, which Kuhn called "paradigmatic shifts," and the other less-important discoveries, which he called "regular science." The people who make paradigmatic shifts are often called geniuses, and those who perform regular science are not. Whereas many people like Kuhn are attracted to dichotomies, the quality of creative acts and the people who are responsible for this creative activity are on a continuum. Although not everyone can perform the type of creative acts that will change civilization (paradigmatic shifts), everyone is capable of performing creative acts. Even people who are employed as secretaries and spend all day typing the messages that others have dictated might spend their weekend selecting furniture or flooring and wallpaper for their home, perhaps not realizing that decorating is a creative act.

The Influences of Society

Many people have observed that during certain ages and in certain places, creativity appears to cluster. The first time I became aware of this is when Bob Joynt, a distinguished behavioral neurologist and former dean of the University of Rochester College of Medicine, was giving his presidential address to the American Academy of Neurology. At one time the National Institutes of Health (NIH) gave training grants that allowed neurology programs to train clinician investigators, but for some reason they decided to cancel this program, Dr. Joynt and others thought that the loss of these funds might be devastating to academic neurology. Having an excellent sense of humor, Dr. Joynt projected a famous picture of Jean Charcot, one the founders of modern neurology and psychiatry. This picture was taken before the NIH was even founded. This picture shows Charcot examining a patient while many of his students—who subsequently became the founders of modern psychiatry, such as Sigmund Freud, and neurology, such as Babinski and Dejerine—watched him. Joynt inserted a letter into this picture. This letter, sent by the NIH, asked Charcot to discharge Drs. Freud, Babinski, Dejerine, and so on, because the funding of his training program was going to be terminated. I was struck by the fact that almost all of these founders of modern neurology and psychiatry had spent time together with Charcot in Paris. Creative people need role models and mentors to teach them the required skills. Even in the United States there were primarily three major mentors who are responsible for modern-day neurology: Derrick Denny-Brown, Raymond Adams, and Houston Merritt. Although these three people developed neurology programs at different medical centers (i.e., Denny-Brown at the Harvard Neurological Unit of Boston City Hospital, Adams at the Massachusetts General Hospital, and Merritt at Columbia Presbyterian Hospital), at one time all three of these founders were together at the Harvard Neurological Unit of Boston City Hospital.

During the time that Charcot taught in Paris, this city was not only a center of creativity in the medical sciences, but also a center of creativity in many other domains, including painting and writing. Several centuries before Paris became a cultural center, Florence was a center of culture. There are many other examples of these phenomena, even going back to ancient times (e.g., 500 BCE) when cities such as Athens were centers of art, architecture, and philosophy. The factors that lead to the development of these creative centers are unknown, but there are several possible explanations. First, it might only be a chance phenomenon, but as I mentioned, when observing an anomaly, if one just attributes this anomaly to chance or to some supernatural power, then observing that anomaly does not lead to creative innovation. A second theory that might help explain the flurry of creativity at these centers is the role of great mentors such as Aristotle, Socrates, and Plato, but the observation that the creativity in these centers was not restricted to a specific domain seems to diminish the importance of this mentor theory.

Earlier I reviewed the evidence that to be highly creative a person probably needs to have sufficient intelligence and that the degree of intelligence needed to be highly creative probably varies according the domain of creativity. Though humans have a high degree of within-organism intelligence, other organisms with very limited brain capacity and low intelligence have excellent environmental adaptability as colonies, and some would call the ability to survive and adapt to the environment a form of intelligence. An excellent example of collective intelligence using these criteria might be an ant colony. In many of the historic centers of creative activity, such as ancient Athens or 19th-century Paris, there was a high degree of communication between people who were being creative in the same domain (perhaps analogous to intrahemispheric communication), but in these centers there was also communication with people who were performing creative acts in other domains (perhaps analogous to interhemispheric communication).

People from other cultures who could share their diverse experiences frequently enriched the environment of these creative centers. For example, in my domain, one of the most important 19th-century Parisian discoveries was reported by Paul Broca, who demonstrated that the left hemisphere of most human brains was dominant for mediating language and that the anterior portion of the left hemisphere was important for the expression of speech. Broca was a surgeon who had a great interest in anthropology, and it was at an anthropological meeting where he heard an outsider Auburtin discuss some of the theories of Gall, who suggested that human knowledge is stored in a modular fashion and that different forms of knowledge are stored in different anatomic areas of the brain.

Another important advance was the invention of printing presses and the development of journals that allowed people who were not living in close proximity to communicate. This form of communication also enhanced creativity. One of the most exciting inventions of our era is the Internet, because—just as the white matter pathways in the brain, such as the corpus callosum, allow modular systems within the brain to communicate—systems such as the Internet allow people from all over the world the ability to communicate rapidly. It is the sharing of knowledge that often leads to paradigmatic shifts.

In the previous chapters of this book I mentioned several factors that appear to be important in creativity, and perhaps for these creative centers to develop they needed to supply the people who lived in these cities the ability to develop their creativity. The first stage in the development of creativity is preparation. The critical part of preparation is education, and in all these historic creative centers, education was excellent.

People who have different experiences, thoughts, and means of expression will not share their differences if the society is intolerant. Germany had a rich history of great composers, writers, scientists, and physicians before the Nazi era. During the time the Nazis were controlling Germany and Austria, in the United States and United Kingdom there were great advances in the science of medicine, such as antibiotics, rapid postsurgical ambulation, and intravenous fluids. While the United States was developing atomic physics, Germany, was experiencing supreme intolerance and, other than the discovery of how many Jews could be killed with one bullet, a paucity of scientific, medical, or artistic advances. Although Heisenberg, the cofounder of quantum mechanics with Nils Bohr, lived in Germany during the Nazi era, he performed most of his important work before this time.

I also suggested that during the act of creative innovation it is helpful if a person is in a low state of arousal. The same principle might be also true for these centers of creativity. During starvation, war, persecution, and plagues, societies and the people who live in these societies are in a state of high arousal and often in a state where they are preparing for flight or fight. Throughout history the centers of creativity were relatively prosperous, without starvation, plagues, or war. Finally, although I previously mentioned that creativity is primarily motivated by endo-incentive drives, exo-incentive rewards might further encourage creative people. Thus, in these creative centers, people who were being creative were recognized, encouraged, and rewarded.

Domains of Creativity

When we think about creative endeavors, we usually think that these creative acts can occur only in a limited number if domains, such as science and art, but people can make creative advances, both small and large, in almost any domain. For example, in Gainesville, I belong to a tennis club that has clay courts. Each morning before the members of the club start playing on the courts, a young man who is developmentally handicapped sweeps each of the courts with a large brush. Sweeping the courts smoothes out the clay so there are no ruts or piles of clay that can alter the trajectory of the ball when it bounces on the clay. In one section of our club, there are three clay courts side by side, without any fences between the courts. This young man would brush one side of each of these three courts, then go to the other side of the court and brush it before going to the next court. One day while we were waiting for him to complete his job before we could start playing, I noticed that he changed his brushing path so that now, rather than brushing each half court before brushing the other half, he brushed all three half courts on the same side before going to the other side and brushing all three half courts on the other side. This change in his procedure saved him time because he did not have to turn as much and since turning slows down the process. When he finished brushing the courts and cleaning the lines, he came over to where I was standing and said in an excited voice, "Doc, did you see how I did that?" I nodded, and he said, "Wow! I am sure glad I discovered this." I recall thinking to myself, even mentally handicapped people performing what appears to be a routine and menial job can experience the joy of discovery and creativity.

Cultural and Religious Influences

One of the strongest and most persistent desires of many people is immortality. About 25 to 30 years ago several laboratories were teaching chimpanzees to communicate with gestural or iconic languages. David Premack, who was teaching chimps an iconic language with great success, came to the University of Florida as a visiting professor. After his lecture and dinner, we attended a party together. We got into a conversation and I asked, "What would happen to your chimps if you or someone in your laboratory provided them knowledge that previously was only available to humans because we are the only verbal animal and this verbal ability allows us to share universal knowledge?" I then said, "I think almost all mammals know that they can die, but only humans, because we can share knowledge, know that we will die. The reason we know about our own mortality is because we have the ability to verbally communicate." I also asked him, "Do you think you could teach your chimps that they are mortal?" He told me that even if it were possible to teach chimps this concept, he would not do so. I asked him why, and he said, with a joking expression, "Perhaps if the chimps in his colony knew for certain they would die they might build a large statue of the Almighty Chimp and after they built the Almighty Chimp, they might spend all their waking hours praying to their deity for their individual immortality and this continuous praying would prohibit them from participating in experiments."

In his book, *Chase, Chance and Creativity,* James Austin quoted Rollo May (1975), who stated, "Creativity is not merely the innocent spontaneity of our youth and childhood; it must also be married to the passion of the adult human being, which is a passion to live beyond ones death." Austin went on to say, "For me, rather, death has become a fact of life, useful because it lends a motivating sense of urgency to my creative efforts. My time is running out."

Although there are many people who are confident that there is an afterlife, many will tell you that they just do not know. Thus, many people want something that they have done on earth to live beyond their time on earth, and performing creative acts is one of the major means a person has of having his or her influence last after he or she is physically gone.

Eysenck in his book *Genius* (1995) noted that only 3% of the U.S. population is Jewish, but that 27% of U.S. Nobel Laureates are Jewish. Thus, according to Eysenck, a person has a much higher chance of winning a Nobel Prize if he or she comes from a Jewish home than from a Christian or Muslim home. To explain this large discrepancy, Eysenck provided two postulates: differences in culture and differences in intelligence. He concluded the discussion of this anomaly by stating that there are studies that show Jewish children have higher IQs than non-Jewish children, and it is this higher intelligence that leads to more Jews being extremely creative. Correlation does not necessarily imply causation. For example, the observation that the pants worn by tall men are longer than those worn by short men does not prove that wearing long pants caused them to be tall. The observation that American Jews appear to be intelligent and creative might be related not to genetic-hereditary factors but rather to cultural factors that induce biological alterations in the brain. In the next few paragraphs I discuss several possible reasons why Jews might have a higher rate of success in creative endeavors. These factors, however, are not limited to Jews.

In regard to intelligence, we know now that the intelligence of a person is not entirely genetically controlled. When I was in medical school, although we knew that the brain changed with maturation and learning, we did not believe that environmental factors could change the structure of the brain. As an indication of this belief, we often used the expression, "The brain is not a muscle." Although literally this expression is still correct, there is now strong evidence that the environment (nurture) can influence the structure of the brain. One of the first dramatic examples of the influence of environment was demonstrated by Rosenzweig and Bennett (1996), who, as I mentioned earlier, found in their classic studies that the animals raised in enriched environments were more intelligent (enhanced problem solving) than those genetically identical animals who were not raised in enriched environments. On their postmortem examination of these animals, Rosenzweig and Bennett found that the experimental animals who were raised in an enriched environment had an increase in the thickness of their cerebral cortex, which reflects an increase in the number of synaptic contacts. On microscopic examination, they found that the number of dendritic spines (the branches off a neuron that connect with other neurons) was also greater in the experimental animals, thereby providing support for the connectivity postulate of intelligence. This increase in neuronal connectivity could increase the potential for the development of the neuronal networks that are important for learning and the storage of knowledge.

In the Jewish religion and culture the ability to read is critical. Even in ancient Israel, before the diaspora, almost all Jewish children were educated, and literacy for boys and men was almost universal because in the synagogue (gathering place) Jews were expected to read the Torah (first five books of the Bible). During the diaspora this tradition continued. Thus, reading and learning have always been an important part of Jewish culture and religion.

Even in the absence of a brain disease, one of the major causes of mental retardation is sensory depravation, and stimulating and educating children causes their brains to grow and their neuronal networks to flourish. Hence, cultures that encourage or require learning, reading, and intellectual stimulation from all its capable children will have many people who are highly intelligent and likely to have creative careers.

The desire to make changes that will influence the course of future generations is also related to the concept of messianism. Jews do not believe that Jesus is the Messiah in the same manner that most Christians believe. Some Jews still await a Messiah who has godly properties, but many others believe that mortals can alter humanity and help us approach a messianic era. Thus, creative acts in science and medicine are still needed, and many Jews who believe in working toward a messianic era are strongly motivated to help create the means to reduce death and suffering. Many Jews, however, envision not only a messianic era where there is the absence of pain, suffering, and death but also an era where people will have a meaningful life that is filled with beauty and joy. Artistic endeavors such as writing plays and books, composing music, and painting can enhance the quality of life. Thus, in many Jewish homes children take all kinds of special lessons and are encouraged to enter creative professions that will help humanity approach the messianic age.

There are other factors that might influence the creativity of Jews. The following is a Jewish joke that I think fairly portrays the culture: A gentile notices that when he asks his Jewish friends questions, they often reply with questions. One of this gentile's friends is a rabbi. He asks the rabbi, "Rabbi, could you tell me why Jews seem to always answer questions with questions?" The rabbi replies, "Why not?" In many Jewish families Jewish children are encouraged to ask questions. For example, one of the most important holidays is Passover, the celebration of freedom. Unlike many other religious holidays that take place in houses of worship and are led by clergy, Passover takes place at home with the family around the dinner table. One of the most important parts of the service is when the youngest child asks, "Why is this day different from all other days?" People who are brought up to ask questions also want to find answers.

Finally, there is one additional reason why there might be a high percentage of Jews who lead creative lives. Earlier I reviewed the evidence that creativity is often associated with affective disorders such as depression and bipolar disorder. Levav, Kohn, Golding, and Weissman (1997) demonstrated that affective disorders are significantly more common in Jews than Catholics or Protestants.

Training Creative People

In this book I mentioned the proposal that there are at least three stages of creative production: (a) preparation, (b) innovation, and (c) verification or production. In this section I discuss some of the strategies that might be helpful in training people for each of these stages.

Preparation

The ability to have a creative career does not appear to be entirely genetic. Talents and even intelligence might be in part genetic, but the parents of most extremely creative people usually did not have careers marked by extreme creativity, and most of the children of extremely creative people also did not have careers marked by extreme creativity. Thus, the development of the creative brain is probably dependent on both nature and nurture.

For many years it was thought that the connectivity of the brain was primarily controlled genetically, and although these connection patterns could be strengthened or weakened by learning, the overall network patterns could not be changed. It was perhaps William James (1890), the late-19th-century physician, psychologist, and philosopher, who first suggested that learning might alter the connectivity of the brain, but this postulate was not addressed until the mid-20th century, when Donald Hebb (1949) suggested that knowledge is stored in neuronal networks by the alterations in the strength of the connections between the neurons in these networks and that the strength of connections between neurons is determined by their firing patterns, such that when two neurons fire at the same time they increase the strength of connections between them. (Neurons that fire together wire together.)

Although William James and Donald Hebb proposed that the brain could be altered by experience, it was not until recently that investigators, using physiological techniques such as recording from neurons in animals and using functional imaging, demonstrated that the organization of the human brain could be altered by sensory experience. For example, in one of the first studies to show this brain plasticity, Merzenich et al. (1984) studied monkeys and mapped the areas of the somatosensory cortex that activated with stimulation of each finger. These investigators then amputated monkeys' fingers and showed that the area of the brain that was previously activated before this finger was amputated is now activated when the finger next to the amputated finger is stimulated. Other studies have shown that with continued stimulation and practice, the cortical region that processes stimuli can grow in size (Recanzone, Schreiner, & Merzenich, 1993).

These studies in monkeys show that training can alter the brain, but to my knowledge there have been no systematic studies of how to best nurture creative minds. Although the type of stimulation that might best help develop creativity in a specific domain is unknown, as I mentioned, we do know the brain needs to be stimulated to fully develop its connectivity. Thus, all people—whether young, middle-aged, or old—need to be stimulated. To be creative people need to be taught the skills that are required in their chosen domain of creativity, but creative people often see problems in a new light because they are able to use alternative stores of knowledge and strategies to solve problems. Thus, a good education is critical for the development of creative potential, and although this education might in part be focused in the domain in which one wants to excel, it must also be broad. Ochse (1990) found that most people who exhibited exceptional creativity came from professional backgrounds. The professional class, in general, values intellectual and artistic pursuits, encourages talented people, and strongly believes in the value of cultural stimulation (reading, conversations, cultural events, and travel) as well as education.

There is evidence that the brains of children are more able to change (plasticity) than are the brains of adults. For example, there have been several reports of children who had left-hemisphere dominance for language, but because they developed serious neurological diseases they had to have their left hemisphere surgically removed (Hoffman, Hendrick, Dennis, & Armstrong, 1979; Smith & Sugar, 1975). After the removal of their left language-dominant hemisphere, these children became aphasic, but they recovered their language, using only their remaining right hemisphere. As people grow older, when they damage their left hemisphere and have impaired language or aphasia, the probability that the undamaged right hemisphere can take over the language functions of the injured left hemisphere decreases.

Puberty seems to be a time when there is a tremendous reduction of the brain's plasticity. Children who move to a country where they must learn a new language appear to learn to speak this new language without any accent, but those who come after puberty often have problems learning this new language and often maintain some accent. In studies of songbirds, investigators have revealed a similar phenomenon. To learn a song, some songbirds must hear their father sing before they can learn their song. If they go through puberty without hearing their father sing, and then hear their father's song afterward, they will not learn the song.

On the basis of these types of studies, investigators believe that the earlier one teaches children skills in a domain, the greater the chance that they will have exceptional talents in this domain. Although the initiation of training at an early age and the focus of a child's learning in one domain can lead to the development of a prodigy, it is overall rare that children who are prodigies have creative careers. It is not known why childhood prodigies are usually not creative, but many prodigies have a limited breath of knowledge that accounts for this failure to be creative. Earlier I mentioned that creative innovation involves the recruitment and association of networks that have different architecture, different forms of stored knowledge, and different means of thinking and problem solving. If a person limits knowledge to a specific domain, that person cannot form associations between separate concepts and ideas.

Many elementary and middle schools focus on reading, writing, and arithmetic. Although it is important to learn these skills, these skills are linear, categorical, and require focused attention. Creative endeavors often require global attentional systems, parallel processing, and continuous reasoning. Reading, writing, and arithmetic are, for most people, mediated by the left hemisphere, but skills such as visual-spatial and emotional processing, global attention, and continuous reasoning, so important in creativity, are mediated by the right hemisphere. For the right hemisphere to fully develop its cognitive capacity, it needs to be stimulated, and it is not clear that the educational methods of most traditional schools stimulate the parts of the brain that mediate these functions.

During times when the school budget must be constrained, school administrators often terminate the teaching of art and music. Because art and music, at least in part, appear to be mediated by the right hemisphere, art and music teachers have reminded the public that they are the ones responsible for educating the right brain. The value of teaching these disciplines in school, however, might be minimal because the children are only infrequently exposed to these types of classes, and both music and art are also, in part, mediated by the left hemisphere. In the past 50 years we have learned much about the functions of the right hemisphere, and there is little doubt that, in association with the left hemisphere, the right hemisphere is critical for many creative endeavors, but we still do not know how to systematically stimulate and educate this hemisphere.

Most of the postdoctoral associates accepted into our program are already prepared because they have graduated from medical school and completed their residency training or have earned their doctorate degree (e.g., psychology, speech therapy, anthropology), but if they need further preparation we can offer this through either didactic courses or tutorials. We can also teach them the methods used for verification (e.g., designing an experiment and analyzing the data) and production (e.g., writing reports and presenting papers). I think we can also develop an environment that leads to creative innovation, but what we cannot do is develop the personality characteristics that are critical for a successful career as a creative scientist. They must have these characteristics when they come to our laboratory, and most of these characteristics are either genetic or taught to young children by their parents.

Personality

Walter Cannon (1965), one of the most brilliant and creative brain scientists, noted that certain personality characteristics are very important for creative careers and that even before a person develops the skills needed for preparation, innovation, and verification-production, a person who desires a creative career should have the following characteristics: (a) The person should be resourceful. In the chapter on the frontal lobes (chapter 9), I described the idea that people with frontal injuries, once they find what they think is a solution to a problem, are unable to shift strategies. To be resourceful a person must have learned or be able to develop multiple strategies and know to use another strategy when one is unsuccessful. (b) The person should be a risk taker. Perhaps the best example of people who cannot take risks are those who suffer with an obsessive-compulsive disorder. They are not willing to take the risk that the door is unlocked and hence will check it on multiple occasions. They are not willing to take the risk that there might be germs on their hands so they will wash their hands multiple times. Many people think that this form of perseverative behavior might also be related to dysfunction of frontal lobe–basal ganglia networks and hence the ability to take risks might depend on the function of these networks. (c) The person should have curiosity. Curiosity and the desire to explore and seek novelty might be a function of a frontal-ventral striatal system. (d) The person should have honesty. Rousseau (1762) stated, "There has never been a wise man who failed to prefer the lie invented by himself, to the truth discovered by someone else." If people do not recognize their own errors and other people's discoveries, their creative career will come an end. (e) The person should be able to delay gratification. Almost every creative work requires an interval between the time that it is initiated and the time when it is successfully completed. As I mentioned in the chapter on the frontal lobes, the ability to perform goal-oriented behaviors, which are often associated with a delay of gratification, is primarily a function of the frontal lobes. (f) The person should have humility. By the term *humility* I suspect that Cannon meant *unpretentiousness*. Although Cannon thought that humility was important, there are many very famous and creative people who are not humble but are pretentious. The goal of every scientific theory, however, is to eventually be proved wrong, and this is the means by which science advances. People who are pretentious and prideful do not want or like to be proved wrong, but sometimes being wrong can allow a person to continue learning. It is the practice of humility that allows a person to learn from errors, which is so critical in creative endeavors.

Leisure

Creative innovation can be enhanced by several factors. The first factor is the environment. As I described earlier, creative innovation often occurs while the creative person is in a low arousal state. When I completed my residency and fellowship at the Harvard Neurological Unit of Boston City Hospital, I was recruited to Dartmouth Medical School and the Hitchcock Clinic in Hanover, NH, which is beautiful, and I liked the people that I met there. When they offered me the position, I asked the director of the Clinic to discuss my clinical duties. He told me that I would have clinic with patients 5 days a week from 8:00 A.M. to 5:00 P.M. and that I could make rounds on my inpatients and see consults before and after clinic. I asked him if I would have any time allocated for research and he said during the weekdays I could use the time before and after rounds. In addition, because there was no clinic on the weekends, I had time to perform research when I was not making rounds. I thanked him for offering me this position, but I explained that I did want to continue to pursue the research that I had started in Boston and I really needed more time for research. He told me that the people at Dartmouth really wanted me to join their faculty and he would see if he could find me more time for research.

The following week he called me again and told me that he had good news. He spoke with the board at the Hitchcock Clinic and the faculty in the medical school, and they suggested that on Thursdays I could complete my clinic at 3:00 P.M. I told him again that I very much appreciated his offer but that I had decided to take a job at another university. He said, "Well, since you are not coming to Dartmouth you must be staying at Harvard. Good luck to you." He then hung up the phone. Although Norman Geschwind had invited me to stay at the Harvard Neurological Unit, I decided to take the position offered to me by Mel Greer at the University of Florida. There were many reasons why the University of Florida appealed to me, but one of the most important ones was that Mel Greer, who was Chief of Neurology at the University of Florida College of Medicine, always made certain that I had sufficient time to pursue research. At that time, I did not know about the relationship between arousal and innovation, but I knew that successful investigators were usually not time pressured.

As I mentioned, since coming to Florida I have developed a postdoctoral fellowship where I attempt to train physicians, psychologists, and speech pathologists to perform neuropsychological research, and I have always attempted to make certain that these peoples' clinical activities occupy less that 25% of their time. Many of our former fellows have had and are having wonderful research careers. Most of their success is related to their hard work and the skills and talents that they brought with them to this fellowship, but prior to starting the fellowship, few of them had innovative ideas, which was probably related to being time pressured during their training. I am not sure that providing our fellows with large amounts of free time where they could study, discuss, and develop innovative ideas was instrumental in their success, but I do not think it hurt.

Anxiety

There is some evidence that people who are creative might be more anxious than people who are not creative (Ludwig, 1994). Schwartz, Wright, Shin, Kagan, and Rauch (2003) found that infants and children with inhibited temperament tend to develop into adults with inhibited temperament and that these people often avoid meeting new people and entering new and unfamiliar situations. In contrast, uninhibited children grow up into adults who spontaneously approach new people and situations. When normal individuals develop the emotion of fear, they demonstrate activation of the amygdala. Schwartz et al. (2003) showed familiar and novel faces to adults who as children appeared to be inhibited (in their second year of life) and compared their functional magnetic resonance imaging activation patterns with those adults who were previously categorized as uninhibited when they were children. They found that the inhibited group showed a greater functional magnetic resonance imaging signal response within the amygdala to novel versus familiar faces.

Many creative authors, artists, composers, and scientists spend many hours each day alone, and it is during these times that they often develop their creative masterpieces. Anxiety is associated with high levels of norepinephrine, and, as I mentioned, high level of norepinephrine might inhibit creative innovation. Perhaps it is this inhibited temperament, induced by a relative hyperactive amygdala, that partly accounts for the tolerance or even joy of solitude. It is during these hours of solitude when there is little anxiety and low levels of norepinephrine that creative innovation becomes possible.

As I mentioned, creative people have a tendency to be anxious, and sometimes anxious children do not explore and have less of a desire for novelty. Learning to enjoy and desire novelty is critical if a person is to have a creative career. L. C. Miller, Bard, Juno, and Nadler (1986) showed that when animals (chimps) or children are placed in a novel situation that causes distress, extreme distress is reported when they are tested alone but is rarely observed when an attachment figure is present. When training an investigator, it is important that this trainee get a feeling of the joy of discovery. Often when people start their research careers, they are anxious about succeeding and feel anxious about attempting to tackle a difficult problem. I think Descartes provided excellent advice when he suggested, "Divide a problem into as many parts as necessary to attack it in the best way and start the analysis by examining the most easy to understand parts before ascending gradually to the most complex." To help students experience the joy, the mentor should not only follow Descartes's advice but also, like the parent of the anxious child, often accompany the trainee and help guide him or her through the discovery process. Initially, during our fellowships we have our new fellows join the more experienced fellows or faculty in a research project where the hypotheses have already been generated but not yet fully tested. This experience not only helps teach the new fellow some of the methods used in our research but also, after the results are analyzed, lets her or him experience the joy of discovery. Because there are not great demands placed on the newcomers, their anxiety is reduced. As I mentioned, Ramón y Cajal (1898/1999) wrote that one of the motives for performing research is "a desire to experience the incomparable gratification associated with the act of discovery itself." Thus, our goal is to get our fellows addicted to research, and, like any "pusher," we cannot get them addicted unless we let them experience the thrill of this expensive habit.

References

Aboitiz, F., Scheibel, A. B., Fisher, R. S., & Zaidel, E. (1992). Individual differences in brain asymmetries and fiber composition in the human corpus callosum. *Brain Research, 598*(1–2), 154–161.

Alajouanine, T. (1948). Aphasia and artistic realization. *Brain, 71,* 229–241.

Albert, R. S., & Runco, M. A. (1999). A history of research on creativity. In J. Sternberg (Ed.), *Handbook of creativity.* New York: Cambridge University Press.

Amabile, T. M. (1983). *Social psychology of creativity.* New York: Springer-Verlag.

American Psychiatric Association. (1980). *Diagnostic and statistical manual of mental disorders* (3rd ed.). Washington, DC: Author.

American Psychiatric Association. (1994). *Diagnostic and statistical manual of mental disorders* (4th ed.). Washington, DC: Author.

Andreasen, N. C. (1987). Creativity and mental illness: Prevalence rates in writers and their first-degree relatives. *American Journal of Psychiatry, 144*(10), 1288–1292.

Andreasen, N. C., & Glick, I. D. (1988). Bipolar affective disorder and creativity: Implications and clinical management. *Comprehensive Psychiatry, 29,* 207–217.

Arnsten, A. F. T., & Goldman-Rakic, P. S. (1984). Selective prefrontal cortical projections to the region of the locus coerulus and raphe nuclei in the rhesus monkey. *Brain Research, 301,* 9–18.

Aston-Jones, G., Chiang, C., & Alexinsky, T. (1991). Discharge of locus coeruleus neurons in behaving rats and monkeys suggests a role in vigilance. *Progress in Brain Research, 88,* 501–520.

Austen, J. H. (2003). *Chase, chance, and creativity.* Cambridge, MA: MIT Press.

Balint, R. (1909). Seelenlahmung des "Schauens" optische Ataxie, raumliche Storung der Aufmerksamkeit. *Monatsschr Psychiatr Neurol, 25,* 57–71.

Banich, M. T., Heller, W., & Levy, J. (1989). Aesthetic preference and picture asymmetries. *Cortex, 25*(2), 187–195.

Bardo, M. T., Donohew, R. L., & Harrington, N. G. (1996). Psycho-biology of novelty seeking and drug seeking behavior. *Behavioural Brain Research, 77*(1–2), 23–43.

Barrett, A. M., Beversdorf, D. Q., Crucian, G. P., & Heilman, K. M. (1998). Neglect after right hemisphere stroke: A smaller floodlight for distributed attention. *Neurology, 51,* 972–978.

Barron, F., & Harrington, D. M. (1981). Creativity, intelligence and personality. *Annual Review of Psychology, 32,* 439–476.

Bauer, R. M. (1984). Autonomic recognition of names and faces in prosopagnosia: A neuropsychological application of the Guilty Knowledge Test. *Neuropsychologia, 22*(4), 457–469.

Bazil, C. W. (1999). Seizures in the life and works of Edgar Allan Poe. *Archives of Neurology, 56*(6), 740–743.

Beals, G. (1996). In Thomas Edison's Home Page: www.thomas-edison.com

Beauvois, M. F., & Saillant, B. (1985). Optic aphasia for colors and color agnosia: A distinction between visual and visual-verbal impairments in the processing of color. *Cognitive Neuropsychology, 2,* 1–48.

Bechara, A., Tranel, D., & Damasio, H. (2000). Characterization of the decision-making deficit of patients with ventromedial prefrontal cortex lesions. *Brain, 123*(11), 2189–2202.

Bechara, A., Tranel, D., Damasio, H., & Damasio, A. R. (1996). Failure to respond automatically to anticipated future outcomes following damage to the prefrontal cortex. *Cerebral Cortex, 6*(2), 215–225.

Benton, A. (1990). Facial recognition. *Cortex, 26*(4), 491–499.

Benton, A., & Tranel, D. (1993). Visuoperceptual, visuospatial, and visuoconstructive disorders. In K. M. Heilman & E. Valenstein (Eds.), *Clinical neuropsychology.* New York: Oxford University Press.

Berg, E. A. (1948). A simple objective test for measuring flexibility in thinking. *Journal of General Psychology, 39,* 15–22.

Berridge, K. C. (2003). Pleasures of the brain. *Brain and Cognition, 52*(1), 106–128.

Beversdorf, D. Q., Hughes, J. D., Steinberg, B. A., Lewis, L. D., & Heilman, K. M. (1999). Noradrenergic modulation of cognitive flexibility in problem solving. *Neuroreport, 10*(13), 2763–2767.

Beversdorf, D. Q., Smith, B. W., Crucian, G., Anderson, J. M., Keillor, J., Barrett, A., Hughes, J., Felopulos, G. L., Bauman, B. L., Nadeau, S. E., & Heilman, K. M. (2000). Increase discrimination of "false memories" in autism spectrum disorder. *Proceedings of the National Academy of Sciences, 97*(15), 8734–8737.

Bihrle, A. M., Brownell, H. H., Powelson, J. A., & Gardner, H. (1986). Comprehension of humorous and nonhumorous materials by left and right brain-damaged patients. *Brain and Cognition, 5*(4), 399–411.

Bisiach, E., & Luzzati, C. (1978). Unilatreral neglect and representational space. *Cortex, 14,* 129–133.

Blonder, L. X., Bowers, D., & Heilman, K. M. (1991). The role of the right hemisphere on emotional communication. *Brain, 114,* 1115–1127.

Bogen, J. E., & Bogen, G. M. (1988). Creativity and the corpus callosum. *Psychiatric Clinics of North America, 11,* 293–301.

Borod, J. C., Rorie, K. D., Pick, L. H., Bloom, R. L., Andelman, F., Campbell, A. L., Obler, L. K., Tweedy, J. R., Welkowitz, J., & Sliwinski, M. (2000). Verbal pragmatics following unilateral stroke: Emotional content and valence. *Neuropsychology, 14*(1), 112–124.

Bowers, D., Bauer, R. M., Coslett, H. B., & Heilman, K. M. (1985). Processing of faces by patients with unilateral hemispheric lesions. I. Dissociation between judgments of facial affect and facial identity. *Brain and Cognition, 4,* 258–272.

Bowers, D., Blonder, L. X., Feinberg, T., & Heilman, K. M. (1991). Differential impact of right and left hemisphere lesions on focal emotion and object imagery. *Brain, 114,* 1593–1609.

Bronowski, J. (1972). *Science and human values.* New York: Harper and Row.

Broome, D. M. W., Cheever, D. C., Hughes, J. D., & Beversdorf, D. Q. (2000). Effects of central and peripheral beta-blockers on noradrenergic modulation of cognitive flexibility. *Journal of Cognitive Neuroscience, 12,* S105.

Brownell, H. H., Potter, H. H., Bihrle, A. M., & Gardner, H. (1986). Inference deficits in right brain damaged subjects. *Brain and Language, 27,* 310–321.

Brownell, H. H., Simpson, T. L., Bihrle, A. M., Potter, H. H., & Gardner, H. (1990). Appreciation of metaphoric alternative word meanings by left and right brain-damaged patients. *Neuropsychologia, 28,* 375–383.

Burgess, P. W., Scott, S. K., & Frith, C. D. (2003). The role of the rostral frontal cortex (area 10) in prospective memory: A lateral versus medial dissociation. *Neuropsychologia, 41*(8), 906–918.

Campbell, D. T. (1960). Blind variation and selective retention in creative thought as in other knowledge processes. *Psychological Review, 67,* 380–400.

Cannon, W. (1965). *The way of an investigator.* New York: Hafner.

Cape, E. G., & Jones, B. E. (1998). Differential modulation of high-frequency gamma-electroencephalogram activity and sleep-wake state by noradrenaline and serotonin microinjections into the region of cholinergic basalis neurons. *Journal of Neuroscience, 18*(7), 2653–2666.

Carlsson, I., Wendt, P. E., & Risberg, J. (2000). On the neurobiology of creativity: Differences in frontal activity between high and low creative subjects. *Neuropsychologia, 38,* 873–885.

Carly, P. G., Golding, S. J. J., & Hall, B. J. D. (1995). Interrelationships among auditory and visual cognitive tasks: An event-related potential (ERP) study. *Intelligence, 21*(3), 297–327.

Casey, M. B., Nuttall, R. L., & Pezaris, E. (1997). Mediators of gender differences in mathematics college entrance test scores: A comparison of spatial skills with internalized beliefs and anxieties. *Developmental Psychology, 33*(4), 669–680.

Cattell, R. B. (1963). The theory of fluid and crystallized intelligence: A critical experiment. *Journal of Educational Psychology, 54,* 1–22.

Cherrier, M. M., Asthana, S., Plymate, S., Baker, L., Matsumoto, A. M., Peskind, E., Raskind, M. A., Brodkin, K., Bremner, W., Petrova, A., LaTendresse, S., & Craft, S. (2001). Testosterone supplementation improves spatial and verbal memory in healthy older men. *Neurology, 57*(1), 80–88.

Choi, J., & Silverman, I. (2002). The relationship between testosterone and route-learning strategies in humans. *Brain and Cognition, 50*(1), 116–120.

Christman, S. (1993). Handedness in musicians: Bimanual constraints on performance. *Brain and Cognition, 22,* 266–272.

Cloninger, C. R., Svrakic, D. M., & Przybeck, T. R. (1993). A psychobiological model of temperament and character. *Archive of General Psychiatry, 50*(12), 975–990.

Collaer, M. L., & Nelson, J. D. (2002). Large visuospatial sex difference in line judgment: Possible role of attentional factors. *Brain Cognition, 49*(1), 1–12.

Contreras, D., & Llinas, R. (2001). Voltage-sensitive dye imaging of neocortical spatiotemporal dynamics to afferent activation frequency. *Journal of Neuroscience, 21*(23), 9403–9413.

Coren, S. (1995). Differences in divergent thinking as a function of handedness and sex. *American Journal of Psychology, 108,* 311–325.

Corkin, S. (1968). Acquistion of motor skill after bilateral medial temporal lobe excision. *Neuropsychologia, 6,* 225–265.

Coslett, H. B. (2002). Simultanagnosia. In T. E. Feinberg & M. Farah (Eds.), *Behavioral neurology and neuropsychology.* New York: McGraw-Hill.

Cox, C. (1926). *The early mental traits of three hundred geniuses.* Stanford, CA: Stanford University Press.

Craig, J., & Baron-Cohen, S. (1999). Creativity and imagination in autism and Asperger syndrome. *Journal of Autism and Developmental Disorders, 29,* 319–326.

Csikszentmihalyi, M. (1996). *Creativity: Flow and the psychology of discovery.* New York: HarperCollins.

Damasio, A. R. (1996). The somatic marker hypothesis and the possible functions of the prefrontal cortex. *Philosophical Transactions of the Royal Society of London. Series B. Biological Science, 351*(1346), 1413–1420.

Damasio, A., Yamada, T., Damasio, H., Corbett, J., & McKee, J. (1980). Central achromatopsia: Behavioral, anatomic, and physiologic aspects. *Neurology, 30*(10), 1064–1071.

de Botton, A. (2001). *The consolations of philosophy.* New York: Vintage Books.

de Courten-Myers, G. M. (1999). The human cerebral cortex: Gender differences in structure and function. *Journal of Neuropathology and Experimental Neurology, 58*(3), 217–226.

Dejerine, J. J. (1891). Sur un cas de cecite verbal avec agraphie suivi d'autopsi. *Mémores de la Societé de Medicine 3,* 197–201.

DeKosky, S. T., Heilman, K. M., Bowers, D., & Valenstein, E. (1980). Recognition and discrimination of emotional faces and pictures. *Brain and Language, 9,* 206–214.

Delis, D. C., Waper, W., Gardner, H., & Moses, J. A., Jr. (1983). The contribution of the right hemisphere to the organization of paragraphs. *Cortex, 19,* 43–50.

Denney, N. W. (1974). Evidence for developmental changes in categorization criteria for children and adults. *Human Development, 17*(1), 41–53.

Denney, N. W., Denney, D. R. (1982). The relationship between classification and questioning strategies among adults. *Journal of Gerontology, 37*(2), 190–196.

Denny-Brown, D., & Chambers, R. A. (1958). The parietal lobe and behavior. *Research Publications—Associations for Research in Nervous and Mental Disease, 36,* 35–117.

DeRenzi, E., & Spinnler, H. (1967). Impaired performance on color tasks in patients with hemispheric lesions. *Cortex, 3,* 194–217.

Deutsch, G., Bourbon, W. T., Papanicolaou, A. C., & Eisenberg, H. M. (1988). Visuospatial tasks compared via activation of regional cerebral blood flow. *Neuropsychologia, 26*(3), 445–452.

Devinsky, O., & Vazquez, B. (1993). Behavioral changes associated with epilepsy. *Neurologic Clinics, 11*(1), 127–149.

Diamond, M. C., Scheibel, A. B., Murphy, G. M., Jr., & Harvey, T. (1985). On the brain of a scientist: Albert Einstein. *Experimental Neurology,* 198–204.

Ditunno, P. L., & Mann, V. A. (1990). Right hemisphere specialization for mental rotation in normals and brain damaged subjects. *Cortex, 26*(2), 177–188.

Dolcos, F., Rice, H. J., & Cabeza, R. (2002). Hemispheric asymmetry and aging: Right hemisphere decline or asymmetry reduction. *Neuroscience and Biobehavioral Review, 26*(7), 819–825.

Drevets, W. C., Videen, T. O., Price, J. L., Preskorn, S. H., Carmichael, S. T., & Raichle, M. E. (1992). A functional anatomical study of unipolar depression. *Journal of Neuroscience, 12*(9), 3628–3641.

Duara, R., Grady, C., Haxby, J., Ingvar, D., Sokoloff, L., Margolin, R. A., Manning, R. G., Cutler, N. R., & Rapoport, S. I. (1984). Human brain glucose utilization and cognitive function in relation to age. *Annals of Neurology, 16*(6), 703–713.

Ducreux, D., Marsot-Dupuch, K., Lasjaunias, P., Oppenheim, C., & Fredy, D. (2003). Lyrical and musical auditive mental imagery in functional MRI. *Journal of Neuroradiology, 30*(1), 18–24.

Duffy, F. H., Albert, M. S., McAnulty, G., & Garvey, A. J. (1984). Age-related differences in brain electrical activity of healthy subjects. *Annals of Neurology, 16*(4), 430–438.

Dulawa, S. C., Grandy, D. K., Low, M. J., Paulus, M. P., & Geyer, M. A. (1999). Dopamine D4 receptor-knock-out mice exhibit reduced exploration of novel stimuli. *Journal of Neuroscience, 19*(21), 9550–9556.

Duncan, J., Seitz, R. J., Kolodny, J., Bor, D., Herzog, H., Ahmed, A., Newell, F. N., & Emslie, H. (2000). A neural basis for general intelligence. *Science, 289*(5478), 457–460.

Easterbrook, E. A. (1959). The effect of emotion on cue utilization and the organization of behavior. *Psychological Review, 66,* 183–201.

Edwards, B. (1999). *Drawing on the right side of the brain.* New York: Penguin-Putman.

Egaas, B., Courchesne, E., & Saitoh, O. (1995). Reduced size of corpus callosum in autism. *Archives of Neurology, 52*(8), 794–801.

Eisen, M. L. (1989). Assessing differences in children with learning disabilities and normally achieving students with a new measure of creativity. *Journal of Learning Disabilities, 22*(7), 462–464.

Eisenman, R., Grossman, J. C., & Goldstein, R. (1980). Undergraduate marijuana use as related to internal sensation novelty seeking and openness to experience. *Journal of Clinical Psychology, 36*(4), 1013–1019.

Elias, L. J., Saucier, D. M., & Guylee, M. J. (2001). Handedness and depression in university students: A sex by handedness interaction. *Brain and Cognition, 46*(1–2), 125–129.

Eysenck, H. L. (1995). *Genius.* New York and Cambridge: Cambridge University Press.

Fankhauser, M. P., Karumanchi, V. C., German, M. L., Yates, A., & Karumanchi, S. D. (1992). A double-blind, placebo-controlled study of the efficacy of transdermal clonidine in autism. *Clinical Psychiatry, 53*(3), 77–82.

Farah, M. J. (1989). The neural basis of mental imagery. *Trends in Neuroscience, 12*(10), 395–399.

Feinberg, T. E., Rothi, L. J. G., & Heilman, K. M. (1986). Multimodal agnosia after a unilateral left hemisphere lesion. *Neurology, 36,* 864–867.

Fellerman, D. J., & Van Essen, D. C. (1991). Distributed hierarchical processing in the primate cerebral cortex. *Cerebral Cortex, 1*(1), 1–47.

Filipek, P. A., Richelme, C., Kennedy, D. N., & Caviness, V. S., Jr. (1994). The young adult human brain: An MRI-based morphometric analysis. *Cerebral Cortex, 4*(4), 344–360.

Foote, S. L., Berridge, C. W., Adams, L. M., & Pineda, J. A. (1991). Electrophysiological evidence for the involvement of the locus coeruleus in alerting, orienting, and attending. *Progress in Brain Research, 88,* 521–532.

Foundas, A. L., Faulhaber, J. R., Kulynych, J. J., Browning, C. A., & Weinberger, D. R. (1999). Hemispheric and gender differences in Sylvian fissure morphology: A quantitative approach using volumetric MRI. *Neuropsychiatry, Neuropsychology, and Behavioral Neurology, 12,* 1–10.

Foundas, A. L., Hong, K., Leonard, C. M., & Heilman, K. M. (1998). Hand preference and MRI asymmetries of the central sulcus. *Neuropsychiatry, Neuropsychology, and Behavioral Neurology, 11,* 65–71.

Foundas, A. L., Leonard, C. M., Gilmore, R. L., Fennell, E. M., & Heilman, K. M. (1994). Planum temporale asymmetry and language dominance. *Neuropsychologia, 32*(10), 1225–1231.

Foundas, A. L., Leonard, C. M., Gilmore, R. L., Fennell, E. M., & Heilman, K. M. (1996). Pars triangularis asymmetry and language dominance. *Proceedings of the National Academy of Sciences, 93,* 719–722.

Freud, S. (1891). *Zur Auffasun der Aphasien. Eine Kritische Studie.* Vienna: Franz Deuticke.

Freud, S. (1959). The relation of the poet to daydreaming. In *Collected papers* (Vol. 4, pp. 173–183). London: Hogarth. (Original work published 1908)

Frost, J. A., Binder, J. R., Springer, J. A., Hammeke, T. A., Bellgowan, P. S., Rao, S. M., & Cox, R. W. (1999). Language processing is strongly left lateralized in both sexes: Evidence from functional MRI. *Brain, 122*(2), 199–208.

Galaburda, A., & Livingstone, M. (1993). Evidence for a magnocellular defect in developmental dyslexia. *Annals of the New York Academy of Sciences, 682,* 70–82.

Galton, F. (1978). *Hereditary genius.* New York: Julian Friedmann. (Original work published 1869)

Gardner, H. (1985). *Frames of mind.* New York: Basic Books.

Gardner, H. (1999). *Intelligence reframed: Multiple intelligences for the 21st century.* New York: Basic Books.

Geary, D. C., Saults, S. J., Liu, F., & Hoard, M. K. (2000). Sex differences in spatial cognition, computational fluency, and arithmetical reasoning. *Journal of Experimental Child Psychology, 77*(4), 337–353.

Geschwind, N. (1979). Behavioral changes in temporal lobe epilepsy. *Psychological Medicine, 9*(2), 217–219.

Geschwind, N., & Galaburda, A. M. (1985). Cerebral lateralization: Biological mechanisms, associations, and pathology. I and II. A hypothesis and a program for research. *Archives of Neurology, 42,* 428–459, 521–552.

Geschwind, N., & Levitsky, W. (1968). Human brain: Left right asymmetries in temporal speech region. *Science, 161,* 186–187.

Ghacibeh, G. A., & Heilman, K. M. (2003). Progressive affective aprosodia and prosoplegia. *Neurology, 60*(7), 1192–1194.

Gillberg, C., & Svennerholm, L. (1987). CSF monoamines in autistic syndromes and other pervasive developmental disorders of early childhood. *British Journal of Psychiatry, 151,* 89–94.

Goldstein, D., Haldane, D., & Mitchell, C. (1990). Sex differences in visual-spatial ability: The role of performance factors. *Memory and Cognition, 18,* 546–550.

Good, C. D., Johnsrude, I., Ashburner, J., Henson, R. N., Friston, K. J., & Frackowiak, R. S. (2001). Cerebral asymmetry and the effects of sex and handedness on brain structure: A voxel-based morphometric analysis of 465 normal adult human brains. *Neuroimage, 14*(3), 685–700.

Goodglass, H., & Kaplan, E. (2000). Boston Naming Test. Philadelphia, PA: Lippincott Williams & Wilkins.

Green, J., McDonald, W. M., Vitek, J. L., Evatt, M., Freeman, A., Haber, M., Bakay, R. A., Triche, S., Sirockman, B., & DeLong, M. R. (2002). Cognitive impairments in advanced PD without dementia. *Neurology, 59*(9), 1320–1324.

Grimshaw, G. M., Bryden, M. P., & Finegan, J. K. (1995). Relations between prenatal testosterone and cerebral lateralization in children. *Neuropsychology, 9*(1), 68–79.

Guilford, J. P. (1967). Creativity: Yesterday, today and tomorrow. *Journal of Creative Behavior, 1,* 3–14.

Guilford, J. P., & Christensen, P. W. (1973). The one way relationship between creative potential and IQ. *Journal of Creative Behavior, 7,* 247–252.

Guilford, J. P , Christensen, P. R., Merrifield, P. R., & Wilson, R. C. (1978). *Alternate uses: Manual of instructions and interpretation.* Orange, CA: Sheridan Psychological Services.

Gur, R. C., Alsop, D., Glahn, D., Petty, R., Swanson, C. L., Maldjian, J. A., Turetsky, B. I., Detre, J. A., Gee, J., & Gur, R. E. (2000). An fMRI study of sex differences in regional activation to a verbal and a spatial task. *Brain and Language, 74*(2), 157–170.

Gur, R. C., Mozley, P. D., Resnick, S. M., Gottlieb, G. L., Kohn, M., Zimmerman, R., Herman, G., Atlas, S., Grossman, R., & Berretta, D. (1991). Gender differences in age effect on brain atrophy measured by magnetic resonance imaging. *Proceeding of the National Academy of Sciences, 88*(7), 2845–2849.

Gur, R. C., Packer, I. K., Hungerbuhler, J. P., Reivich, M., Obrist, W. D., Amarnek, W. S., & Sackeim, H. A. (1980). Differences in the distribution of gray and white matter in human cerebral hemispheres. *Science, 207*(4436), 1226–1228.

Halpern, A. R. (2001). Cerebral substrates of musical imagery. *Annals of the New York Academy of Sciences, 930,* 179–192.

Halpern, D. F., Haviland, M. G., & Killian, C. D. (1998). Handedness and sex differences in intelligence: Evidence from the Medical College Admission Test. *Brain and Cognition, 38*(1), 87–101.

Hamsher, K., Capruso, D. X., & Benton, A. (1992). Visuospatial judgment and right hemisphere disease. *Cortex, 28*(3), 493–495.

Hamsher, K., Levin, H. S., & Benton, A. L. (1979). Facial recognition in patients with focal brain lesions. *Archives of Neurology, 36*(13), 837–839.

Happe, F., & Frith, U. (1996). "Theory of mind" in the brain: Evidence from a PET scan study of Asperger syndrome. *Neuroreport, 8*(1), 197–201.

Harlow, J. M. (1868). Recovery from passage of an iron bar through the head. *Proceedings of the Massachusetts Medical Society, 2*, 327–347.

Harris, I. M., Egan, G. F., Sonkkila, C., Tochon-Danguy, H. J., Paxinos, G., & Watson, J. D. (2000). Selective right parietal lobe activation during mental rotation: A parametric PET study. *Brain, 123*(1), 65–73.

Hasselmo, M. E., Linster, C., Patil, M., Ma, D., & Cekic, M. (1997). Noradrenergic suppression of synaptic transmission may influence cortical signal to noise ratio. *Journal of Neurophysiology, 77*, 3326–3339.

Hassler, M., & Gupta, D. (1993). Functional brain organization, handedness, and immune vulnerability in musicians and non-musicians. *Neuropsychologia, 31*(7), 655–660.

Head, H. (1926). *Aphasia and kindred disorders of speech.* New York: Macmillan Press.

Hebb, D. O. (1949). *The organization of behavior.* New York: Wiley.

Heilman, K. M. (2002). *Matter of mind.* New York: Oxford University Press.

Heilman, K. M., Nadeau, S. E., & Beversdorf, D. O. (2003). Creative innovation: Possible brain mechanisms. *Neurocase, 9*, 369–379.

Heilman, K. M., Schwartz, H. F., & Watson, R. T. (1978). Hypoarousal in patients with the neglect syndrome and emotional indifference. *Neurology, 28*, 229–232.

Heilman, K. M., & Valenstein, E. (2003). *Clinical neuropsychology.* New York: Oxford University Press.

Heilman, K. M., & Van den Abell, R. (1980). Right hemisphere dominance for attention: The mechanism underlying hemispheric asymmetries of inattention. *Neurology, 30*, 327–330.

Heilman, K. M., Watson, R. T., & Valenstein, E. (2003). Neglect and related disorders. In *Clinical neuropsychology.* New York: Oxford University Press.

Hering, R., Catarci, T., & Steiner, T. (1995). Handedness in musicians. *Functional Neurology, 10*, 23–26.

Herr, E. L., Moore, G. D., & Hasen, J. S. (1965). Creativity, intelligence and values: A study of relationships. *Exceptional Children, 32*, 414–415.

Hines, T. (1998). Further on Einstein's brain. *Experimental Neurology, 150*, 343–344.

Hoffman, B., & Dukas, H. (1972). *Albert Einstein: Creator and rebel.* New York: Viking Press.

Hoffman, H. J., Hendrick, E. B., Dennis, M., & Armstrong, D. (1979). Hemispherectomy for Sturge-Weber syndrome. *Childs Brain, 5*(3), 233–248.

Hopper, K. D., Patel, S., Cann, T. S., Wilcox, T., & Schaeffer, J. M. (1994). The relationship of age, gender, handedness and sidedness to the size of the corpus callosum. *Academic Radiology, 1*(3), 243–248.

Hou, C., Miller, B. L., Cummings, J. L., Goldberg, M., Mychack, P., Bottino, V., & Benson, D. F. (2000). Artistic savants. *Neuropsychiatry, Neuropsychology, and Behavioral Neurology, 13*(1), 29–38.

Hutt, S. J., Hutt, C., Lee, D., & Ounsted, C. (1965). A behavioral and electroencephalographic study of autistic children. *Journal of Psychiatric Research, 3*, 181–197.

Ishai, A., Ungerleider, L. G., & Haxby, J. V. (2000). Distributed neural systems for the generation of visual images. *Neuron, 28*(3), 979–990.

Jacobs, D. H., Adair, J. C., Williamson, D. J. G., Cibula, D. J., Na, D. L., Gold, M. G., Shuren, J., Foundas, A., & Heilman, K. M. (1999). Apraxia and motor-skill acquisition in Alzheimer's disease are dissociable. *Neuropsychologia, 37*, 875–880.

Jaeger, J. J., Lockwood, A. H., Van Valin, R. D., Jr., Kemmerer, D. L., Murphy, B. W., & Wack, D. S. (1998). Sex differences in brain regions activated by grammatical and reading tasks. *Neuroreport, 9*(12), 2803–2807.

James, W. (1890). *The Principle of psychology.* New York: Dover.

Jamison, K. R. (1989). Mood disorders and patterns of creativity in British writers and artists. *Psychiatry, 52*(2), 125–134.

Jancke, L., Schlaug, G., & Steinmetz, H. (1997). Hand skill asymmetry in professional musicians. *Brain and Cognition, 34*(3), 424–432.

Jausovec, N., & Jausovec, K. (2000). Differences in resting EEG related to ability. *Brain Topography, 12*, 229–240.

Johnson, M. K., & Raye, K. L. (1981). Reality monitoring. *Psychological Review, 88*(1), 67–85.

Kantha, S. S. (1992). Albert Einstein's dyslexia and the significance of Brodmann area 39 of his left cerebral cortex. *Medical Hypotheses, 37*, 119–122.

Kaplan, J. A., Brownell, H. H., Jacobs, J. R., & Gardner, H. (1990). The effects of right hemisphere damage on the pragmatic interpretation of conversational remarks. *Brain and Language, 38*, 315–333.

Kapur, N. (1996). Paradoxical functional facilitation in brain behavior research: A critical review. *Brain, 119*, 1775–1790.

Katusic, S. K., Colligan, R. C., Barbaresi, W. J., Schaid, D. J., & Jacobsen, S. J. (2001). Incidence of reading disability in a population-based birth cohort, 1976–1982, Rochester, Minn. *Mayo Clinic Proceedings, 76*(11), 1081–1092.

Keenan, P. A., Ezzat, W. H., Ginsburg, K., & Moore, G. J. (2001). Prefrontal cortex as the site of estrogen's effect on cognition. *Psychoneuroendocrinology, 26*(6), 577–590.

Kegel-Flom, P., & Didion, C. J. (1995). Women, math, and test scores. *Science, 270*(5235), 364–365.

Kester, D. B., Saykin, A. J., Sperling, M. R., & O'Conner, M. J. (1991). Acute effect of anterior temporal lobectomy on musical processing. *Neuropsychologia, 29*(7), 703–708.

Kiloh, L. G. (1986). The epilepsy of Dostoevsky. *Psychiatric Developments, 4*(1), 31–44.

Kimura, D. (1999). *Sex and cognition.* Cambridge, MA: MIT Press.

Kimura, D. (2002). Sex hormones influence human cognitive pattern. *Neuroendocrinology Letters, 23*(Suppl. 4), 67–77.

Kinsbourne, M. (1970). A model for the mechanism of unilateral neglect of space. *Transactions of the American Neurological Association, 95,* 143–146.

Kischka, U., Kammer, T., Maier, S., Weisbrod, M., Thimm, M., & Spitzer, M. (1996). Dopaminergic modulation of semantic network activation. *Neuropsychologia, 34,* 1107–1113.

Knott, V., Mahoney, C., & Evans, K. (2000). Pre-treatment EEG and its relationship to depression severity and paroxetine treatment outcome. *Pharmacopsychiatry, 6,* 201–205.

Koss, E., Haxby, J. V., DeCarli, C., & Schapiro, M. C. (1991). Patterns of performance preservation and loss in healthy aging. *Developmental Neuropsychology, 7*(1), 99–113.

Kosslyn, S. M. (1999). *Image and the brain.* Cambridge, MA: MIT Press.

Kuhn, T. S. (1996). *The structure of scientific revolutions* (3rd ed.). Chicago: University of Chicago Press.

Kulynych, J. J., Vladar, K., Jones, D. W., & Weinberger, D. R. (1994). Gender differences in the normal lateralization of the supratemporal cortex: MRI surface-rendering morphometry of Heschl's gyrus and the planum temporale. *Cerebral Cortex, 4*(2), 107–118.

Lang, A. R., Verret, L. D., & Watt, C. (1984). Drinking and creativity: Objective and subjective effects. *Addictive Behaviors, 9*(4), 395–399.

Lanthony, P. (1995). Left-handed painters. *Revue Neurologique, 151*(3), 165–170.

Lawrence, D. G., & Kuypers, H. G. (1968). The functional organization of the motor system in the monkey. I. and II. The effects of bilateral pyramidal lesions. *Brain, 91*(1), 1–14, 15–36.

LeBoutillier, N., & Marks, D. F. (2003). Mental imagery and creativity: A meta-analytic review study. *British Journal of Psychology, 94*(1), 29–44.

Lee, D. J., Chen, Y., & Schlaug, G. (2003). Corpus callosum: Musician and gender effects. *Neuroreport, 14*(2), 205–209.

Leon, S., Heilman, K. M., Fuller, R., Kendall, D., Nadeau, S. E., Spevack, A. A., & Roth, L. J. G. (2003). Cognitive-cholinergic therapy of anomia in 6 cases of Alzheimer's disease. Presented at the Thirty-First Annual International Neuropsychological Society Conference, February 5–8, 2003, Honolulu, Hawaii. *Journal of the International Neuropsychological Society, 9*(2), 194.

Levav, I., Kohn, R., Golding, J. M., & Weissman, M. M. (1997). Vulnerability of Jews to affective disorders. *American Journal of Psychiatry, 154*(7), 941–947.

Levine, D. N., Warach, J., & Farah, M. J. (1985). Two visual systems in mental imagery: Dissociations of what and where in imagery disorders due to posterior bilateral lesions. *Neurology, 35,* 1010–1018.

Lewin, C., & Herlitz, A. (2002). Sex differences in facial recognition. *Brain and Cognition, 50*(1), 121–128.

Lewis, R. T. (1979). Organic signs, creativity, and personality characteristics of patients following cerebral commissurotomy. *Clinical Neuropsychologist, 1,* 29–33.

Lhermitte, F. (1986). Human autonomy and the frontal lobes. Part II. Patient behavior in complex and social situations: The "environmental dependency syndrome." *Annals of Neurology, 19*(4), 335–343.

Liepmann, H. (1920). Apraxia Ergebn. *Ges. Med., 1,* 516–543.

Liotti, M., & Mayberg, H. S. (2001). The role of functional neuroimaging in the neuropsychology of depression. *Journal of Clinical and Experimental Neuropsychology, 23,* 121–126.

Lissauer, H. (1890). Ein Fall von Seelenblindheit nebst einem Beitrage zur Theori derselben. *Archiv fur Psychiatrie und Nervenkrankheiten, 21,* 222–270.

Livingstone, M. (2002). *Vision and art: The biology of seeing.* New York: Abrams.

Ludwig, A. M. (1994). Mental illness and creative activity in female writers. *American Journal of Psychiatry, 151*(11), 1650–1656.

Luria, A. R. (1968). *The mind of a mnemonist.* Cambridge, MA: Harvard University Press.

Luria, A. R. (1969). Frontal lobe syndrome. In P. J. Vinkin & G. W. Bruyn (Eds.), *Handbook of clinical neurology* (Vol. 2). Amsterdam: North Holland Publishing.

Lynn, R. (1994). Sex differences in intelligence and brain size: A paradox resolved. *Personality and Individual Differences, 17,* 257–272.

Maki, P. M., Rich, J. B., & Rosenbaum, R. S. (2002). Implicit memory varies across the menstrual cycle: Estrogen effects in young women. *Neuropsychologia, 40*(5), 518–529.

Marr, D. (1982). *Vision: A computational investigation into the human representation and processing of visual information.* New York: Freeman.

Marshall, J. C., & Halligan, P. W. (1988). Blindsight and insight in visuo-spatial neglect. *Nature, 336*(6201), 766–767.

Martindale, C., & Greenough, J. (1973). The differential effect of increased arousal on creative and intellectual performance. *Journal of Genetic Psychology, 123,* 329–335.

Martindale, C., & Hasenfus, N. (1978). EEG differences as a function of creativity, stage of creative process and effort to be original. *Biological Psychiatry, 6,* 157–167.

Masure, M. C., & Benton, A. L. (1983). Visuospatial performance in left-handed patients with unilateral brain lesions. *Neuropsychologia, 21*(2), 179–181.

May, R. (1975). *The courage to create.* New York: Norton.

McCarley, R. W. (1982). REM sleep and depression: Common neurobiological control mechanisms. *American Journal of Psychiatry, 139,* 565–570.

McGlone, J. (1977). Sex differences in the cerebral organization of verbal functions in patients with unilateral brain lesions. *Brain, 100*(4), 775–793.

Meador, K. J., Ray, P. G., Echauz, J. R., Loring, D. W., & Vachtsevanos, G. J. (2002). Gamma coherence and conscious perception. *Neurology, 59*(6), 847–854.

Mednick, S. A. (1962). The associative basis of the creative process. *Psychological Review, 9,* 220–232.

Mellet, E., Tzourio-Mazoyer, N., Bricogne, S., Mazoyer, B., Kosslyn, S. M., & Denis, M. (2000). Functional anatomy of high-resolution visual mental imagery. *Journal of Cognitive Neuroscience, 12*(1), 98–109.

Merzenich, M. M., Nelson, R. J., Stryker, M. P., Cynader, M. S., Schoppmann, A., & Zook, J. M. (1984). Somatosensory cortical map changes following digit amputation in adult monkeys. *Journal of Comparative Neurology, 224*(4), 591–605.

Miller, A. I. (2000). *Insights of genius.* Cambridge, MA: MIT Press.

Miller, B. L., Boone, K., Cummings, J., Read, S. L., & Mishkin, M. D. (2000). Functional correlates of musical and visual ability in frontotemporal dementia. *British Journal of Psychiatry, 176,* 458–463.

Miller, B. L., Cummings, J., Mishkin, M. D., Boone, K., Prince, F., Ponton, M., & Cotman, C. (1998). Emergence of artistic talent in frontotemporal dementia. *Neurology, 51,* 978–982.

Miller, G. (2000). Evolution of human music through sexual selection. In N. L. Wallin, B. Merker, & S. Brown (Eds.), *The origins of music* (pp. 329–360). Cambridge, MA: MIT Press.

Miller, L. C., Bard, K. A., Juno, C. J., & Nadler, R. D. (1986). Behavioral responsiveness of young chimpanzees (*Pan troglodytes*) to a novel environment. *Folia Primatologica, 47,* 128–142.

Milner, B. (1962). Laterality effects on audition. In V. B. Mountcastle (Ed.), *Interhemispheric relations and cerebral dominance.* Baltimore: Johns Hopkins University Press.

Milner, B. (1974). *Hemispheric specialization: Scope and limits.* In F. O. Schmidt & F. G. Worten (Eds.), *The neuroscience third study program.* Cambridge, MA: MIT Press.

Milner, B. (1984). Behavioural effects of frontal-lobe lesions in man. *Trends in Neurosciences, 7,* 403–407.

Mishkin, M., & Ungerleider, L. G. (1982). Contribution of striate inputs to the visuospatial functions of parieto-preoccipital cortex in monkeys. *Behavioural Brain Research, 6*(1), 57–77.

Mittenberg, W., Seidenberg, M., O'Leary, D. S., & DiGiulio, D. V. (1989). Changes in cerebral functioning associated with normal aging. *Journal of Clinical and Experimental Neuropsychology, 11*(6), 918–932.

Morrison, J., & Foote, S. (1986). Noradrenergic and serotonergic innervation of cortical, thalamic and tectal visual structures in old and new world monkeys. *Journal of Comparative Neurology, 243,* 117–128.

Nauta, W. J. (1971). The problem of the frontal lobe: A reinterpretation. *Journal of Psychiatric Research, 8*(3), 167–187.

Newland, A. G. (1981). Differences between left- and right-handers on a measure of creativity. *Perceptual and Motor Skills, 53,* 787–792.

Nieber, D., & Schlegel, S. (1992). Relationships between psychomotor retardation and EEG power spectrum in major depression. *Neuropsychobiology, 25,* 20–23.

Nudo, R. J., Milliken, G. W., Jenkins, W. M., & Merzenich, M. M. (1996). Use-dependent alterations of movement representations in primary motor cortex of adult squirrel monkeys. *Journal of Neuroscience, 16*(2), 785–807.

Ochse, R. (1990). *Before the gates of excellence: The determinants of creative genius.* Cambridge, UK: Cambridge University Press.

Ongur, D., Ferry, A. T., & Price, J. L. (2003). Architectonic subdivision of the human orbital and medial prefrontal cortex. *Journal of Comparative Neurology, 460*(3), 425–449.

Ozturk, A. H., Tascioglu, B., Aktekin, M., Kurtoglu, Z., & Erden, I. (2002). Morphometric comparison of the human corpus callosum in professional musicians and non-musicians by using in vivo magnetic resonance imaging. *Journal of Neuroradiology, 29*(1), 29–34.

Pakkenberg, B., Pelvig, D., Marner, L., Bundgaard, M. J., Gundersen, H. J., Nyengaard, J. R., & Regeur, L. (2003). Aging and the human neocortex. *Experimental Gerontology, 38*(1–2), 95–99.

Paradiso, S., Hermann, B. P., Blumer, D., Davies, K., & Robinson, R. G. (2001). Impact of depressed mood on neuropsychological status in temporal lobe epilepsy. *Journal of Neurology Neurosurgery Psychiatry, 70*(2), 180–185.

Parsons, L. M., & Osherson, D. (2001). New evidence for distinct right and left brain systems for deductive versus probabilistic reasoning. *Cerebral Cortex, 11*(10), 954–965.

Peterson, J. M. (1979). Left handedness: Differences between student artists and scientists. *Perceptual and Motor Skills, 48,* 961–962.

Pham, T. M., Ickes, B., Albeck, D., Soderstrom, S., Granholm, A. C., & Mohammed, A. H. (1999). Changes in brain nerve growth factor levels and nerve growth factor receptors in rats exposed to environmental enrichment for one year. *Neuroscience, 94*(1), 279–286.

Poincare, H. (1913). *The Foundations of science.* Lancaster PA: Science Press. Quoted by Martinbdale, C. (1999). Biological basis of creativity. In R. J. Sternberg (Ed.), *Handbook of creativity.* New York: Cambridge University Press.

Plucker, J. A., & Renzulli, J. S. (1999). Experimental studies of creativity. In R. J. Sternberg (Ed.), *Handbook of creativity.* Cambridge, UK: Cambridge University Press.

Poldinger, W. (1986). The relation between depression and art. *Psychopathology, 19,* 263–268.

Post, F. (1994). Creativity and psychopathology: A study of 291 world-famous men. *British Journal of Psychiatry, 165*(2), 22–34.

Post, F. (1996). Verbal creativity, depression and alcoholism: An investigation of 100 American and British writers. *British Journal of Psychiatry, 168,* 545–555.

Potzl, O. (1928). *Die Optisch-agnostischen Storungen. Die verschieden Formen der Seelenblindheit.* Leipzig, Vienna: Deutticke.

Pozzilli, C., Bastianello, S., Bozzao, A., Pierallini, A., Giubilei, F., Argentino, C., & Bozzao, L. (1994). No differences in corpus callosum size by sex and aging. A quantitative study using magnetic resonance imaging. *Journal of Neuroimaging, 4*(4), 218–221.

Rabinowicz, T., Dean, D. E., Petetot, J. M., & de Courten-Myers, G. M. (1999). Gender differences in the human cerebral cortex: More neurons in males; more processes in females. *Journal of Child Neurology, 14,* 98–107.

Ramachandran, V. S., & Hubbard, E. M. (2001). Synaesthesia: A window into perception, thought and language. *Journal of Consciousness Studies, 8*(12), 3–34.

Ramón y Cajal, S. (1999). *Advice for a young investigator* (N. Swanson & L. W. Swanson, Trans.). Cambridge, MA: MIT Press. (Original work published in 1898)

Rapcsak, S. Z., Gonzalez-Rothi, L. J., & Heilman, K. M. (1987). Apraxia in a patient with atypical cerebral dominance. *Brain and Cognition, 6,* 450–463.

Ratey, J. J., Bemporad, J., Sorgi, P., Bick, P., Polakoff, S., O'Driscoll, G., & Mikkelsen, E. (1987). Open trial effects of beta-blockers on speech and social behaviors in 8 autistic adults. *Journal of Autism and Developmental Disorders, 17,* 439–446.

Raymond, G. V., Bauman, M. L., & Kemper, T. L. (1996). Hippocampus in autism: A Golgi analysis. *Acta Neuropathologica, 91,* 117–119.

Read, D. E. (1988). Age-related changes in performance on a visual-closure task. *Journal of Clinical and Experimental Neuropsychology, 10*(4), 451–466.

Recanzone, G. H., Schreiner, C. E., & Merzenich, M. M. (1993). Plasticity in the frequency representation of primary auditory cortex following discrimination training in adult owl monkeys. *Journal of Neuroscience, 13*(1), 87–103.

Reuter-Lorenz, P. A., & Stanczak, L. (2000). Differential effects of aging on the functions of the corpus callosum. *Developmental Neuropsychology, 18,* 113–137.

Richards, R., Kinney, D. K., Lunde, I., Benet, M., & Merzel, A. P. (1988). Creativity in manic-depressives, cyclothymes, their normal relatives, and control subjects. *Journal of Abnormal Psychology, 97,* 281–288.

Ridderinkhof, K. R., Span, M. M., & van der Molen, M. W. (2002). Perseverative behavior and adaptive control in older adults: Performance monitoring, rule induction, and set shifting. *Brain and Cognition, 49*(3), 382–401.

Robertson, L. C., & Lamb, M. R. (1991). Neuropsychological contributions to theories of part/whole organization. *Cognitive Psychology, 23*(2), 299–330.

Rosenzweig, M. R. (1972). Brain changes in response to experience. *Scientific American, 226*(2), 22–29.

Rosenzweig, M. R., & Bennett, E. L. (1996). Psychobiology of plasticity: Effects of training and experience on brain and behavior. *Behavioural Brain Research, 78,* 57–65.

Ross, E. D. (1981). The aprosodias: Functional-anatomic organization of the affective components of language in the right hemisphere. *Archives of Neurology, 38*(9), 561–569.

Rousseau, J. J. (1762). *The social contract. Or principles of political right.* Translated by G. D. H. Cole, public domain.

Ryan, J. J., Sattler, J. M., & Lopez, S. J. (2000). Age effects on Wechsler Adult Intelligence Scale–III subtests. *Archives of Clinical Neuropsychology, 15*(4), 311–317.

Sachdev, H. S., & Waxman, S. G. (1981). Frequency of hypergraphia in temporal lobe epilepsy: An index of interictal behaviour syndrome. *Journal of Neurology, Neurosurgery and Psychiatry, 44*(4), 358–360.

Sackeim, H. A., Gur, R. C., & Saucy, M. C. (1978). Emotions are expressed more intensely on the left side of the face. *Science, 202*(4366), 434–436.

Saigusa, T., Tuinstra, T., Koshikawa, N., & Cools, A. R. (1999). High and low responders to novelty: Effects of a catecholamine synthesis inhibitor on novelty-induced changes in behaviour and release of accumbal dopamine. *Neuroscience, 88*(4), 1153–1163.

Schacter, D. L., Verfaellie, M., & Anes, M. (1997). Illusory memories in amnesic patients: Conceptual and perceptual false recognition. *Neuropsychology, 3,* 331–342.

Schacter, S., & Singer, J. E. (1962). Cognitive, social and physiological determinants of emotional state. *Psychology Review, 69,* 379–399.

Schinka, J. A., Letsch, E. A., & Crawford, F. C. (2002). DRD4 and novelty seeking: Results of meta-analyses. *American Journal of Medical Genetics, 114*(6), 643–648.

Schirillo, J. A. (2000). Hemispheric asymmetries and gender influence Rembrandt's portrait orientations. *Neuropsychologia, 38*(12), 1593–1606.

Schlaug, G., Jancke, L., Huang, Y., & Steinmetz, H. (1995). In vivo evidence of structural brain asymmetry is musicians. *Science, 267,* 699–701.

Schott, G. D. (1979). Some neurological observations on Leonardo da Vinci's handwriting. *Journal of the Neurological Sciences, 42*(3), 321–329.

Schultz, W., Tremblay, L., & Hollerman, J. R. (1998). Reward prediction in primate basal ganglia and frontal cortex. *Neuropharmacology, 37*(4–5), 421–429.

Schwartz, C. E., Wright, C. I., Shin, L. M., Kagan, J., & Rauch, S. L. (2003). Inhibited and uninhibited infants "grown up": Adult amygdalar response to novelty. *Science, 300*(5627), 1952–1953.

Segundo, J. P., Naguet, R., & Buser, P. (1955). Effects of cortical stimulation on electrocortical activity in the monkey. *Neurophysiology, 18,* 236–245.

Sergent, J. (1993). Music, the brain and Ravel. *Trends in Neuroscience, 16,* 168–171.

Servan-Schreiber, D., Printz, H., & Cohen, J. D. (1990). A network model of catecholamine effects gain signal to noise ratio and behavior. *Science, 249,* 892–895.

Shaywitz, B. A., Shaywitz, S. E., Pugh, K. R., Constable, R. T., Skudlarski, P., Fulbright, R. K., Bronen, R. A., Fletcher, J. M., Shankweiler, D. P., & Katz, L. (1995). Sex differences in the functional organization of the brain for language. *Nature, 373*(6515), 607–609.

Shepard, R. N., & Metzler, J. (1971). Mental rotation of three-dimensional objects. *Science, 171,* 701–703.

Simonton, D. K. (1994). *Greatness: Who makes history and why?* New York: Guilford.

Simonton, D. K. (1999). *Origins of genius: Darwinian perspectives on creativity.* New York: Oxford University Press.

Slaby, A. E. (1992). Creativity, depression and suicide. *Suicide and Life-Threatening Behavior, 22,* 157–166.

Smith, A., & Sugar, O. (1975). Development of above normal language and intelligence 21 years after left hemispherectomy. *Neurology, 25*(9), 813–818.

Soukhanov, A. H., & Ellis, K. (1988). *Webster's II: New Riverside university dictionary.* Boston: Houghton Mifflin.

Spearman, C. (1905). General intelligence: Objectively determined and measured. *American Journal of Psychology, 15,* 210–293.

Spearman, C. (1927). *The abilities of man.* London: Macmillian.

Speedie, L. J., Wertman, E., Tair, J., & Heilman, K. M. (1993). Disruption of automatic speech following a right basal ganglia lesion. *Neurology, 43,* 1768–1774.

Spitzka, E. A. (1907). A study of the brains of six eminent scientists and scholars belonging to the American Anthropometric Society: Together with a description of the skull of Professor E. D. Cope. *Transactions of the American Philosophical Society, 21,* 175–308.

Stanley, J. C. (1993). Boys and girls who reason well mathematically. *Ciba Foundation Symposium, 178,* 119–134.

Steinmetz, H., Staiger, J. F., Schlaug, G., Huang, Y., & Jancke, L. (1995). Corpus callosum and brain volume in women and men. *Neuroreport, 6*(7), 1002–1004.

Sternberg, R. J., & Lubert, T. I. (1995). *Defying the crowd: Cultivating creativity in a culture of conformity.* New York: Free Press.

Sternberg, R. J., & O'Hara, L. A. (1999). Creativity and intelligence. In R. J. Sternberg (Ed.), *Handbook of creativity* (pp. 251–272). New York: Cambridge University Press.

Stewart, C. A., & Clayson, D. (1980). A note on change in creativity by handedness over maturational time period. *Journal of Psychology, 104,* 39–42.

Storandt, M. (1977). Age, ability level, and method of administering and scoring the WAIS. *Journal of Gerontology, 32*(2), 175–178.

Strunz, F. (1993). Preconscious mental activity and scientific problem-solving: A critique of the Kekule dream controversy. *Journal of the Association for the Study of Dreams, 3*(4), 281–294.

Sullivan, E. V., Pfefferbaum, A., Adalsteinsson, E., Swan, G. E., & Carmelli, F. (2002). Differential rates of regional brain change in callosal and ventricular size. *Cerebral Cortex, 12,* 438–445.

Tang, Y. P., Shimizu, E., Dube, G. R., Rampon, C., Kerchner, G. A., Zhuo, M., Liu, G., & Tsien, J. Z. (1999). Genetic enhancement of learning and memory in mice. *Nature, 401*(6748), 63–69.

Tang, Y., Whitman, G. T., Lopez, I., & Baloh, R. W. (2001). Brain volume changes on longitudinal magnetic resonance imaging in normal older people. *Journal of Neuroimaging, 11*(4), 393–400.

Tankle, R. S., & Heilman, K. M. (1983). Mirror writing in right-handers and in left-handers. *Brain and Language, 19,* 115–123.

Tekin, S., & Cummings, J. L. (2003). Hallucinations and related conditions. In K. M. Heilman & E. Valenstein (Eds.), *Clinical neuropsychology* (4th ed., pp. 479–494). New York: Oxford University Press.

Terman, L. M. (1954). The discovery and encouragement of exceptional talent. *American Psychologist, 9,* 221–230.

Thayer, R. E. (1996). *The origins of everyday moods.* New York: Oxford University Press.

Thurstone, L. L. (1938). *Primary mental abilities.* Chicago: University of Chicago Press.

Torrance, E. P. (1974). The Torrance Test of Creative Thinking. Bensenville, IL: Scholastic Testing Service.

Torrance, E. P. (1975). Creativity research in education: Still alive. In I. A. Taylor (Ed.), *Perspectives in creativity* (pp. 278–296). Zurich: Aldine de Gruyter.

Torrance, E. P. (1988). The nature of creativity as manifest in its testing. In R. J. Sternberg (Ed.), *The nature of creativity* (pp. 43–74). New York: Cambridge University Press.

Tramo, M. J., Loftus, W. C., Stukel, T. A., Green, R. L., Weaver, J. B., & Gazzaniga, M. S. (1998). Brain size, head size and intelligence quotient in monozygotic twins. *Neurology, 50,* 1246–1252.

Treffert, D. A., & Wallace, G. L. (2002). Islands of genius. *Scientific American, 286,* 76–85.

Triggs, W. J., Calvanio, R., Macdonell, R. A., Cros, D., & Chiappa, K. H. (1994). Physiological motor asymmetry in human handedness: Evidence from transcranial magnetic stimulation. *Brain Research, 14; 636*(2), 270–276.

Trimble, M. R. (2000). Charles Lloyd: Epilepsy and poetry. *History of Psychiatry, 11*(Pt. 3, 43), 273–289.

Tucker, D. M., Watson, R. T., & Heilman, K. M. (1977). Discrimination and evocation of affectively intoned speech in patients with right parietal disease. *Neurology, 27,* 947–950.

Tupala, E., Kuikka, J. T., Hall, H., Bergstrom, K., Sarkioja, T., Rasanen, P., Mantere, T., Hiltunen, J., Vepsalainen, J., & Tiihonen, J. (2001). Measurement of the striatal dopamine transporter density and heterogeneity in type 1 alcoholics using human whole hemisphere autoradiography. *Neuroimage, 14*(Pt. 1, 1), 87–94.

Underwood, A. (2003, December 1). Real rhapsody in blue. *Newsweek,* p. 67.

Valenstein, E. S. (1973). *Brain control.* New York: Wiley Interscience.

Vargha-Khadem, F., Gadian, D. G., Watkins, K. E., Connelly, A., Van Paesschen, W., & Mishkin, M. (1997). Differential effects of early hippocampal pathology on episodic and semantic memory. *Science, 277*(5324), 376–380.

Volkow, N. D., Logan, J., Fowler, J. S., Wang, G. J., Gur, R. C., Wong, C., Felder, C., Gatley, S. J., Ding, Y. S., Hitzemann, R., & Pappas, N. (2000). Association between age-related decline in brain dopamine activity and impairment in frontal and cingulate metabolism. *American Journal of Psychiatry, 157*(1), 75–80.

von Helmholz, H. (1896). *Vortrage und Reden.* Brunswick, Germany: Friedrich Vieweg.

Voyer, D., Voyer, S., & Bryden, M. P. (1995). Magnitude of sex differences in spatial abilities: A meta-analysis and consideration of critical variables. *Psychological Bulletin, 117*(2), 250–270.

Wallas, G. (1926). *The art of thought.* New York: Harcourt Brace.

Warrington, E. K., & James, M. (1988). Visual apperceptive agnosia: A clinico-anatomical study of three cases. *Cortex, 24*(1), 13–32.

Waterhouse, B. D., & Woodward, D. J. (1980). Interaction of norepi-nephrine with cerebrocortical activity evoked by stimulation of somatosensory afferent pathways in the rat. *Experimental Neurology, 67,* 11–34.

Watson, R. T., & Heilman, K. M. (1981). Callosal apraxia. *Brain, 106,* 391–404.

Watson, R. T., Valenstein, E., Day, A., & Heilman, K. M. (1994). Posterior neocortical systems subserving awareness and neglect: Neglect after superior temporal sulcus but not area 7 lesions. *Archives of Neurology, 51,* 1014–1021.

Wechsler, D. (1981). *WAIS-R manual.* New York: Psychological Corporation.

Weinberger, D. R., Berman, K. F., & Zee, R. F. (1986). Physiologic dysfunction of dorsolateral prefontal cortex in schizophrenia. *Archives of General Psychiatry, 43,* 114–124.

Weisberg, R. W. (1986). *Creativity: Genius and other myths.* New York: W. H. Freeman.

Weisberg, R. W. (1994). Genius and madness? A quasi-experimental test of the hypothesis that manic depression increases creativity. *Psychological Science, 5,* 365–367.

Wilson, E. O. (1999). *Consilience.* New York: Random House.

Winner, E., von Karolyi, C., Malinsky, D., French, L., Seliger, C., Ross, E., & Weber, C. (2001). Dyslexia and visual-spatial talents: Compensation vs. deficit model. *Brain and Language, 76*(2), 81–110.

Wisniewski, A. B. (1998). Sexually-dimorphic patterns of cortical asymmetry, and the role for sex steroid hormones in determining cortical patterns of lateralization. *Psychoneuroendocrinology, 23*(5), 519–547.

Witelson, S. F. (1985). The brain connection: The corpus callosum is larger in left-handers. *Science, 229*(4714), 665–668.

Witelson, S. F. (1991). Neural sexual mosaicism: Sexual differentiation of the human temporo-parietal region for functional asymmetry. *Psychoneuroendocrinology, 16*(1–3), 131–153.

Witelson, S. F., & Kigar, D. L. (1992). Sylvian fissure morphology and asymmetry in men and women: Bilateral differences in the relationship to handedness in men. *Journal of Comparative Neurology, 323,* 326–340.

Witelson, S. F., Kigar, D. L., & Harvey, T. (1999). The exceptional brain of Albert Einstein. *Lancet, 353,* 2149–2153.

Wolff, U., & Lundberg, I. (2002). The prevalence of dyslexia among art students. *Dyslexia, 8*(1), 34–42.

Zangwell, O. L. (1966). Psychological deficits associated with frontal lobe lesions. *International Journal of Neurology, 5,* 395–402.

Zeki, S., Watson, J. D., Lueck, C. J., Friston, K. J., Kennard, C., & Frackowiak, R. S. (1991). A direct demonstration of functional specialization in human visual cortex. *Journal of Neuroscience, 11*(3), 641–649.

Zihl, J., von Cramon, D., & Mai, N. (1983). Selective disturbance of movement vision after bilateral brain damage. *Brain, 106*(2), 313–340.

Zuckerman, M. (1977). *Scientific elite: Nobel laureates in the United States.* New York: Free Press.

Index